From

Absurd

to

ZEITGEIST

From
Absurd
to
ZEITGEIST

The
Compact
Guide to
Literary
Terms

Kathleen Morner   **Ralph Rausch**

NTC Publishing Group
NTC/Contemporary Publishing Company

Library of Congress Cataloging-in-Publication Data

Morner, Kathleen.
    [NTC's dictionary of literary terms]
    From absurd to Zeitgeist : the compact guide to literary terms / Kathleen
Morner, Ralph Rausch.
        p.   cm.
    Originally published under title: NTC's dictionary of literary terms. 1991.
    ISBN 0-8442-0401-3
    1. Criticism—Terminology.   2. Literature—Terminology.   3. English
language—Terms and phrases.   I. Rausch, Ralph.   II. Title.
PN44.5.M58   1997
803—dc21   97-15379
                                                                        CIP

Originally published as *NTC's Dictionary of Literary Terms.*

This edition published 1997 by NTC Publishing Group
An imprint of NTC/Contemporary Publishing Company
4255 West Touhy Avenue, Lincolnwood (Chicago), Illinois 60646-1975 U.S.A.
Copyright © 1991 by NTC/Contemporary Publishing Company
Manufactured in the United States of America
International Standard Book Number: 0-8442-0401-3
18   17   16   15   14   13   12   11   10   9   8   7   6   5   4   3   2   1

Acknowledgments

Excerpt from *The Myth of Sisyphus and Other Essays* by Albert Camus, translated by Justin O'Brien. Copyright © 1955 by Alfred A. Knopf Inc. Reprinted by permission of the publisher. In the UK and Commonwealth, reproduced by permission of Hamish Hamilton Ltd. and Editions Gallimard.

"November Night," reprinted from *The Complete Poems and Collected Letters of Adelaide Crapsey,* ed. by Susan B. Smith, by permission of the State University of New York Press. © 1977 by the State University of New York Press.

"!" is reprinted from *Complete Poems, 1913-1962* by E. E. Cummings, by permission of Liveright Publishing Corporation. Copyright © 1923, 1925, 1931, 1935, 1938, 1939, 1940, 1944, 1945, 1946, 1947, 1948, 1949, 1950, 1951, 1952, 1953, 1954, 1955, 1956, 1957, 1958, 1959, 1960, 1961, 1962 by the Trustees for the E. E. Cummings Trust. Copyright © 1961, 1963, 1968 by Marion Morehouse Cummings. UK and Commonwealth permissions granted by Grafton Books, a division of the Collins Publishing Group.

From "On the Mall" from *The White Album* by Joan Didion. Copyright © 1975, 1979, 1989 by Joan Didion. Reprinted by permission of Farrar, Straus and Giroux, Inc., and The Wallace Agency.

"Oread" by H. D., reprinted from *Collected Poems 1912-1944.* Copyright © 1982 by The Estate of Hilda Doolittle. Reprinted by permission of New Directions. UK and Commonwealth permissions granted by Carcanet Press Limited.

Excerpt from "Tradition and the Individual Talent" from *Selected Essays* by T. S. Eliot, copyright 1950 by Harcourt Brace Jovanovich, Inc., and renewed 1978 by Esme Valerie Eliot. Reprinted by permission of the publisher. World permissions (other than the United States) granted by Faber and Faber Ltd.

"Whose Canon Is It, Anyway?" by Henry Louis Gates, Jr. Copyright © 1989 by Henry Louis Gates, Jr. Reprinted by permission of Brandt & Brandt Literary Agents, Inc.

"Hawk Roosting" by Ted Hughes. Copyright © 1959 by Ted Hughes. Taken from *Selected Poems 1957-1967* by Ted Hughes. Copyright © 1972 by Ted Hughes. Reprinted by permission of Harper & Row, Publishers, Inc. World permissions (other than the United States) granted by Faber and Faber Ltd.

Excerpt from "Number 3 on the Docket" and "Tanka" from *The Complete Poetical Works of Amy Lowell* by Amy Lowell. Copyright © 1955 by Houghton Mifflin Company. Copyright © renewed 1983 by Houghton Mifflin Company, Brinton P. Roberts, Esquire, and G. D'Andelot Belin, Esquire. Reprinted by permission of Houghton Mifflin Company.

To the User

In *From Absurd to Zeitgeist: The Compact Guide to Literary Terms*, we have aimed both at satisfying immediate curiosity about terms such as *irony, graveyard school, omniscient point of view, intentional fallacy,* and *conceit* and at stimulating interest in the individual works of literature that such terms help to categorize, analyze, and describe. In compiling a list of literary genres, forms, styles, movements, periods, and technical terms, as well as critical theories and approaches, we have been selective, concerned more with making this guide generally useful than with making it all-inclusive. Toward that end, we surveyed widely used high-school and college texts to identify those terms most likely to be encountered by the student of literature. Our list is comprehensive in that it represents what we believe to be the basic literary and critical vocabulary that students, teachers, and other interested readers of literature must be able to understand and apply. This guide, therefore, can be used both as a supplementary text in literature courses and as a general reference book.

Looking up a literary term can be a vicious circle. To comprehend fully the definition of any one term, one usually needs to be familiar with several other terms. Although there is no escaping the use of terms within definitions, we have attempted to lighten the semantic burden of our entries by using plain language and concrete description wherever possible and by illustrating terms with quotations from or references to familiar works of American, British, and world literature.

The entries are cross-referenced so that the reader can move easily from one term to a related term. Terms referred to within an entry that are discussed more fully elsewhere in the guide are printed in SMALL CAPITAL LETTERS. For example, the entry on *figurative language* mentions METAPHOR, SIMILE, PERSONIFICATION, and HYPERBOLE. Terms defined and explained within entries as subtypes or subcategories are printed in **boldface**, as are close synonyms. To enrich the reader's understanding of individual terms and their relationships, we have clustered closely related terms in extended entries under the most general term. For instance, in the entry on *metaphor,* the terms *extended metaphor, dead metaphor,* and *mixed metaphor* are also introduced and discussed.

Because we feel that the reader deserves at least some immediate information as a reward for having looked up a term, we have included no empty entries, no mere cross-references instructing the reader, for instance, to "See CHARACTER." Instead, for every term listed, there is a brief definition. For example, rather than simply stating "**dirge**. See ELEGY," the guide provides

dirge. A funeral song of lamentation; a short LYRIC of mourning. See ELEGY.

Each entry has received the space we feel it requires. If a term is relatively current and familiar and can be made clear in a few lines, we do not elaborate. The entry for *biography,* for example, is shorter than the entry for *epic theater.* For terms that have two or more distinct definitions, applicable in their use as literary terms, we have numbered the definitions. Where there has been disagreement or confusion over the meaning of a term—*catharsis, negative capability, rhetoric, sarcasm*—or a term has changed its meaning or its significance over time—*humor, imagination, sentimental novel, wit*—we sort out the variations and lead the reader to accurate and historically appropriate uses of the term.

How to Use This Guide

All entries are listed in alphabetical order. The sample entries below illustrate the kinds of information provided in the guide.

entry head

run-on lines. VERSE in which the thought of one line runs into the next line with no punctuation or grammatical break; also called **enjambment**, and the opposite of END-STOPPED LINES. These lines from William Wordsworth's "Westminster Bridge" are run-on lines:

ubtype, ubcategory, or ose synonym

term discussed more fully in separate entry

example or excerpt

> This City now doth, like a garment, wear
> The beauty of the morning.

ss-reference to ated terms

See END-STOPPED LINES, ENJAMBMENT.

terms discussed more fully in separate entries

ntry head

scene. 1. In DRAMA, a subdivision of an act that usually does not involve a change of locale or a shift in time. However, there seems to be no universal agreement about what constitutes a scene. Changes of scene may be signaled by CHARACTERS entering or leaving the stage or by a clearing of the stage, as in ELIZABETHAN drama, which made no clear division of scenes, and in RESTORATION drama, in which new scenes were numbered with each entrance or exit. Modern playwrights generally consider a scene to be a continuous EPISODE, a unit of action without interruption or break in continuity. The end of a scene is often marked by dimming the stage lights or by dropping the curtain.

umbered efinitions for erm with hore than one istinct meaning

2. A part of a drama featuring a single, specific INCIDENT or segment of DIALOGUE, for example, a death scene or a mad scene.

3. In NARRATIVE FICTION, the place in which the action is set.

4. In Kenneth D. Burke's system of analyzing LITERATURE, one of the five items in his "pentad," elements he considers essential to all literary works: Act (what happened), Scene (where), Agent (who did it), Agency (how), and Purpose (why). Burke's system, which centers on the idea that literature is a form of action, is called DRAMATISM.

absurd, theater of the. A kind of DRAMA growing out of the philosophy of EXISTENTIALISM and flourishing in Europe and America in the 1950s and 1960s. Absurdist dramas present CHARACTERS struggling to find order and purpose in irrational and incomprehensible situations. In the dramas of Eugène Ionesco, Samuel Beckett, Jean Genet, Harold Pinter, Fernando Arrabal, Edward Albee, and Arthur Kopit, characters find themselves buried in sand up to their armpits, submerged in a room full of proliferating furniture, standing interminably and for no purpose in a line, worked over by an interrogation team for no reason, or visited by friends who insist on staying with them indefinitely. Influenced by DADA, EXPRESSIONISM, and SURREALISM, the FORM and STYLE of absurdist plays reflect their subject matter. INCIDENTS do not tell a connected story; characters lack motivation; even the language is cryptic. There is an odd kinship between absurdist drama and FARCE—as if, in the theater of the absurd, the merciless and abusive situations of farce have been transformed into nightmares about the human condition. Like farces, absurdist plays are terribly funny—until they are suddenly profoundly sad.

See DADA, DRAMA, EXISTENTIALISM, EXPRESSIONISM, FARCE, SURREALISM.

accent. In POETRY, the vocal force or emphasis placed on a syllable or a word. See STRESS.

adaptation. **1.** A re-rendering of a work originally written in one GENRE or medium into another genre or medium; for example, the adaptation of Sir Walter Scott's HISTORICAL NOVEL *The Bride of Lammermoor* into Gaetano Donizetti's opera *Lucia di Lammermoor,* the adaptation of Shirley Jackson's SHORT STORY *The Lottery* into a stage PLAY, or the adaptation of E. M. Forster's NOVEL *A Passage to India* into a movie.

2. A TRANSLATION from one language to another that derives its inspiration from the original work—retaining the general features of PLOT, CHARACTERS, and TONE—but that is essentially a rewriting.

See GENRE, TRANSLATION.

adventure story. A type of popular LITERATURE that centers on exciting action and danger, heroic derring-do, and happy endings, often to the detriment of solid CHARACTERIZATION. Richard Connell's SHORT STORY *The Most Dangerous Game* and Robert Louis Stevenson's NOVEL *Treasure Island* are classic examples. See ROMANCE.

aesthetic distance. Standing apart from a work of art as a reader or viewer; recognizing that it is art and not real life. See DISTANCE.

aestheticism. Reverence for beauty; for "art for art's sake." The term also refers to a nineteenth-century movement in art and literature that held that beautiful form is more to be valued than morally instructive content, and even that morality is irrelevant to art. An early expression of aestheticism is found in John Keats's lines from "Ode on a Grecian Urn":

> "Beauty is truth, truth beauty"—that is all
> Ye know on earth, and all ye need to know.

In part a reaction against the ugliness and mere usefulness of the products of industrialization, the movement reached its peak in the 1890s and is usually associated with Walter Pater, Oscar Wilde, and Aubrey Beardsley, who aspired to live their very lives as art, to live lives of beauty and intensity and brilliance rather than lives of goodness or usefulness. The tendency of the followers of aestheticism to focus on sensational subject matter and surface polish led Alfred, Lord Tennyson to satirize the ideals of the movement:

> The filthiest of all paintings painted well
> Is mightier than the purest painted ill!

See AESTHETICS, DECADENCE.

aesthetics. The philosophy of art; the study of the nature of beauty in literature and the arts, and the development of criteria for judging beauty.

See AESTHETICISM, LITERARY CRITICISM, NEW CRITICISM.

affective fallacy. A term introduced by W. K. Wimsatt and M. C. Beardsley to describe the critical approach of evaluating a work of literature by the emotional effect it produces in the reader. Proponents of the OBJECTIVE THEORY OF ART, especially followers of NEW CRITICISM, regard such an approach as misguided because they feel it confuses the work with its results, what it *is* with what it *does*.

Supporters of IMPRESSIONISTIC CRITICISM, however, insist that the reader's response to a work of literature is the ultimate criterion for judging its worth. They point to a long list of champions of the affective approach, from Aristotle to Emily Dickinson. Aristotle asserted that the purpose of TRAGEDY is to evoke "pity and fear" and then to offer a therapeutic release from these emotions (CATHARSIS). Dickinson said, "If I feel physically as if the top of my head were taken off, I know that is poetry."

The affective fallacy is considered the converse of the INTENTIONAL FALLACY, the "error" of judging a work primarily in terms of the author's intention.

See INTENTIONAL FALLACY, NEW CRITICISM, OBJECTIVE THEORY OF ART.

Age of Sensibility. The period in the history of English LITERATURE roughly between 1744 and 1798; also called the **Age of Johnson.** See SENSIBILITY.

alexandrine.   A twelve-syllable poetic line. The original French alexandrine, containing four accented syllables, became the standard verse FORM of seventeenth-century French TRAGEDY. The English alexandrine, an iambic HEXAMETER line, has been used more sparingly because its six accents make it seem overly long. In the second line of this COUPLET, Alexander Pope illustrates the alexandrine as he criticizes it:

> A needless Alexandrine ends the song,
> That, like a wounded snake, drags its slow length along.

Edmund Spenser used the alexandrine effectively as the ninth and final line in an otherwise IAMBIC PENTAMETER STANZA he invented, known as the SPENSERIAN STANZA.

See HEXAMETER, IAMBIC PENTAMETER, METER.

allegory.   An extended NARRATIVE in PROSE or VERSE in which CHARACTERS, events, and SETTINGS represent abstract qualities and in which the writer intends a second meaning to be read beneath the surface story. The underlying meaning may be moral, religious, political, social, or satiric. The characters are often PERSONIFICATIONS of such abstractions as greed, envy, hope, charity, or fortitude.

Thus, allegory sustains interest on two levels: first, in the characters and actions described by the surface story; second, in the ideas symbolized by them. For example, John Bunyan's *The Pilgrim's Progress* allegorizes a Christian's journey from the City of Destruction (his conversion) to the Celestial City (his death and salvation). He carries a heavy bundle (his sins) on his back, he struggles with giants (doubts), and he is guided by a chart (his Bible). Other well-known allegories include *Everyman* (a MORAL-ITY PLAY), Edmund Spenser's *The Faerie Queene* and Alfred, Lord Tennyson's *Idylls of the King* (CHIVALRIC ROMANCES), John Dryden's *Absalom and Achitophel* (a political SATIRE), and Jonathan Swift's *Gulliver's Travels* (a social satire).

While allegory makes use of SYMBOLS, it differs from other fiction that suggests several levels of meaning in that *everything*—PLOT, setting, characterization—is specifically structured to convey both a concrete surface story and abstract meanings that lie outside the narrative itself.

See APOLOGUE, EXEMPLUM, FABLE, PARABLE.

alliteration. The repetition of consonant sounds at the beginning of words or within words, as in Macbeth's phrase "*after life's fitful fever.*" Alliteration is used in both POETRY and PROSE for UNITY, EMPHASIS, and musical effect. An especially musical example is Samuel Taylor Coleridge's famous DESCRIPTION of the sacred river Alph in his poem *Kubla Khan:*

> Five *m*iles *m*eandering with *m*azy *m*otion

Alliteration for ludicrous effect is common in NONSENSE VERSE, jingles, and tongue twisters:

> Betty Botter bought some butter,
> But, said she, the butter's bitter;
> If I put it in my batter
> It will make my batter bitter,
> But a bit of better butter,
> That would make my batter better.

In English poetry, alliteration is a very old device, predating RHYME. The alliterative VERSE FORM used in the Old English poem *Beowulf,* in other early Germanic literature, and in much Middle English NARRATIVE poetry features alternating patterns of alliteration on the accented words in the line, as in the following lines from *Piers the Plowman,* a Middle English poem by William Langland:

> In a *s*omer *s*eson whan *s*oft was the *s*onne,
> I *sh*ope me in *sh*roudes as I a *sh*epe were,
> In *h*abite as an *h*eremite un*h*oly of workes,
> Went *w*yde in this *w*orld *w*ondres to here.

See ASSONANCE, CONSONANCE.

allusion. A passing reference to historical or fictional CHARACTERS, places, or events, or to other works that the writer assumes the reader will recognize. Allusions to the Bible and to William Shakespeare's works are common because both enjoy a vast readership. Older LITERATURE contains many allusions to Greek and Roman literature, which formerly played an important role in education.

Allusions may refer to mythology, religion, literature, history, or art. Their power lies in suggestion and CONNOTATION.

They serve to evoke emotions, convey information concisely, and establish character, MOOD, and SETTING. Often in POETRY an allusion may be central to the reader's understanding and response.

"Out, Out—" is a poem by Robert Frost about the accidental death of a young boy. Its THEME is the unpredictability of life, the waste of premature death. Frost's title is an allusion to the key phrase of a famous speech in Act V, scene 5, of *Macbeth:* "Out, out, brief candle!" Frost's brief allusion evokes the SCENE in which Macbeth mourns the death of his wife and the brevity, uncertainty, and meaninglessness of life:

> She should have died hereafter;
> There would have been time for such a word.
> Tomorrow, and tomorrow, and tomorrow,
> Creeps in this petty pace from day to day,
> To the last syllable of recorded time,
> And all our yesterdays have lighted fools
> The way to dusty death. Out, out, brief candle!
> Life's but a walking shadow, a poor player
> That struts and frets his hour upon the stage
> And then is heard no more; it is a tale
> Told by an idiot, full of sound and fury,
> Signifying nothing.

William Faulkner alludes to this same passage in the title of his NOVEL *The Sound and the Fury,* part of which is "a tale/Told by an idiot."

ambiguity. Double or even multiple meaning. Unintentional ambiguity is considered a defect in scientific writing and wherever clarity is prized, as in the following telegram:

> Ship sails today.

Intentional ambiguity in the form of a PUN, or play on words, is a source of HUMOR much used by stand-up comics and writers of DIALOGUE for situation COMEDIES:

> "Your cousin is a well-digger?"
> "Yes, he really gets to the bottom of things."

The term *ambiguity* has also been applied to the richness of association valued in POETRY. Critic I. A. Richards pointed out in *Practical Criticism* that ambiguity is a natural characteristic of language that becomes heightened in poetry, partly because the language of poetry is compressed. Wrote Richards,

> A word...can equally and simultaneously represent vastly different things. It can effect extraordinary combinations of feelings. A word is a point at which many different influences may cross or unite. Hence its dangers in prose discussions and its treacherousness for careless readers of poetry, but hence at the same time the peculiar quasi-magical sway of words in the hands of a master.

A classification of kinds of ambiguity was provided by another critic, William Empson. In his famous and controversial book, *Seven Types of Ambiguity,* Empson uses the following line from William Shakespeare's Sonnet 73 to illustrate his first and most useful category of ambiguity, "language simultaneously effective in several ways":

> Upon those boughs which shake against the cold

According to Empson, *shake* simultaneously suggests that the boughs are shaking in the sense of shivering and in the sense of making a defiant gesture toward the cold, similar to shaking a fist.

See CONNOTATION.

anachronism. An event, object, custom, person, or thing that is out of its natural order in time. Anachronisms abound in Shakespeare. A striking clock chimes in *Julius Caesar,* a PLAY set long before such clocks were invented. There is a reference to billiards in *Antony and Cleopatra;* the game did not appear until about the middle of the fifteenth century. Cannons are mentioned in *King John,* a play set in a time before they were in use. While these anachronisms are unintentional, others are consciously used to achieve humorous or satirical effects. For example, Mark Twain builds an entire novel on the sustained anachronism of *A Connecticut Yankee in King Arthur's Court.*

analogy. A comparison of similar things, often for the purpose of using something familiar to explain something unfamiliar. For example, the branching of a river system is often explained by comparing it to a tree. The work of the heart is explained by comparing it to a pump. Although the two items being compared in an analogy may be similar in a number of ways, they are not identical. The whole truth about one is not the whole truth about the other. An analogy pushed beyond the points of similarity thus breaks down and loses its effectiveness.

An effective METAPHOR or SIMILE differs from an analogy in that a metaphor or a simile makes an imaginative, often unexpected, comparison between basically dissimilar things, as in these lines from Christina Rossetti's *Goblin Market:*

> Her locks streamed like a torch
> Borne by a racer at full speed.

See METAPHOR, SIMILE.

analytical criticism.   A type of OBJECTIVE CRITICISM that employs detailed verbal analysis (EXPLICATION, or "close reading") of a work, its elements, and their relationship, in order to clarify the author's meaning.

See EXPLICATION, LITERARY CRITICISM, OBJECTIVE CRITICISM, OBJECTIVE THEORY OF ART.

anapest.   A metrical FOOT consisting of three syllables: two unaccented syllables followed by one accented syllable, as in *interfere*. Originally a Greek martial rhythm, the galloping anapest creates a sense of speed and action, as in Lord Byron's *The Destruction of Sennacherib,* which begins:

> The Assyr | ian came down | like a wolf | on the fold,
> And his co | horts were gleam | ing in pur | ple and gold;
> And the sheen | of their spears | was like stars | on the
> sea,
> When the blue | wave rolls night | ly on deep | Galilee.

A musical equivalent of anapestic rhythm is found in Gioacchino Rossini's *William Tell* Overture, known to millions as the theme song of "The Lone Ranger."

See FOOT, METER.

anastrophe.   A rhetorical term for the inversion of the normal order of the parts of a sentence. Writers, especially poets, use anastrophe to place emphasis on a word or idea or to create or accommodate a certain RHYME, RHYTHM, or EUPHONY. Notice what is lost when normal word order replaces the anastrophe in these lines of poetry:

> After great pain a formal feeling comes—
> The nerves sit ceremonious like tombs.
>
> —Emily Dickinson
>
> *A formal feeling comes after great pain—*
> The nerves sit ceremonious like tombs.

> I will arise and go now, and go to Innisfree,
> And a small cabin build there, of clay and wattles made.
> —William Butler Yeats
>
> I will arise and go now, and go to Innisfree,
> *And build a small cabin there made of clay and wattles.*

anecdote.   A brief NARRATIVE of an entertaining and presumably true incident. Anecdotes are used in biographical writing, ESSAYS, and speeches to reveal a personality trait or to illustrate a point. In this excerpt from a newspaper article, Henry Louis Gates, Jr., uses an anecdote to illustrate a point about how culture critics view the predictions they make:

> We make dire predictions, and when they come true, we think we've changed the world.
>
> It's a tendency that puts me in mind of my father's favorite story about Father Divine, that historic con man of the cloth. In the 1930s, he was put on trial and convicted for using the mails to defraud. At sentencing, Father Divine stood up and told the judge: "I'm warning you, you send me to jail, something terrible is going to happen to you." Father Divine, of course, was sent to prison, and a week later, by sheer coincidence, the judge had a heart attack and died. When the warden and the guards found out about it in the middle of the night, they raced to Father Divine's cell and woke him up. "Father Divine," they said, "your judge just dropped dead of a heart attack." Without missing a beat, Father Divine lifted his head and told them: "I *hated* to do it."

As writers, teachers, or intellectuals, most of us would like
to claim greater efficacy for our labors than we're entitled to.

antagonist.   Usually, the CHARACTER in FICTION or DRAMA who
stands in direct opposition to or in conflict with the central character. For example, John Claggart is the antagonist in Herman
Melville's *Billy Budd;* Madame Merle is the antagonist in Henry
James's *The Portrait of a Lady.* In some instances the antagonist
may be a group of people, some force in nature, or some aspect
of the central character's personality or psyche.

See CHARACTER, PROTAGONIST.

anticlimax.   An effect that spoils a CLIMAX. Used deliberately, anticlimax is a stylistic device involving a witty descent from something serious or lofty to something frivolous or trivial.
Anticlimax is especially effective if a sudden descent follows a
gradual ascent, as in William Thackeray's *Vanity Fair,* when the
NARRATOR tells what Becky Sharp has to put up with in taking
care of the ailing Miss Crawley:

> Picture her to yourself, oh fair young reader, a worldly, self-
> ish, graceless, thankless, religionless old woman, writhing in
> pain and fear, and without her wig.

Unintentional anticlimax, known as BATHOS, can result if, in
trying to be sublime, a writer ends up sounding absurd, a fault
of these lines from Ann Radcliffe's *The Mysteries of Udolpho:*

> But, if between some hideous chasm yawn,
> Where the cleft pine a doubtful bridge displays,
> In dreadful silence, on the brink, forlorn
> He stands, and views in the faint rays
> Far, far below, the torrent's rising surge,
> And listens to the wild impetuous roar;
> Still eyes the depth, still shudders on the verge,
> Fears to return, nor dares to venture o'er.
> Desperate, at length the tottering plank he tries,
> His weak steps slide, he shrieks, he sinks—he dies!

In DRAMA or other FICTION, a weak or unnecessary conclusion following a strong climax is another form of unintentional
anticlimax. In a murder mystery that builds toward a climax in

which the murderer is finally revealed, a SCENE showing the murderer being routinely sentenced and sent to prison would be anticlimactic.

See BATHOS, CLIMAX.

antihero. A central CHARACTER, or PROTAGONIST, who lacks traditional heroic qualities and virtues (such as idealism, courage, and steadfastness). An antihero may be comic, antisocial, inept, or even pathetic, while retaining the sympathy of the reader. Antiheroes are typically in conflict with a world they cannot control or whose values they reject. Although elements of the antihero may be found in Miguel de Cervantes' *Don Quixote* (1605), the type is more often found in modern FICTION and DRAMA. Representative antiheroes include James Joyce's Leopold Bloom in *Ulysses;* Edith Wharton's Lily Bart in *The House of Mirth;* Clyde Griffiths in Theodore Dreiser's *An American Tragedy;* Arthur Miller's Willy Loman in *Death of a Salesman;* and Yossarian in Joseph Heller's *Catch-22.*

See CHARACTER.

antiphrasis. Verbal IRONY, in which what is said contrasts sharply with what is actually meant. See IRONY.

antithesis. **1.** A figure of speech in which opposing or contrasting ideas are balanced against each other in grammatically parallel syntax, as in the following sentence from *The Story of My Life* by Helen Keller:

> There is no king who has not had a slave among his ancestors, and no slave who has not had a king among his.

2. In reasoning by means of ARGUMENT, known as dialectic, the antithesis is the statement of the opposing viewpoint:

> *Thesis:* The money should be spent on a new gymnasium large enough to host tournaments.
> *Antithesis:* No, the money should be spent on an auditorium.
> *Synthesis:* Let's build a new gymnasium and make the old gym into an auditorium.

See EPIGRAM, OXYMORON.

anxiety of influence.   A phrase used by critic Harold Bloom to identify his theory that a poet, in attempting to preserve a sense of artistic autonomy and originality, "misreads" the work of a predecessor to avoid being influenced by it. See INFLUENCE.

aphorism.   A terse statement of a principle or truth, usually an observation about life; a maxim. Aphorisms can be witty as well as insightful, as this aphorism by George Eliot demonstrates: "The happiest women, like the happiest nations, have no history." Hippocrates, who first used the term in his *Aphorisms,* provides perhaps the most famous example:

> Life is short, art is long, opportunity fleeting,
> experimenting dangerous, reasoning difficult.

The essays of Francis Bacon are known for their aphoristic style. In "Of Studies" he writes:

> Reading maketh a full man; conference [conversation] a ready man; and writing an exact man.

See EPIGRAM.

apologue.   Any story, short or long, designed to illustrate the truth of a statement. The statement might be a moral lesson, such as "It is better to ask some of the questions than to know all the answers," illustrated by James Thurber's "The Scotty Who Knew Too Much," from *Fables for Our Time.* The statement also might be a philosophical conclusion, such as the opinion that human happiness is an impossible ideal, illustrated by Samuel Johnson's *Rasselas.* Among the different kinds of apologues are the FABLE, in which the CHARACTERS are usually animals; the ALLEGORY, in which the characters are often abstract qualities, such as virtues and vices; and the PARABLE, in which the characters are human beings, sometimes actual persons.

See ALLEGORY, EXEMPLUM, FABLE, PARABLE.

apostrophe.   The device, usually in POETRY, of calling out to an imaginary, dead, or absent person, or to a place, thing, or personified abstraction either to begin a poem or to make a dramatic break in thought somewhere within the poem. In these lines from *Childe Harold's Pilgrimage,* Lord Byron twice breaks into his description of a stormy night in the Alps to call out to the night:

> The sky is changed!—and such a change! Oh night,
> And storm, and darkness, ye are wondrous strong,
> Yet lovely in your strength, as is the light
> Of a dark eye in woman! Far along,
> From peak to peak, the rattling crags among
> Leaps the live thunder! Not from one lone cloud,
> But every mountain now hath found a tongue
> And Jura answers, through her misty shroud,
> Back to the joyous Alps, who call to her aloud!
>
> And this is in the night—most glorious night!
> Thou wert not sent for slumber! let me be
> A sharer in thy fierce and far delight—
> A portion of the tempest and of thee!

An apostrophe asking a god or goddess for inspiration, especially at the beginning of an EPIC, is an **invocation.** John Milton begins *Paradise Lost* with the invocation, "Sing, Heavenly Muse."

applied criticism.   The analysis, interpretation, and evaluation of particular works of LITERATURE, also called PRACTICAL CRITICISM. See PRACTICAL CRITICISM.

archetypal criticism.   A critical approach that describes, interprets, or evaluates a work in terms of its relationship to all other works centered on a basic situation (such as coming of age), CHARACTER type (the jealous husband), PLOT pattern (boy meets girl—girl resists—boy wins girl), IMAGE (the lily for purity), or THEME (the conflict between free will and destiny) that recurs consistently enough to be considered universal. According to critic Northrop Frye, an ARCHETYPE "recurs often enough to be recognizable as an element of one's literary experience as a whole."

See ARCHETYPE, LITERARY CRITICISM.

archetype.   A pattern or model of an action (such as lamenting the dead), a CHARACTER type (rebellious youth), or an IMAGE (paradise as a garden) that recurs consistently enough in life and LITERATURE to be considered universal. Although the term *archetype* has long been used in its most general sense, the psychoanalyst C. G. Jung gave it new meaning. He theorized that certain ideas, actions, and images—rivalry between brothers, for example—arose out of early experiences of the human race, passed along through the "collective unconscious of mankind," and are present in the subconscious of every individual. According to Jung, these archetypes emerge in the IMAGERY of dreams and also in MYTHS and other literature.

Some archetypes are used so often in certain literary GENRES that they become CONVENTIONS, or distinguishing features of the genre. For example, it is conventional for the dying hero of a folk BALLAD to announce his or her last will and testament.

See ARCHETYPAL CRITICISM, CONVENTION, SYMBOL.

argument. **1.** DISCOURSE intended to convince or persuade through appeals to reason or to the emotions, the objective being to influence belief or to motivate action.

2. A prose summary of the PLOT or idea of a work. Each of the books of John Milton's *Paradise Lost* begins with an "Argument," like this one from *Book I:*

> This first book proposes, first in brief, the whole subject, man's disobedience, and the loss thereupon of Paradise wherein he was placed: then touches the prime cause of his fall, the Serpent, or rather Satan in the Serpent; who, revolting from God, and drawing to his side many legions of angels, was by the command of God driven out of Heaven with all his crew into the great Deep.

See DESCRIPTION, DISCOURSE, EXPOSITION, NARRATION.

argumentation. A mode of writing, the purpose of which is to prove a point or to persuade the reader to accept a proposal; one of the four major types of DISCOURSE. See ARGUMENT.

Aristotelian criticism. The type of inductive, analytical LITERARY CRITICISM originated by Aristotle in his *Poetics.* Plato had charged that POETRY (by which he meant all types of LITERATURE) lacked value because it was not true, and that it was harmful because, instead of appealing to people's reason, it excited their passions. Aristotle responded by examining the literary works of his day scientifically. He analyzed the elements of each and described how the elements functioned as parts of the whole work. He took into consideration the subject matter of the work (the aspect of life that the work imitated), the means and the manner of presentation, and the effect of the work on the audience or reader. In this way he was able to discover the essential nature and function of each GENRE, or type, of literature—TRAGEDY, COMEDY, and EPIC were the major genres in which poets wrote at the time. This gave him a basis for evaluating individual works, for showing what different genres had in common and how they differed from one another, and for defending literature as a whole against Plato's condemnation.

Aristotle's defense consisted of three key ideas: (1) Literature is an IMITATION of life, combining universal psychological truths with probable events, not a literal account of actual events; (2) the beginning-middle-ending structure of a literary work engages and satisfies the mind; and (3) rather than exciting people's emotions, experiencing literature offers people a therapeutic release of emotion (CATHARSIS).

See IMITATION, LITERARY CRITICISM, PLATONIC CRITICISM.

art ballad. Another term for LITERARY BALLAD, a form of NARRATIVE POETRY that imitates the general RHYTHM and STANZA patterns of traditional FOLK BALLADS. See BALLAD.

aside. In DRAMA, a CONVENTION by which actors speak briefly to the audience, supposedly without being heard by the other actors on stage. Asides provide information to the audience about a CHARACTER's thoughts, inner feelings, and private interpretations of ongoing action. These "spoken thoughts" are sometimes used for melodramatic or comic effect. Here is an example of an aside from *The Busie Body* by Susanna Centlivre, a popular RESTORATION dramatist:

> **Miranda:** You know my father's will runs that I am not to possess my estate, without your consent, till I'm five-and-twenty; you shall only abate the odd seven years, and make me mistress of my estate today, and I'll make you

	master of my person tomorrow.
Sir Francis *(aside):*	Humph? That may not be safe.... *(To Miranda)* No, "Chargy," I'll settle it upon thee for pin-money, and that will be every bit as well, thou know'st.
Miranda *(aside):*	Unconscionable old wretch, bribe me with my own money—which way shall I get out of his hands?

See CONVENTION, MONOLOGUE, SOLILOQUY.

assonance. The close repetition of middle vowel sounds between different consonant sounds: fade/pale. Assonance is usually used within a line of POETRY for UNITY or rhythmic effect, as Edith Sitwell uses it in this line from "The Drum":

Whinnying, neighed the maned blue wind

Sitwell is famous for her experiments with carefully arranged assonant and dissonant vowels.

Assonance is sometimes used to create **near rhymes** in place of END RHYMES. FOLK BALLADS, which may have been hurriedly improvised, often rely on the near rhyme of assonance:

He had horses and harness for them all.
    Their goodly steeds were all milk-white.
O the golden bands all about their necks!
    Their weapons, they were all alike.

—from "Johnny Armstrong"

See ALLITERATION, CONSONANCE, END RHYME.

atmosphere. The pervasive MOOD or TONE of a literary work—gloom, foreboding, joyful expectation—often created and sustained by the author's treatment of landscape or SETTING and use of SYMBOLISM. For example, Emily Brontë's descriptions of the moorland setting of *Wuthering Heights* establish the powerful sense of thwarted passion and unavoidable tragedy that is sustained throughout the NOVEL. Edgar Allan Poe creates an atmosphere of foreboding in the opening sentence of his SHORT STORY "The Fall of the House of Usher":

> During the whole of a dull, dark, and soundless day in the autumn of the year, when the clouds hung oppressively low in the heavens, I had been passing alone, on horseback, through a singularly dreary tract of country, and at length found myself, as the shades of the evening drew on, within view of the melancholy House of Usher.

See MOOD, TONE.

autobiography. An account of all or a part of a person's life written by that person, usually with publication in mind. Typically, an autobiography takes the form of a continuous NARRATIVE of significant events, in which memory and introspection and even IMAGINATION are blended. The *Confessions* of St. Augustine, for example, considered the first real autobiography, presents the events of Augustine's early life as a spiritual journey and as an opportunity for self-analysis.

Although often unreliable as a record of facts, an autobiography offers unique insight into its author's personality, attitudes, and impressions. Many of the greatest autobiographies—the *Autobiography* of Benvenuto Cellini (1562), Margaret Cavendish's *True Relation of My Birth, Breeding and Life* (1656), Benjamin Franklin's *Autobiography* (1766), Jean-Jacques Rousseau's *Confessions* (1781, 1788), and Henry Adams's *The Education of Henry Adams* (1906)—also offer insight into the times in which their author-subjects lived.

Diaries, JOURNALS, and letters are autobiographical writings, but they differ from an autobiography in not being continuous narratives. A **memoir** differs from an autobiography in that it tends to focus on a single period in the writer's life—often a time that coincides with important events—and on notable people known to the writer. An example is Lillian Hellman's *Pentimento* (1973).

See BIOGRAPHY.

autotelic. A critical term used by the New Critics to describe a work of LITERATURE that is significant in and of itself. An autotelic work is one whose purpose and meaning lie wholly within itself.

See BELIEF, PROBLEM OF; NEW CRITICISM; OBJECTIVE THEORY OF ART.

B

ballad. A FORM of NARRATIVE POETRY that presents a single dramatic EPISODE, which is often tragic or violent. Ballads typically tell stories of unhappy love affairs; domestic tragedies, especially family feuds or murders; popular outlaws and rebels, such as Jesse James or Robin Hood; historical events like battles, shipwrecks, and mine disasters; and occupational heroes, such as John Henry and Casey Jones.

There are two types of ballads. The **folk ballad** is one of the earliest forms of LITERATURE. Composed anonymously and transmitted orally from generation to generation, folk ballads were originally sung or recited. They have been set down in writing only in fairly recent times. Folk ballads share several characteristics: They deal with common people rather than nobility; the supernatural plays an important role in events; the story line often develops through DIALOGUE; action, rather than CHARACTERIZATION or DESCRIPTION, is emphasized; a REFRAIN and INCREMENTAL REPETITION are common elements; the language is simple, and the RHYTHM pronounced.

Many Scottish and English ballads have survived from the MIDDLE AGES. In America the folk-ballad tradition has been kept alive in the Appalachian Mountains, among the cowboys of the Old West, and within some of the early labor movements. Here is an early Scottish folk ballad, which may recount an incident involving a clan feud or a border raid.

Bonnie George Campbell

High upon the Highlands,
  and low upon the Tay,
Bonnie George Campbell
  rade out on a day.

Saddled and bridled
  and gallant rade he;
Hame cam his guid horse,
  but never cam he.

Out cam his auld mither
  greeting fu' sair,
And out cam his bonnie bride
  riving her hair.

Saddled and bridled
  and booted rade he;
Toom hame cam the saddle,
  but never cam he.

"My meadow lies green,
  and my corn is unshorn,
My barn is to build,
  and my babe is unborn."

Saddled and bridled
  and booted rade he;
Toom hame cam the saddle,
  but never cam he.

Written by known authors, the **literary ballad** is a studied imitation of the general rhythmic pattern and STANZA form of the folk ballad. These **art ballads,** as they are sometimes called, are more polished and consciously artful than folk ballads and often contain the more elevated language and poetic DICTION of the professional poet. Some well-known English literary ballads are "La Belle Dame sans Merci" by John Keats, *The Rime of the Ancient Mariner* by Samuel Taylor Coleridge, and Sir Walter Scott's "Rosabelle." American literary ballads include Henry Wadsworth Longfellow's "The Skeleton in Armor," Stephen Vincent Benet's "The Ballad of William Sycamore," and Ernest Thayer's "Casey at the Bat."

See BALLAD STANZA, INCREMENTAL REPETITION, REFRAIN.

ballad stanza.   The STANZA form of the BALLAD, usually four lines rhyming *abcb.* The first and third lines typically contain four accented syllables; the second and fourth lines, three accented syllables. The number of unaccented syllables varies widely. A REFRAIN, usually at the end of the stanza, is common. A representative example is this stanza from "The Douglas Tragedy," a FOLK BALLAD:

He's mounted her on a milk-white steed   a

And himself on a dapple grey,   b

With a buglet horn hung down by his side,   c

And lightly they rode away.   b

See BALLAD, METER, REFRAIN, RHYME SCHEME, STANZA.

baroque.   Possessing a grand and exuberantly ornamented style. First applied to seventeenth-century art (the paintings of Caravaggio, Van Dyck, Rembrandt), architecture (St. Peter's in Rome; St. Paul's in London), and music (the *Passions* of J. S. Bach; operas by Claudio Monteverdi), the term *baroque* has gradually been adopted by literary critics. The CONCEITS of John Donne and the other METAPHYSICAL POETS have been called baroque, as have the extravagant and even bizarre IMAGES of Richard Vaughan, as well as the rich yet grandly coherent STYLE of John Milton's *Paradise Lost.* Some literary historians have joined art and music historians in giving the name **baroque era** to the years between the RENAISSANCE and the Enlightenment, 1580 to 1680.

See CONCEIT.

bathos.   Excessive sentimentality or ludicrousness. Bathos is produced by an unsuccessful attempt to elicit pity or sorrow from the reader. Bathos also results when elevated language and style are used inappropriately in treating a commonplace subject. These lines from William Wordsworth's poem "Simon Lee" provide an example of writing that attempts to wring tears from the reader but unintentionally produces laughter instead:

Few months of life has he in store
As he to you will tell,
For still, the more he works, the more
Do his weak ankles swell.

Used intentionally for humorous or satiric effect, the juxtaposition of the elevated with the trivial is an ANTICLIMAX, as in this COUPLET from Alexander Pope's *Rape of the Lock:*

Not louder shrieks to pitying Heaven are cast,
When husbands or when lap dogs breathe their last.

See ANTICLIMAX, PATHOS.

beat generation.   A group of poets and other writers of the 1950s and early 1960s, who expressed their alienation from society by rebelling against both social and literary CONVENTIONS. They grew beards, wore blue jeans and sandals, experimented with Zen Buddhist meditation and hallucinogens, and spoke and wrote in private slang, all of which was startling behavior in the conformist 1950s.

The word *beat* might be assumed to imply that these writers were weary of life. However, Jack Kerouac, whose loosely structured novel *On the Road* made him the most widely known of the group, pointed out that *beat,* short for *beatific,* suggested that the beat generation was "basically a religious generation," on a new spiritual quest. Beat poets Allen Ginsberg, Gregory Corso, and Lawrence Ferlinghetti found their audience in the San Francisco coffeehouses of the late 1950s, where they read their works aloud, sometimes to the accompaniment of jazz drumbeats. Ginsberg's long poem *Howl* is considered the major work of the movement.

belief, problem of.   The question of to what degree a reader's response to a literary work is affected by that reader's belief or disbelief in the version of "truth" (doctrines, religious or philosophical assumptions) set forth in the work. Can a reader value a poem as a work of art if he or she finds the poem's implicit or explicit doctrine unacceptable? Or more generally, if literature presents statements of truth, what is the reader to make of two excellent works whose worldviews are mutually exclusive?

Traditionally, the relation between "the truth" expounded by the work and "the actual truth" as held by the reader was considered crucial to the reader's valuing of the work. During the twentieth century, however, this position has been attacked by critics, among them advocates of NEW CRITICISM, who hold that the AESTHETIC value of a work and the acceptability of its "truth" are totally independent of each other.

See AUTOTELIC, NEW CRITICISM.

bildungsroman. A German word that, translated literally, means "development NOVEL." Coined by German critics to describe Johann Wolfgang von Goethe's novel *Wilhelm Meisters Lehrjahre* ("Wilhelm Meister's Apprenticeship"), the term *bildungsroman* is applied to a novel that traces the early education of its HERO from youth to experience. Examples are Charles Dickens' *David Copperfield,* Charlotte Brontë's *Jane Eyre,* Hermann Hesse's *Demian,* Saul Bellow's *The Adventures of Augie March,* and Doris Lessing's five-volume *Children of Violence.*

A novel telling the story of an artist's development, such as Thomas Mann's *Tonio Kröger* or James Joyce's *A Portrait of the Artist as a Young Man,* is a type of bildungsroman known as a **Künstlerroman** ("artist-novel").

See NOVEL.

biographical fallacy. The error of relying on an understanding of an author's life as the chief means of analyzing and interpreting his or her work. The heavy use of biographical information as an approach to CRITICISM is considered a fallacy by advocates of NEW CRITICISM, who maintain that the meaning and significance of a literary work reside within the work itself, without reference to the author's intention or life.

See INTENTIONAL FALLACY, LITERARY CRITICISM.

biography. A written account of a person's life that focuses on the character and career of the subject. Ideally, a biography is an accurate life history of a particular person, placed in the times in which he or she lived, but centered on a well-rounded and factual portrait of personality, character, and habits of mind. Elizabeth Gaskell's *Life of Charlotte Brontë* is an example of such a biography. Perhaps the most famous biography in English is James Boswell's *The Life of Samuel Johnson, LL.D.* Even today, to be an admiring biographer is to be a "Boswell."

Some biographies are attempts to debunk the false reputations that have built up around their subjects. The first and most famous of such critical biographies is Lytton Strachey's collection of four biographical sketches, *Eminent Victorians.*

An AUTOBIOGRAPHY is a life written by the subject; a biography is a life written by someone other than the subject.

See AUTOBIOGRAPHY.

black humor.   Humorous effects resulting largely from GROTESQUE, morbid, or macabre situations dealing with a horrifying and disoriented world. Characteristic chiefly of modern DRAMA and FICTION, such as the works of Eugène Ionesco (*The Lesson*), Vladimir Nabokov (*Lolita*), Joseph Heller (*Catch-22*), and Kurt Vonnegut, Jr. (*Slaughterhouse Five*), black humor aims to shock and disorient readers, making them laugh in the face of anxiety, suffering, or death. Sometimes also called **black comedy,** it is an important element in plays of the THEATER OF THE ABSURD. The controversial comedian Lenny Bruce brought black humor to the nightclub circuit, and Stanley Kubrick (*Dr. Strangelove*) took it to the movies.

blank verse.   POETRY written in unrhymed IAMBIC PENTAMETER. Blank verse should not be confused with FREE VERSE. It is "blank" only in the sense that its lines do not RHYME; it is not metrically blank.

These famous lines from Christopher Marlowe's *Dr. Faustus* exemplify the qualities of blank verse:

> Was this the face that launched a thousand ships
> And burned the topless towers of Ilium?
> Sweet Helen, make me immortal with a kiss.

Blank verse is uniquely suitable for poetic DRAMA and other long NARRATIVE or reflective poems because of its closeness to natural speech RHYTHMS, its lack of rhyme, and its rhythmic flexibility.

Employed extensively and brilliantly in dramatic DIALOGUE by Marlowe, William Shakespeare, and the other ELIZABETHAN playwrights, developed by John Milton into a vehicle for his great EPIC *Paradise Lost,* rediscovered by the nineteenth-century romantic poets, and revived in a freer form by T. S. Eliot and Maxwell Anderson in their verse plays, blank verse has been used for serious poetry more than any other English VERSE FORM.

See IAMBIC PENTAMETER.

blend.   A word formed by combining two or more words, for example, *brunch* (*br*eakfast + l*unch*). See PORTMANTEAU WORDS.

bluestocking. A nickname for intellectual and literary women in eighteenth-century English society, especially those who gathered for conversation with literary men instead of for the more usual cardplaying. The group that met at the home of Elizabeth Montague was called "The Blue Stocking Society" after one of its male members happened to wear blue stockings instead of black. In addition to Montague, famous bluestockings included Fanny Burney and Hannah More.

book. A division in a long NOVEL or NARRATIVE POEM. Also, another term for LIBRETTO; the text or words of an opera, oratorio, cantata, musical comedy, or similar musical work. See LIBRETTO.

bourgeois tragedy. Another term for **domestic tragedy;** a TRAGEDY concerning a middle- or lower-class PROTAGONIST who suffers a personal disaster. See TRAGEDY.

bowdlerize. To remove immoral or indecent passages from a NOVEL, PLAY, or other piece of writing. The practice is named after Thomas Bowdler, who in 1818 published an edition of William Shakespeare's plays called *The Family Shakespeare.* Bowdler's editing of Shakespeare included removing whatever he thought was "unfit to be read by a gentleman in a company of ladies."

See CENSORSHIP.

Breton lay. A NARRATIVE adventure poem written in fourteenth-century England that imitated the LAIS of Marie de France (*Breton* means "from Brittany," a region of France). See LAI.

broadside. A large sheet of paper printed on one side only and meant for distribution or posting. BALLADS published in this manner in England (especially during the sixteenth century) were called **broadside ballads,** or simply **broadsides.** Their quality and subject matter varied widely: hack-written accounts of executions or disasters, reproductions of traditional ballads, religious and political attacks, satires, and personal attacks. They were popular in England well into the nineteenth century.

burlesque. In general, any kind of satiric imitation. Used more precisely, the term *burlesque* usually refers to a theater piece, poem, or work of FICTION that spoofs a literary or theatrical GENRE, often poking fun at customs, institutions, and personages in the process. Geoffrey Chaucer's "Tale of Sir Topaz" and Miguel de Cervantes' *Don Quixote* are burlesques of the CHIVALRIC RO-MANCE. John Gay's *The Beggar's Opera* spoofs eighteenth-century Italian opera. One of the most famous burlesques is the rustics' performance of the TRAGEDY of "Pyramis and Thisbe" in William Shakespeare's *A Midsummer Night's Dream,* and another is Charles Dickens' takeoff on amateur productions of Shakespeare in *Nicholas Nickleby.*

The most important characteristic of burlesque is the discrepancy between its STYLE and its content. **High burlesque** presents trivial content in an ironically lofty style, often as a MOCK EPIC. In Alexander Pope's *Rape of the Lock*, for example, the stealing of a lock of a young woman's hair is presented as an event of epic proportions and consequences. **Low burlesque** treats serious content lightly or even grotesquely. "Springtime for Hitler," the musical comedy being planned in Mel Brooks's film *The Producers* is an example of low burlesque, also known, when it is GROTESQUE enough, as **travesty.**

PARODY differs from burlesque by being a satiric imitation of an author's style or of the style of an individual work, rather than of a genre. CARICATURE is DESCRIPTION of CHARACTER that exaggerates traits of appearance or personality for comic effect.

See CARICATURE, MOCK EPIC, PARODY, SATIRE.

C

cacophony. Harsh, clashing, or dissonant sounds, often produced by combinations of words that require a clipped, explosive delivery, or words that contain a number of plosive consonants such as *b, d, g, k, p,* and *t;* the opposite of EUPHONY.

The following lines from Edgar Allan Poe's "The Bells" are cacophonous:

> Hear the loud alarum bells—
> Brazen bells!
> What a tale of terror, now, their turbulency tells!

See EUPHONY, SOUND DEVICES.

caesura. A pause within a line of POETRY, often resulting from the natural RHYTHM of language and not necessarily indicated by punctuation. Skillful poets use the caesura to ease the stiffness of a metrical line without changing the metrical count. A caesura usually occurs near the middle of the line. Sometimes there is more than one caesura in a line. The last four lines of Elizabeth Barrett Browning's famous SONNET demonstrate subtle variation in the placement of the caesura:

> I love thee // with a love I seemed to lose
> With my lost saints. // I love thee with the breath,
> Smiles, tears, // of all my life! // and, if God choose,
> I shall but love thee better // after death.

See METER, RHYTHM.

canon.   Generally, any group of writings that has been established as authentic; more specifically, those books of the Christian Bible that are accepted as Scripture.

The term is used to describe collectively those works of a particular author that have been proven or are considered genuine, such as the canon made up of William Shakespeare's thirty-seven plays. Currently *canon* is often used to identify the classical and contemporary literature "authorized" by schools and universities as the core of literary study.

canto.   A subdivision of an EPIC or other long NARRATIVE poem. Originally meaning "a song singable in one sitting," a canto is comparable to a chapter of a NOVEL. In *The Divine Comedy,* for example, Dante typically devotes one or two cantos to the journey through each circle of the Inferno. The canto is also used as a subdivision in Edmund Spenser's *The Faerie Queene,* Alexander Pope's *Rape of the Lock,* and Lord Byron's *Childe Harold's Pilgrimage.*
See EPIC.

caricature.   Descriptive writing that exaggerates specific features of appearance or personality, usually for comic effect; also, a CHARACTER developed in such a manner. Many of Charles Dickens' characters are caricatures, for example: Jerry Cruncher, the "Resurrection Man" in *A Tale of Two Cities;* Uriah Heep, the " 'umble" clerk in *David Copperfield;* and Sairey Gamp in *Martin Chuzzlewit.* Caricatures are sometimes labeled by their names, as is Lydia Languish, a character in Richard Brinsley Sheridan's *The Rivals.*
See BURLESQUE, CHARACTER, CHARACTERIZATION, PARODY.

Caroline.   From *Carolus,* the Latin form of Charles, the term refers to the reign of Charles I of England (1625–1649). During this period the conflict between supporters of the king (CAVALIERS) and their Puritan opponents erupted into civil war. The era came to an end when a victorious Puritan Parliament removed Charles from the throne and closed the theaters. LYRIC POETRY flourished during the reign of Charles I, while DRAMA declined. Applied to the writers of the period, the term *Caroline* is usually reserved for those who supported the king and who were known as the Cavalier poets—Thomas Carew, Richard Lovelace, Sir John Suckling, and Robert Herrick. The great Puritan poet, John Milton, was also writing during this period, as were John Donne, George Herbert, Richard Crashaw, and Henry Vaughan.

See CAVALIER.

carpe diem.   A Latin phrase meaning "seize the day," used to designate a THEME or MOTIF, especially in LYRIC POETRY, that warns about the brevity of life and the finality of death. The origin of the phrase is Horace's *Odes*.

A common example of the *carpe diem* theme is the rose motif, in which the blooming and fading of the rose symbolizes the brevity of life. The rose motif was used by CAVALIER poet Robert Herrick:

> Gather ye rosebuds while ye may,
>> Old time is still a-flying;
> And this same flower that smiles today,
>> Tomorrow will be dying.

The concern with the passing of time, which is a basic element of the *carpe diem* theme, has continued in LITERATURE up to the present. It is evident in the poetry of John Keats, Emily Dickinson, and Dylan Thomas, among others.

catalog.   A long list of anything; an inventory (such as of an important person's ancestors, of the names of the Greek ships that sailed to Troy, of the physical charms of one's beloved) used to emphasize quantity or inclusiveness. A conventional feature of ancient sacred texts, classical EPICS, and African praise songs, the catalog is also used by modern writers. Poets Walt Whitman, Vachel Lindsay, and Carl Sandburg are particularly known for accumulating details in lengthy catalogs. Among Sandburg's catalogs are lists of TALL TALES and of definitions of poetry. Richard Wright's autobiographical NOVEL *Black Boy* includes a catalog of twenty-five superstitions. The catalogs of modern writers usually do not attempt to provide complete inventories but rather to suggest the proliferation of something—a certain type of name for shopping malls, for example, as in Joan Didion's essay:

> They float on the landscape like pyramids to the boom years, all those Plazas and Malls and Esplanades. All those Squares and Fairs. All those Towns and Dales, all those Villages, all those Forests and Parks and Lands. Stonestown. Hillsdale. Valley Fair, Mayfair, Northgate, Southgate, Eastgate, Westgate, Gulfgate. They are toy garden cities in which no one lives but everyone consumes.

See EPIC.

catastrophe. The final action that brings a PLAY, particularly a TRAGEDY, to its conclusion. Ancient DRAMA divided the structure of classical tragedy into five parts: EXPOSITION (introduction), RISING ACTION, CLIMAX, FALLING ACTION, and catastrophe. The catastrophe presents the tragic downfall—usually the death—of the HERO as a natural consequence of the preceding action. For example, the catastrophe in *Macbeth* occurs in Act V with the coming of Birnam wood to Dunsinane and the deaths of Lady Macbeth and Macbeth. In modern drama the term DENOUEMENT, applied to both tragedy and COMEDY, has replaced *catastrophe* to identify the concluding action of a play.

See DRAMATURGY, FREYTAG'S PYRAMID.

catharsis. According to Aristotle, the power of TRAGEDY to purge the emotions of pity and fear that its incidents have aroused. Critics have long debated what Aristotle may have meant by the term *catharsis*. The traditional viewpoint is that he was referring to the emotional release that watching a tragedy offers the audience. An alternative interpretation is that the catharsis, or purification, takes place within the world of the PLAY's action. Most critics agree that tragic catharsis ultimately affects the audience and that it has something to do with the sense of awe and deep satisfaction, even exaltation, that the audience feels at the tremendous force of the CONFLICT, at the HERO's recognition of tragic waste, and at the return to order in the tragic universe.

See ARISTOTELIAN CRITICISM, TRAGEDY.

Cavalier. The name given to Royalist supporters of Charles I of England (1624–1649). Most of the **Cavalier poets**—chief among them Robert Herrick, Thomas Carew, Sir John Suckling, and Richard Lovelace—were soldiers and courtiers who wrote light-hearted LYRIC POETRY that celebrated love, loyalty, CHIVALRY, and bravery. Because they were influenced by the poetic principles and style of Ben Jonson, poets of the Cavalier school were also called the "sons of Ben."

Cavalier poetry consisted of lyrics marked by their gaiety, gracefulness, melodiousness, and polish, and by their art in exhibiting classical Latin influences. Like Lovelace's "To Althea from Prison" and Carew's "Epitaph on the Lady Mary Villers," many of the poems were OCCASIONAL VERSE.

As an illustration of Cavalier STYLE, TONE, and subject matter, here is Lovelace's "To Lucasta, on Going to the Wars":

Tell me not, sweet, I am unkind,
  That from the nunnery
Of thy chaste breast and quiet mind
  To war and arms I fly,

True, a new mistress now I chase,
  The first foe in the field;
And with a stronger faith embrace
  A sword, a horse, a shield.

Yet this inconstancy is such
  As thou too shalt adore;
I could not love thee, dear, so much,
  Loved I not honor more.

See CAROLINE, LYRIC.

censorship. Suppressing or deleting portions of books, PLAYS, films, newspapers, magazines, radio and television programs, and other art forms or communications media that are considered irreligious, immoral, or politically dangerous. Most obvious during wartime, in puritanical societies, and under totalitarian governments, where even personal letters are inspected by an official censor, censorship is also at work in subtle ways in freer times and places, often with profit as the motive. Movie producers, for example, sometimes remove potentially objectionable material from scripts to make sure the movie will receive a PG rating and the greater money-making potential the PG brings with it. Newspaper and magazine publishers and radio and television producers practice a similar form of self-censorship to avoid losing advertisers; book publishers are wary of manuscripts that may offend a large portion of their market.

Censorship has had a long and sporadic history. Many authors, ranging from Aristophanes in the fifth century B.C. to Salman Rushdie in the twentieth century, have fought for freedom of expression against the threat of censorship. The most famous argument against the suppression of books is contained in a few lines from John Milton's ESSAY on censorship, *Areopagitica:*

> As good almost kill a man as kill a good book: who kills a man kills a reasonable creature, God's image; but he who destroys a good book, kills reason itself.

See BOWDLERIZE, PORNOGRAPHY.

character.   A person in a literary work. Unlike a person in real life, a literary character's personal qualities and actions are limited by his or her function in the story, whether the character seems designed to fit the PLOT or the plot is derived from the character. At the center of the plot is the **hero,** or **protagonist.** The hero is usually an admirable figure. An exception is the **antihero,** an inept or otherwise ridiculous character who is presented sympathetically. The plot follows what happens to the hero and is determined by the hero's characteristics and choices as well as by circumstance.

The **antagonist** is a character in conflict with the hero and is usually less admirable than the hero. Sometimes the antagonist is a **villain** (a completely unadmirable figure), as in MELODRAMAS, some westerns, DETECTIVE STORIES, and ROMANCES.

In many PLAYS and in some stories, the hero has a **confidant** to talk to, enabling the audience or reader to become aware of the hero's MOTIVATION. In westerns, the confidant is called a *sidekick.* Tonto is the confidant of the Lone Ranger. The confidant, the antagonist, or some other character may also serve as a **foil** to the hero. A foil contrasts with the hero in a way that illuminates one or more significant traits, attitudes, or actions of the hero. In *Vanity Fair,* Amelia's goodness, faith in people, and mediocre intelligence make her a foil for the wicked, cynical, and brilliant Becky Sharp.

A **choral character,** a remnant of the CHORUS in Greek DRAMA, is a character whose role is to comment on the actions of the main characters. Often used in plays to substitute for NARRATIVE comment, a choral character may represent conventional wisdom or the author's own views. In Molière's *Tartuffe,* for example, Cleante is the voice of reason and wisdom.

A **narrator** who tells a story from the FIRST-PERSON POINT OF VIEW is also a character in that story, either a main-character narrator like Jane Eyre or a minor-character observer narrator like Mrs. Dean in *Wuthering Heights.*

Even though fictional characters do not have a life beyond the story, they carry with them the illusion of being real people. Some characters seem real because they possess a recognizably universal personality trait, such as stinginess, naiveté, deceitfulness, or loyalty. Known as **type** characters, they derive from and appeal to the human habit of stereotyping, of seeing people in terms of one prominent trait. Greek COMEDY established several of these types as **stock characters**, characters who have kept turning up in literary works through the centuries: the naive country bumpkin; the imposter; the boasting soldier; the self-effacing trickster; and the scapegoat. More stock characters developed from the PERSONIFICATIONS of virtues and vices and other abstract qualities who peopled the MORALITY PLAYS and other ALLEGORIES of the MIDDLE AGES. One of the most popular of these was, in fact, called Vice. Ancestor of William Shakespeare's Puck in *A Midsummer Night's Dream* and of Ariel in *The Tempest,* Vice was a comic mischief-maker.

More lifelike than single-trait characters are characters who are collections of universal and particular traits. They give the illusion of individuality and depth. Shakespeare's Falstaff is based on a stock character—the bragging soldier who is really a coward. But many particular traits are incorporated in his character: He is old, fat, charming, witty, conniving, affectionate, sentimental, at times merely clever, but elsewhere wise; a gentleman and an officer, a rogue, a philosopher, a drunkard, a womanizer, a skillful orator, a father figure for Prince Hal, a liar...the list goes on. Falstaff may be the most lifelike fictional character in English literature.

Dynamic characters, characters who change significantly during the course of a story, carry with them the reality of human growth and decline. This is especially true of heroes and heroines with whom readers identify. Dynamic characters are not necessarily more true-to-life than **static,** or unchanging, **characters,** however. As author and critic Mary McCarthy pointed out, in many works the comic characters—Falstaff, Mr. and Mrs. Micawber, Molly Bloom—seem far more real than the hero or heroine because they do not change: "What we recognize as reality in these figures," argued McCarthy, "is their implacable resistance to change."

See ANTAGONIST, ANTIHERO, CHARACTERIZATION, HERO, NARRATOR, PLOT, PROTAGONIST.

characterization. The method by which an author creates the appearance and personality of imaginary persons and reveals their CHARACTER. Characterization—the ability to bring the people of his or her imagination to life for the reader—is judged one of the most important attributes of a writer of FICTION. Successful characterization is also crucial to the development of a NARRATIVE, since the events that move the story forward are often strongly influenced by the natures of the persons involved.

Basically, there are three methods of characterization:

1. Direct DESCRIPTION of physical appearance and explanation of character traits and attributes. This description may occur either in an introduction or in statements distributed throughout the work. Essentially, the author *tells* the reader what sort of person the character is.

2. Presentation of the character in action, without interpretive comment by the author. Essentially, the author *shows* the reader what sort of person the character is through what the character says and does and what is said by other characters. As a "witness" to the character's actions, the reader is free to draw his or her own conclusions.

3. Representation of the character's inner self. Essentially, the author describes the thoughts and emotions triggered in the character by external events. A classic example is Molly Bloom's STREAM-OF-CONSCIOUSNESS SOLILOQUY in James Joyce's *Ulysses*.

In extended fiction, such as the NOVEL, all three of these approaches may be used. However, the method of characterization is often the result of an author's choice of POINT OF VIEW. Direct description (method 1) usually occurs when the story is told from the FIRST-PERSON POINT OF VIEW or the OMNISCIENT POINT OF VIEW. Representation of a character's inner self (method 3) results when an author chooses a THIRD-PERSON POINT OF VIEW that is limited to the internal responses of a single person, often revealed through INTERIOR MONOLOGUE.

A character that is fully developed as a complex, three-dimensional person is called a **round character.** Generally, major characters in fiction are presented as fully rounded personalities. If, instead, the author chooses to focus a characterization on a single dominant trait, the result is a **flat** or **thin character.** Such a two-dimensional character becomes a CARICATURE if the trait is exaggerated and is specific to a particular person, or a STEREOTYPE if the characterization represents a universal type or a **stock character.** Minor characters in fiction are often flat and frequently function as FOILS for major characters.

Finally, a character may be either static or dynamic. A **static character** changes little or not at all through the course of the narrative. While things happen to and around static characters, things do not happen within them. A **dynamic character** is changed by the actions in which he or she is involved. In fact, authors often create dynamic characters in order to reveal the effects of events on their development as human beings. George Eliot's Silas Marner is both round and dynamic; he is a fully developed character that changes in response to a series of events. Dunstan Cass, a minor character in the same novel, is flat and static, entering the novel a wild, reckless, and dissolute bully and leaving it unchanged.

See CHARACTER, PLOT.

chiasmus. A form of ANTITHESIS (a grammatically balanced statement of contrasting or opposing ideas) in which the second half of the statement inverts the word order of the first half:

> Ask not what your country can do for you; ask what you can do for your country.
> —John F. Kennedy

See ANTITHESIS.

chivalric romance. An episodic ADVENTURE STORY of the MIDDLE AGES, usually in VERSE, in which the main CHARACTER is a *cheva-*

lier, or knight on horseback, who fights monsters, dragons, and evil knights and saves damsels in distress. In the course of these adventures, or quests, the knight is expected to follow the codes of CHIVALRY and COURTLY LOVE, serving his lord and, especially, his lady bravely and with devoted loyalty. Often he operates in a world in which MEDIEVAL Christian values are imposed on magical events and supernatural figures, remnants of the pagan sources of the chivalric romance.

Ancestors of the NOVEL, most chivalric romances are loosely structured tales based on stories of the legendary HEROES of Greece and Rome (as in "The Knight's Tale" from *Canterbury Tales* and *Troilus and Criseyde* by Geoffrey Chaucer), and on the legends growing out of British folklore about King Arthur and the knights of the Round Table. In England, the best known Arthurian works are *Sir Gawain and the Green Knight* and Sir Thomas Malory's *Le Morte d'Arthur.* Chrétien de Troyes's *Yvain,* Wolfram von Eschenbach's *Parzifal,* and Gottfried von Strassburg's *Tristan und Isolde* are well-known French and German stories of Arthurian knights.

See CHIVALRY, COURTLY LOVE, NOVEL, ROMANCE.

chivalry. The code of conduct of the feudal court, especially of the MEDIEVAL knight. Originating in France and Spain and spreading to England, this system of manners and morals reached its height during the twelfth and thirteenth centuries. Bound by the conventions of chivalry and COURTLY LOVE, knights were expected to practice the virtues of loyalty, bravery, piety, and honor. They were pledged to champion ladies in distress, to defend the weak, to be absolutely faithful to their king, and to be devoted to a single, unattainable ladylove. The familiar portrait of the medieval knight in action is idealized, more the product of literature than of real life.

Chivalry has provided the subject matter for medieval RO-MANCES; HISTORICAL NOVELS, such as Sir Walter Scott's *Ivanhoe;* and the many renderings of the Arthurian LEGEND, including Sir Thomas Malory's *Le Morte d'Arthur,* Alfred, Lord Tennyson's *Idylls of the King,* T. H. White's *The Once and Future King,* and Mary Stewart's *Hollow Hills* series.

See CHIVALRIC ROMANCE, ROMANCE.

choral character. A CHARACTER whose role is to comment on the actions of the main characters; derived from the CHORUS in Greek DRAMA. See CHARACTER.

chorus. 1. In Greek DRAMA, a group of CHARACTERS whose lines, originally sung, comment on the action of each EPISODE or serve as a break between episodes.

In the great Greek TRAGEDIES of Aeschylus, Sophocles, and Euripides, the role of the chorus shifted from participating in the action of the PLAY to serving as concerned but objective bystanders whose reactions created emotional ATMOSPHERE and FORESHADOWING. The chorus also provided moral judgments on the actions of the main characters.

Although in later times the chorus gradually disappeared from most drama, it survives in opera and musical comedy. Some plays and NOVELS include one or more characters, known as **choral characters,** who comment on the action. The group of good wives at the beginning of Nathaniel Hawthorne's *The Scarlet Letter,* the rustic characters in George Eliot's *Silas Marner,* Seth Beckwith in Eugene O'Neill's *Mourning Becomes Electra,* the Stage Manager in Thornton Wilder's *Our Town,* and the group narrator of Mary McCarthy's *The Group* are all examples of choral characters.

2. In songs, another term for a REFRAIN, a phrase, line, or group of lines repeated at intervals.

See CHARACTER, REFRAIN, TRAGEDY.

chronicle play. Generally, a play having a historical THEME, with SCENES loosely connected by the chronology of historical events. Specifically, a type of DRAMA popular during the time of Elizabeth I, based on the events of a particular king's or queen's reign and characterized by large casts and such pageantry as onstage battles. William Shakespeare's *Henry VI, Richard III,* and *King Henry IV, Part 1* and *Part 2* are representative of the type.

chronological primitivism. An attitude or belief that values the past over the present. See PRIMITIVISM.

cinquain. In general, any five-line STANZA. A cinquain is also a single-stanza poem invented by the American poet Adelaide Crapsey while she was translating Japanese poetry. Similar to the

Japanese TANKA, her cinquain consists of five unrhymed lines with, in order, two, four, six, eight, and two syllables. "November Night" is a cinquain by Crapsey:

Listen...
With faint dry sound,
Like steps of passing ghosts,
The leaves, frost-crisped, break from the trees
And fall.

See HAIKU, TANKA.

classic. **1.** A work of LITERATURE that is universally acknowledged to be superior to other works of the same type and to be of enduring value and appeal. In this sense, Jane Austen's *Pride and Prejudice* is a classic of English literature. The origin of the term can be traced to the Romans, who called their best authors *classici auctores,* meaning "authors of the first or highest class."

2. The literature of ancient Greece and Rome; also **classical.** In this sense, it can be said that William Shakespeare's plays demonstrate his knowledge of the classics.

3. A description applied to any work or literary period that exhibits the qualities found in the literature of Greece and Rome, especially technical precision, balance, clarity, restraint, rationality, and the emphasis of FORM over content; also **classical, neoclassic.** In this sense, John Dryden's ode "Alexander's Feast; or, The Power of Music" is a neoclassic masterpiece.

See NEOCLASSICISM.

classicism (in criticism). Discussing and ultimately judging a literary work in terms of principles derived from admired qualities in the CLASSICS of Greek and Roman LITERATURE. The list of qualities varies but usually includes well-proportioned, unified FORM, emotional restraint, OBJECTIVITY, and lack of eccentricity. Classicism is often contrasted with, even pitted against, ROMANTICISM. Johann Wolfgang von Goethe went so far as to equate classicism with health and romanticism with sickness.

See CLASSIC, LITERARY CRITICISM, NEOCLASSICISM, ROMANTICISM.

cliché. Any expression that has been used so often it has lost its freshness and precision. Expressions like "tried and true," "sharp as a tack," "nipped in the bud," "the last straw," and "sadder but wiser" are clichés. By extension, *cliché* has also come to mean any hackneyed, or timeworn, PLOT, THEME, or situation in FICTION or DRAMA.

climax. The moment of highest intensity and interest in a DRAMA or story. The climax is usually also the **crisis** or TURNING POINT of the fortunes of the PROTAGONIST, the peak of the RISING ACTION. In some works the climax follows closely upon the turning point. The murder of Desdemona is the climax of William Shakespeare's *Othello;* the turning point is Othello's vow to kill her.

    See FREYTAG'S PYRAMID, PLOT, RISING ACTION, TURNING POINT.

closed couplet. A pair of rhymed lines of POETRY in which thought and grammatical structure are complete; called a HEROIC COUPLET when the lines are in IAMBIC PENTAMETER. See COUPLET, HEROIC COUPLET.

coherence. A quality of composition in which the parts or ideas of a piece of writing are so logically and clearly arranged and presented that the reader can follow the progression from one part or idea to the next without difficulty. A coherent sentence is one in which words, phrases, and clauses are logically related, a sentence that "holds together." Similarly, a longer work is coherent when its parts—sentences, paragraphs, chapters, STANZAS, SCENES, acts—form a clearly sequential, cohesive whole. Coherence is often linked with UNITY and EMPHASIS as the basic requirements of composition.

colloquialism. A word or phrase in everyday use in conversation and informal writing, but sometimes inappropriate in a formal ESSAY.

> Carol *won't let on,* but I know she had *a lot* of trouble getting her car *fixed.*

Bergen Evans pointed out that a colloquialism has often been compared to a good business suit, appropriate dress for almost any occasion, while formal language, like formal wear, has only restricted use.

comedy. In general, any literary work that aims to amuse by dealing with humorous, familiar situations involving ordinary people speaking everyday language. In particular, a PLAY written primarily to amuse or entertain and usually having a happy ending. While TRAGEDY often begins in happy circumstances and ends in disaster, comedy often begins with its CHARACTERS in difficult but amusing situations that are happily resolved at the end. While the characters of tragedy tend to be idealized, noble, or almost godlike, the characters of comedy are—more realistically—average (or worse) human beings.

It is sometimes difficult to distinguish comedy from other dramatic forms because comedy can have a serious purpose and tone and because a happy ending is not mandatory. It differs from BURLESQUE and FARCE in having a more carefully structured PLOT, more subtle and sensible DIALOGUE, more natural characters, and less slapstick humor. Crude, boisterous comedy filled with buffoonery and coarse jokes is called **low comedy.** In contrast, witty, subtle, polished comedy that appeals to the intellect is called **high comedy.**

There are many different kinds of comedy. The **comedy of humors,** written by Ben Jonson and John Fletcher among others, is a play in which each character's actions are dictated by some exaggerated trait, or HUMOR. The characters are PERSONIFICATIONS of particular humors and, like George Downright in Jonson's *Every Man in His Humour,* are often given characterizing names.

The **comedy of intrigue** is a play in which plot manipulation is more important than CHARACTERIZATION. A writer of such comedies in seventeenth-century England was Aphra Behn, whose most popular plays were *The Rover* and *The City Heiress.*

The **comedy of manners** presents the manners and social code of a sophisticated society in which WIT and polished behavior are valued over fundamental morality. Molière, William Congreve, Oliver Goldsmith, Richard Brinsley Sheridan, Susanna Centlivre, Oscar Wilde, Somerset Maugham, Noël Coward, and Philip Barry all wrote comedies of manners.

See HUMOR; HUMORS, THEORY OF; RESTORATION COMEDY; TRAGEDY.

comedy of humors. A FORM of COMEDY in which each CHARAC-
TER's actions are dictated by some exaggerated trait, or HUMOR.
See COMEDY; HUMORS, THEORY OF.

comedy of intrigue. A FORM of COMEDY in which PLOT is more important than CHARACTERIZATION. See COMEDY.

comedy of manners. A FORM of COMEDY set in sophisticated society, where WIT and polished behavior are valued over morality.
See COMEDY, RESTORATION COMEDY.

comic relief. In a TRAGEDY or other serious work, a humorous INCI-
DENT, action, or remark that relieves emotional tension. The
contrast offered by comic relief can actually heighten the emotional impact of a dramatic SCENE or broaden its implications.
The witty remarks of the dying Mercutio in *Romeo and Juliet*
make his death harder to bear. In *Macbeth* the drunken porter's
grumbling response to the knocking at the gate provides a mo-
mentary return to the ordinary world, in which Macbeth will ultimately have to face the consequences of his murder of Duncan.

comparative literature. A field of literary study that explores the
relationships between the literatures of different national cultures
or languages. Comparative literature investigates mutual influences, STYLES, movements, sources, THEMES, ARCHETYPES, and
MOTIFS. It is also concerned with the interrelationships of MYTHS,
LEGENDS, and EPICS and with the development of literary forms
and GENRES.

complication. An entangling of affairs early in the development of
the PLOT of a PLAY or NARRATIVE that must be unraveled in the
RESOLUTION at the end. See RISING ACTION.

computational stylistics. The analysis of measurable aspects of an
author's STYLE—such as sentence length and structure, or the
frequency of use of certain words or phrases—usually with the
goal of revealing the unconscious stylistic choices and preoccupa-
tions of the author. In the past, this kind of analysis was rare. A
scholar like T. C. Mendenhall, who in 1887 published calcula-
tions of word length in William Thackeray's and Charles Dickens' works, labored long indeed. Because computers have taken

the drudgery out of counting, computational style studies are increasingly common.

See STYLISTICS.

conceit. An elaborate figure of speech comparing two very dissimilar things. The comparison may be startling, farfetched, fanciful, or highly intellectual and may develop an ANALOGY or METAPHOR to its logical limits and beyond.

There are two types of conceits. The **Petrarchan conceit,** borrowed from Italian love poetry, compares the subject of the poem to a rose, the sun, a statue, or some other object. Skin is alabaster, teeth are pearls, and so on. Petrarchan conceits were widely used in ELIZABETHAN love poems and SONNETS. In this sonnet William Shakespeare employs conceits to satirize their abuse:

> My mistress' eyes are nothing like the sun;
> Coral is far more red than her lips' red;
> If snow be white, why then her breasts are dun;
> If hairs be wires, black wires grow on her head.

The **metaphysical conceit,** a common feature of the META-PHYSICAL POETRY of the seventeenth century, is more startling, ingenious, and intellectual, sometimes carried to the point of absurdity. In *A Valediction Forbidding Mourning,* John Donne compares the union of two lovers' souls to a drafting compass:

> If they be two, they are two so
> As stiff twin compasses are two;
> Thy soul, the fix'd foot, makes no show
> To move, but doth, if th'other do.
> And though it in the centre sit,
> Yet when the other far doth roam,
> It leans and hearkens after it,
> And grows erect as that comes home.

Though conceits fell out of favor during the eighteenth and nineteenth centuries, they have regained respectability in the poems of such modern poets as T. S. Eliot, Allen Tate, John Crowe Ransom, and Emily Dickinson, who wrote:

> Remembrance has a Rear and Front —
> 'Tis something like a House —

> It has a Garret also
> For Refuse and the Mouse.

concrete poetry. POETRY in which the visual arrangement of words or letters suggests something about the subject of the poem. Many concrete poems consist of a single word—for example, the word *shrink* printed with gradually smaller letters. Other concrete poems offer more subtle or more complicated visualizations of their subject matter, as does this poem by Eve Merriam:

fog smog	fog smog
tissue paper	tissue paper
clear the blear	clear the smear
fog more	fog more
splat splat	downpour
rubber scraper	rubber scraper
overshoes	macintosh
bumbershoot	muddle on
slosh through	slosh through
drying up	drying up
sky lighter	sky lighter
nearly clear	nearly clear

clearing clearing veer
clear here clear

confessional literature. A type of autobiographical writing in which the author discusses highly personal and private experiences normally withheld. Early examples of the type are St.

Augustine's *Confessions,* Jean-Jacques Rousseau's *Confessions,* and Thomas DeQuincey's *Confessions of an English Opium-Eater.* Fictionalized forms can be found in the "true confessions" of today's pulp magazines and in **confessional novels,** from Fyodor Dostoevsky's *Notes from the Underground* to Sylvia Plath's *The Bell Jar* and Saul Bellow's *Herzog.* Several contemporary poets, including Plath, Anne Sexton, Robert Lowell, and John Berryman, are known for their **confessional poetry,** which reveals intensely personal, often painful, emotions and experiences.

confidant/confidante. In DRAMA and other FICTION, someone that the HERO talks to, enabling the audience or reader to become aware of the hero's MOTIVATION. See CHARACTER.

conflict. The struggle between opposing forces that determines the action in DRAMA and most NARRATIVE FICTION. The earliest type of story conflict pits a CHARACTER *against nature*—storms at sea, wild beasts, or even insects, as in Carl Stephenson's ADVENTURE STORY, "Leiningen Versus the Ants." A variation of the physical struggle against nature is the *conflict with natural law or with fate.* In the *Epic of Gilgamesh,* the main character undertakes a perilous journey in the hope of overcoming death, his human destiny.

The PLOTS of many stories and most dramas are based on the struggle of the main character *against another character* (the PROTAGONIST versus the ANTAGONIST). Edgar Allan Poe's story "The Cask of Amontillado" grows out of the simplest kind of character-against-character conflict: Montresor carries out a plan of revenge against Fortunato. Sometimes the main character is in conflict with a group of other people, even a whole society, as in Henrik Ibsen's *An Enemy of the People.*

A character's struggle against nature or against another character is an **external conflict;** the main character is in conflict with an outside force. The focus in some stories, however, is on an **internal conflict.** The main character struggles *against himself or herself.* James Joyce's "Eveline" is an example of a story that takes place entirely inside the mind of a character making a difficult decision.

The greatest works of fiction offer rich combinations of external and internal conflicts. In William Shakespeare's *Macbeth,* the murder of Duncan is given psychological significance by the internal conflicts that torture Macbeth before and after the murder; Macbeth's inner turmoil is fueled by his external conflict with Lady Macbeth.

See ANTAGONIST, PLOT, PROTAGONIST.

connotation.   The associations, images, or impressions carried by a word, as opposed to the word's literal meaning. For example, the word *mother* means literally "a female parent," but it usually connotes warmth, love, sympathy, security, and nurture. Connotations may be individual (resulting from personal experience), group (shared by people with the same professional, national, linguistic, or racial background), or general (common to everyone). Scientists attempt to hold words to their precise meanings; writers, especially poets, rely on connotations to evoke responses in their readers.

See DENOTATION.

consonance.   The close repetition of identical consonant sounds before and after differing vowel sounds: *leave/love, short/shirt.* A number of familiar compound words are consonant: *pingpong, fulfill, tiptop.* Like ALLITERATION, consonance is used in POETRY to create EMPHASIS and UNITY.

A few poets have experimented with substituting consonance for END RHYME. These lines from Wilfred Owen's poem "Insensibility" show the subtle effect of consonant rhyme:

> Having seen all things *red,*
> Their eyes are *rid*
> Of the hurt of the colour of blood fore*ver,*
> And terror's constriction *over,*
> Their hearts remain small-drawn.

See ALLITERATION, ASSONANCE, END RHYME.

context.   The part of a work of LITERATURE that precedes or follows a given word, phrase, or passage. Context is important in clarifying, specifying, extending, or changing meaning. Removed from its surroundings, a word or passage may easily take on meanings unintended by the writer and, as a consequence, may not be properly understood or judged. "Quoting out of context" and "reading out of context" are considered serious faults by a number of schools of LITERARY CRITICISM.

convention. In general, an accepted way of doing things. A literary convention is an element of FORM, STYLE, or content in standard use. RHYME SCHEMES, EPIC SIMILES, happy endings in COMEDY, and wicked stepmothers in fairy tales are all conventions. Each literary GENRE—such as historical NOVEL, BALLAD, MELODRAMA—has its own set of recognizable characteristics, and is defined by those characteristics or conventions. When a group of writers follows a set of conventions, the group may establish a TRADITION, for example, the tradition during the RENAISSANCE of writing a SONNET to praise the virtues of a ladylove. Originality often consists in manipulating the conventions of a particular genre in a fresh way.

See GENRE, TRADITION.

counterplot. A SUBPLOT that presents a contrast to the main story in a PLAY, SHORT STORY, or NOVEL. See SUBPLOT.

couplet. Two consecutive lines of POETRY that RHYME and that are written to the same METER, or pattern of stressed and unstressed syllables. For example, here is a couplet from "Inventory," a poem by Dorothy Parker:

> Three be the things I shall have till I die:
> Laughter and hope and a sock in the eye.

A **closed couplet,** like the example above, is one that is grammatically and logically complete in itself. It is composed of END-STOPPED LINES (ending with a syntactical pause) rather than RUN-ON LINES (sense continuing into next line without a pause).

See HEROIC COUPLET.

courtly love. In the LITERATURE of the MIDDLE AGES, the emotion that a knight was expected to feel toward a noble lady. Ideally, the knight loved from a distance the wife of the knight's lord or some other married noblewoman, was faithful to her, and was inspired by his love to perform noble deeds in her honor. Geoffrey Chaucer's Squire is on his way to becoming such a courtly lover.

The concept of courtly love apparently originated in the troubadour POETRY of eleventh-century Provence. Sometimes courtly love rose to a form of religious veneration, as in Dante's veneration of Beatrice. His love for her led him to a vision of God. More often, the love remained on the human plane—involving secrecy; dalliance; unrequited passion with its telltale signs of sleeplessness, pallor, sighs, and trembling; and adultery. Famous examples of this kind of courtly love are the stories of Lancelot and Guinevere, Tristan and Isolde, and Paolo and Francesca.

crisis. The point at which the action turns and the fortune of the PROTAGONIST changes for better or worse; a structural element of PLOT. See TURNING POINT.

criticism. The classification, interpretation, analysis, and evaluation of works of LITERATURE. See LITERARY CRITICISM.

cubist poetry. POETRY that presents an experience as fragmented elements rearranged to form a new synthesis, or whole. Such poetry is influenced by **cubism,** an abstract style of painting and sculpture (developed by Pablo Picasso and Georges Braque) that presents natural objects as collections of geometric shapes and figures. Many of the poems of E. E. Cummings and Kenneth Rexroth are cubist poetry. This poem by Cummings is an example:

!

o(rounD)moon,how
do
you(rouNd
er
than roUnd)float;
who
lly &(rOunder than)
go
:ldenly(Round
est)

?

cultural primitivism. The belief that the natural, the simple, the spontaneous and free is superior to the artificial, the sophisticated, the consciously crafted and controlled. See PRIMITIVISM.

D

dactyl. A metrical FOOT consisting of three syllables, one accented syllable followed by two unaccented syllables, as in the word *time-lessly*. Each of the feet in the opening lines of Henry Wadsworth Longfellow's *Evangeline* are dactyls:

This is the | forest pri|meval. The | murmuring | pines
and the | hemlocks...

See FOOT, METER, SCANSION.

Dada. A phase of the modernist movement in art and LITERATURE that occurred in Europe and New York City between 1916 and 1922. Dada officially began in February of 1916 at the Cabaret Voltaire in Zurich, Switzerland. A number of young artists and writers, including Tristan Tzara, Jean (Hans) Arp, Richard Huelsenbeck, Hugo Ball, Emmy Hennings, and Sophie Tauber, decided to protest the insanity of World War I, as well as the values of middle-class society, rationalism, and representational art, by creating deliberately meaningless, formless works. A glance at the top of a page of an open German-French dictionary produced the word *dada,* baby talk in French for *hobbyhorse,* which was hailed by the group as a suitable name for their "nonsense"—collages of street debris as art and poems composed of random syllables or words pulled out of a paper bag, or of several unrelated passages read aloud simultaneously. At public events they tried to goad spectators into becoming themselves Dadaists. One time the public was given hatchets so that they could destroy collages and other constructions.

Dada caught on in other cities. Marcel Duchamp, who, among his accomplishments, originated the Mona Lisa with a mustache, led Dada activities in Paris and, with Francis Picabia and Man Ray, established Dada in New York. German Dada produced the painters Max Ernst and Kurt Schwitters, whose photomontages reflected the more specifically political concerns of the German Dadaists, especially in Berlin.

Dada reportedly came to an end as abruptly as it began. A number of Paris Dadaists had already become Surrealists by May 1921, when Dada was drowned in effigy in the Seine. There are also reports that Dada lives.

See MODERNISM, SURREALISM.

dead metaphor.   A METAPHOR that, through repeated and customary use, has lost its figurativeness and is taken literally, like "the heart of the matter." See METAPHOR.

decadence.   A term used in LITERARY CRITICISM to indicate the decline of quality that often accompanies the end of a great period of LITERATURE or art; a lowering of values, moral tone, and poetic power. Decadent literature tends to be sensational, morbid, and often morally dissolute.

The **decadents** were groups of late nineteenth- and early twentieth-century writers, especially in France and England, who felt that art is superior to nature, who found beauty in decay, and who rebelled against the accepted social and moral standards of the time. These groups included Paul Verlaine, Arthur Rimbaud, and Charles Baudelaire in France, and Oscar Wilde, Aubrey Beardsley, and Frank Harris in England. Some modern critics hold that many of today's NOVELS and films are decadent.

See AESTHETICISM.

deconstruction.   A mode of analytical reading based on the radically skeptical assumption that the language of written DIS-

COURSE is inherently unreliable. The goal of deconstruction is thus to search out the contradictions in a given text and prove that the text lacks both UNITY and COHERENCE. An analysis is made of all the ways the possible meanings of the words and phrases are at odds. The point of deconstruction is not to show that the text means the opposite of what it appears to mean, but that there can be no final interpretation of the text's meaning.

The French philosopher Jacques Derrida invented both the term *deconstruction* and the activity in the 1960s. According to Derrida, deconstruction is an outgrowth of the recognition by Friedrich Nietzsche and Martin Heidegger that the writer's and reader's desire for certainty of meaning results in the repression of other possible meanings (which are ferreted out by the act of deconstruction). Deconstruction also reflects the Structuralists' (notably Ferdinand de Saussure's) characterization of language as a collection of signs in which meaning is transient and arbitrary and therefore uncertain.

Although deconstruction is primarily applied to written texts, some practitioners, including Derrida himself, use deconstructive procedures to analyze concepts, systems, and institutions. They often refer to whatever it is that they are deconstructing as a "text." For example, in their view reality itself is a text, a collection of contradictory signs without certain meaning that we spend our lives struggling to "read" or interpret.

As Robert Scholes points out in *Textual Power: Literary Theory and the Teaching of English,* deconstruction theory can correct the naive assumptions (1) that a piece of written discourse can necessarily be made to yield up a single, paraphrasable meaning, and (2) that language reproduces reality transparently—that it does not, by its very nature, distort reality. Used sensibly, deconstruction can be a useful analytical tool. But, continues Scholes, deconstructive theory ventures into philosophical absurdity when it insists that words do not refer to concrete facts and when it overlooks the fact that language operates as a system, a network of meaning, not as a jumble of unconnected words.

See DECONSTRUCTIVE CRITICISM, LITERARY CRITICISM, POSTSTRUCTURALISM, STRUCTURALISM.

deconstructive criticism. An approach to LITERARY CRITICISM based on the views and procedures of the French thinker Jacques

Derrida. Deconstructive criticism utilizes reader-centered theories of meaning that ignore reference to the author's intention and deny the possibility of a determinate meaning or "correct" interpretation for any text. Deconstructive criticism makes possible innumerable contradictory but "undecidable" meanings. First becoming prominent in the 1970s, deconstructive criticism is central to POST-STRUCTURALISM.

See DECONSTRUCTION, POST-STRUCTURALISM, STRUCTURALISM.

decorum. The principle of literary propriety, of suiting STYLE to CHARACTER, situation, subject, or GENRE; of making all the elements in a written work or speech appropriate to each other. Derived from the CLASSICS of Greece and Rome, in which a lofty style was reserved for TRAGEDY and the style of everyday speech was used in COMEDY, the idea of decorum grew in importance during the RENAISSANCE. It became the central principle of the neoclassicists, by whom it was applied somewhat too mechanically as a standard of judgment. A famous example is Samuel Johnson's objection to William Shakespeare's practice of intruding comic characters—the gravediggers in Hamlet, for instance—into a TRAGEDY.

In the romantic period, William Wordsworth rebelled against so restrictive a notion of appropriate style, finding nobility and dignity in the speech of common people. Since then speakers and writers have continued to be sensitive to what is appropriate but have interpreted decorum flexibly.

See NEOCLASSICISM.

denotation. The precise, literal meaning of a word, without emotional associations or overtones. For example, although the word *gold* may suggest riches, power, and greed, its denotative meaning is precisely "a malleable, ductile, yellow trivalent and univalent metallic element."

See CONNOTATION.

denouement. Literally, unravelling, as of a knot. The final RESOLUTION of the CONFLICTS and COMPLICATIONS of a PLAY. While roughly synonymous with CATASTROPHE, the term *denouement* has traditionally been used in speaking about COMEDIES and MELO-

DRAMAS, while *catastrophe* has been reserved for TRAGEDY. Of the two, *denouement* is the more general term, applicable to tragedy in a way that *catastrophe* is not applicable to comedy. The resolution of a NOVEL or SHORT STORY is also called a denouement.

Because the kind of denouement common in the plays of previous centuries often seems artificial—long-lost relatives mysteriously arriving, misunderstandings suddenly set straight, a troublemaker conveniently leaving town, Aunt Bessie finally dying and leaving her money to the heroine—many modern playwrights aim for a more lifelike ending in which there is perhaps only a temporary resolution of the main conflict.

See CATASTROPHE.

description.   The picturing in words of people, places, and activities through detailed observations of color, sound, smells, touch, and motion. Description is one of the four modes of DISCOURSE, or major classifications of PROSE. The others are ARGUMENT (or ARGUMENTATION), EXPOSITION, and NARRATION. While it may stand alone and be used for its own sake, description appears most frequently as an element in the other types of writing. For example, in NARRATIVES such as NOVELS and SHORT STORIES, description figures importantly in creating SETTING and ATMOSPHERE and in CHARACTERIZATION.

Here is a passage of description from Richard Wright's short story "The Man Who Saw the Flood":

> The front room was dark and silent. The damp smell of flood silt came fresh and sharp to their nostrils. Only one-half of the upper window was clear, and through it fell a rectangle of dingy light. The floors swam in ooze. Like a mute warning, a wavering flood mark went high around the walls of the room. A dresser sat cater-cornered, its drawers and sides bulging like a bloated corpse. The bed, with the mattress still on it, was like a giant casket forged of mud. Two smashed chairs lay in a corner, as though huddled together for protection.

See DISCOURSE.

detective story.   A SHORT STORY or a NOVEL in which a mystery or crime (usually a theft or a murder) is solved by a detective who cleverly gathers and interprets clues. Elements common to such stories are an apparently perfect crime; an obvious but wrongly accused culprit; inept police; a brilliant, persistent, and often eccentric detective; an admiring associate who sometimes acts as NARRATOR; and a surprise ending. A basic rule of detective stories is that the reader be presented clues that lead to a solution at the same time the detective uncovers them, and that the detective use only such shared evidence in solving the crime.

While the emphasis in detective stories is usually on PLOT, the most enduring detective stories also develop unique and strongly characterized PROTAGONISTS, such as Sir Arthur Conan Doyle's Sherlock Holmes, Agatha Christie's Miss Jane Marple and Hercule Poirot, M. B. Lee's Ellery Queen, Dorothy Sayers' Lord Peter Wimsey, Erle Stanley Gardner's Perry Mason, Raymond Chandler's Phillip Marlowe, and Mickey Spillane's Mike Hammer.

It is commonly agreed that Edgar Allan Poe originated the detective story in 1841 with his "The Murders in the Rue Morgue." It has grown in popularity and variety ever since. One of its more recent forms, the mystery-espionage novel, first appeared in the 1960s and, with the works of Ian Fleming, John Le Carré, and Helen MacInnes, remains popular today.

determinism.   A persistent philosophy that people's actions and all other events are determined, or set in motion, by forces over which human beings have no control. People's concept of the nature of the outside force has varied over time. CHARACTERS in the LITERATURE of the ancients struggle in vain to avoid their fate—that which has been predestined for them by the gods. Christian thinkers have debated the precise balance between the free will of human beings and God's foreknowledge of events. In some Christian thought, notably in Calvinism, the balance is tipped toward the deterministic idea that God has predestined events, including human actions. The precariousness of the balance between human free will and predestination is reflected in Shakespearean TRAGEDY. William Shakespeare's tragic HEROES make tragic choices; they are the agents of their own tragic fall, yet often seem the victims of mysterious forces. Macbeth falls victim to the predictions of the witches. What they tell him is both predestination and temptation.

At the end of the nineteenth century, theological predestination was replaced by scientific and social determinism, in which heredity and environment were seen as the determining forces. The PROTAGONIST of Henrik Ibsen's play *Ghosts* is a victim of his heredity. The NOVELS of Émile Zola and other writers in the literary movement called NATURALISM are grim accounts of characters trapped in their animal natures and sordid environment. Literature influenced by Marxist SOCIALIST REALISM presents characters who are products of the conflicts between economic systems.

See NATURALISM.

deus ex machina.   In modern DRAMA and FICTION, any forced or artificial device introduced by an author to solve some difficult problem with the RESOLUTION of a PLOT. For example, a last-minute reprieve saves the HERO from wrongful execution. An unexpected inheritance from a long-lost aunt rescues the family business from bankruptcy. An outlaw holsters his gun when he recognizes a birthmark that identifies the sheriff as his twin brother. Considered a weakness in serious drama, the deus ex machina is a common element in MELODRAMA.

Literally, the Latin phrase means "god from the machine." In ancient Greek drama, when the gods were introduced to intervene in a difficult situation, they were lowered to the stage by a mechanical device, or "machine."

dialect.   The version of a language spoken by people of a particular region or social group—for example, the American Southern dialect found in the DIALOGUE of many works by Southern writers, such as Tennessee Williams and Flannery O'Connor, or the Cockney dialect that figures in George Bernard Shaw's play *Pygmalion.* Differing in vocabulary and grammar as well as in pronunciation, the dialects of a language develop when groups of people are separated from each other for a long time by natural or social barriers. People speaking one dialect are usually, but not always, able to understand the speakers of another dialect of the same language. There is greater similarity among the three major dialects—Southern, Central, and Northeastern—found in the United States, than among the dialects of most European languages or even among the dialects of the British Isles.

dialogue.   1. The conversation of two or more people as represented in writing, especially in PLAYS, NOVELS, SHORT STORIES, and NARRATIVE POEMS. Dialogue is important in forwarding the action, developing CHARACTERS, and intensifying a sense of reality and immediacy. Characters often reveal themselves more by what they say than by what they do or by what is said about them. To be effective, dialogue must be true to the personalities, social positions, and outlooks of the speakers. It must present the exchange of ideas in a conversational give-and-take, not merely record the remarks of alternating speakers. And it must *seem* true to life without being a verbatim account of what was said.

2. A form of literature in which two or more people, through invented conversation, discuss or reason about questions of philosophy or ethics; for example, the dialogues of Plato.

See DRAMA.

diction.   Word choice. There are two basic standards—not mutually exclusive—by which a speaker's or writer's diction is usually judged: clarity and appropriateness. Clear diction is both precise and concrete, including a high proportion (approximately one out of every six words) of strong verbs and verbals. Appropriate diction is diction at a level—formal, informal, colloquial, slang—suitable to the occasion.

See COLLOQUIALISM, DECORUM, STYLE.

didactic literature.   POETRY, PLAYS, NOVELS, and stories whose primary purpose is to guide, instruct, or teach. Since all literature communicates ideas, whether a particular work is didactic or not depends largely on the author's intention, so far as it can be known or inferred by the reader or critic. If an author intends to instruct, then the work is didactic.

The place and value of didactic literature has been a subject of debate among literary critics over the years. While **didacticism** has generally been considered an acceptable aspect of literature, many modern critics use the term in a derogatory sense. These critics feel that if carried too far, didacticism results in

PROPAGANDA. They also contend that the significant meaning of a work resides in the work itself, not in some goal external to it. On the other hand, MORAL CRITICISM and MARXIST CRITICISM continue to demand didactic purposes in literature.

See AUTOTELIC, LITERARY CRITICISM, NEW CRITICISM.

digression. A portion of a speech or written work that interrupts the development of the THEME or PLOT. Although out of place in FORMAL ESSAYS and tightly structured PLAYS and stories, digressions are common in loosely structured NARRATIVES, such as EPICS and PICARESQUE NOVELS. The NARRATORS of these works pause in their story to present a list, or CATALOG; to preach or philosophize; to describe in detail; or to make an extended comparison (the EPIC SIMILE is a digression). The leisurely pace of such works invites digression. Digressions are also acceptable, even desirable, in INFORMAL ESSAYS and STREAM-OF-CONSCIOUSNESS FICTION, where digressive lapses into memory and daydream suggest the free association of thoughts. Such digressions usually bear some relation to the main subject or story.

See ESSAY.

dimeter. A line of POETRY consisting of two metrical feet. These lines from Emily Dickinson's poem "I Went to Heaven" are in dimeter:

> Í wĕnt tŏ | Héavĕn,—
> 'Twás ă smăll | tówn,
> Lít wĭth ă | rúbў,
> Láthĕd wĭth | dówn.

See FOOT, METER, RHYTHM, SCANSION.

direct satire. Another term for FORMAL SATIRE, in which the author or a NARRATOR speaks directly to the reader. See SATIRE.

dirge. A funeral song of lamentation; a short LYRIC of mourning. See ELEGY.

discourse. **1.** Spoken or written language, including literary works. Discourse has traditionally been classified in either of two ways: according to mode and according to the writer's or speaker's purpose. Mode includes NARRATION, DESCRIPTION, EXPOSITION, and ARGUMENT. (Some scholars agree with Aristotle that argument is not itself a mode, but rather subsumes, or makes use of, the true modes—narration, description, and exposition.) The writer's or speaker's purpose might be to express, to inform, to persuade, to entertain (or to create a form or to imitate life). The aim of the literary artist is noticeably difficult to pinpoint.

Recent studies of discourse range from detailed analyses of conversation and dramatic DIALOGUE to studies of the social context of communication to philosophical and historical studies questioning traditional assumptions about the nature of discourse, authorship, and intention.

2. A treatise or dissertation or other learned, formal written work or lecture, for example, *A Discourse on Method* by René Descartes.

discovery. That moment, near the end of a PLAY, when the PROTAGONIST finally realizes a truth or gains an understanding previously unrecognized or disregarded; also called RECOGNITION. See RECOGNITION.

distance. The "standing apart" of a reader or viewer from a work of art by being aware that it *is* a work of art and not actual life; sometimes called **aesthetic distance** or **psychic distance** in LITERARY CRITICISM. Critical readers must maintain a degree of detachment and OBJECTIVITY, or distance, if they are to fully understand and evaluate what they are reading. The term is also used to describe the degree of objectivity an author displays in presenting CHARACTERS and actions without expressing personal views or judgments or revealing his or her own personality.

See NEGATIVE CAPABILITY, OBJECTIVE CORRELATIVE, OBJECTIVITY.

documentary fiction. FICTION built around current news events, such as sensational trials, acts of heroism, disasters, serial murders, and the like. An example is Truman Capote's *In Cold Blood.* See FICTION.

doggerel.　Rhyming VERSE that is trite, sentimental, and not quite funny. Its METER is often monotonously strict or clumsily loose. The verse of greeting cards and advertising jingles is often doggerel. Able writers occasionally use doggerel for satiric or comic effect. The fifteenth-century English writer John Skelton made his brand of short-line doggerel famous enough to be named after him. In the following lines he comments on his **Skeltonics:**

> For though my rhyme be ragged,
> Tattered and jagged,
> Rudely rain-beaten,
> Rusty and moth-eaten,
> If ye take well therewith,
> It hath in it some pith.

domestic tragedy.　A TRAGEDY of domestic life concerning a middle- or lower-class PROTAGONIST who suffers a personal disaster. Also called **bourgeois tragedy.** See TRAGEDY.

double rhyme.　A RHYME consisting of two syllables, the first accented and the second unaccented, as in *sénding* and *blénding*. See FEMININE RHYME.

drama.　Generally, a literary work written in DIALOGUE to be performed before an audience by actors on a stage. Essential to all forms of drama are a story, action that develops the story, and actors who impersonate the CHARACTERS of the story. In this sense, the term *drama* identifies anything from TRAGEDY to MELODRAMA, from HIGH COMEDY to FARCE. More specifically, a *drama* is a serious, generally realistic PLAY that, while not of the magnitude of a grand tragedy, cannot be categorized as a comedy. And in the broadest sense, *drama* refers to the composition and performance of plays.

　　Drama had its origins in religious ceremonies. Greek comedy evolved from Dionysian fertility rites; Greek tragedy, from rites concerned with life and death. MEDIEVAL drama evolved from rites commemorating the birth and resurrection of Jesus Christ. Beginning with the RENAISSANCE, drama has continued to develop new FORMS and STYLES. For example, early drama was poetic; PROSE dialogue was introduced in the sixteenth century.

By the eighteenth century prose had become dominant, due largely to the demands of a rising middle-class audience for more contemporary subjects and THEMES. Despite continuing experimentation and innovation, however, the basic elements of drama have remained essentially unchanged. Drama is still, as Aristotle called it, "imitated human action" presented through dialogue for the entertainment and instruction of an audience.

See ABSURD, THEATER OF THE; CHRONICLE PLAY; COMEDY; DRAMATURGY; EPIC THEATER; MASQUE; MELODRAMA; MIRACLE PLAY; MORALITY PLAY; NO DRAMA; ONE-ACT PLAY; TRAGEDY.

dramatic irony. A situation in a PLAY or other FICTION in which a CHARACTER unwittingly makes a remark that the audience is intended to understand as ironic, or in contradiction to the full truth. In Euripides' *Medea,* Creon postpones Medea's banishment until morning, asking, "What harm could she do in the tail of one day?" The Greek audience, who already knew the legend of Medea, must have shivered in recognition of the terrible irony of his question—they knew, as Creon could not, that Medea would destroy both Creon's daughter and Creon himself.

For audiences new to a play and for first-time readers of fiction, dramatic irony can serve as FORESHADOWING. In Henrik Ibsen's *Hedda Gabler,* Judge Brack's complacent remark to Hedda about suicide, "People say such things—but they don't do them," would not have struck the original audience as ironic until the end of the play, when Hedda shoots herself and the shocked Brack says again, "Good God! People don't do such things."

One of the satisfactions of seeing certain plays again or of re-reading fiction comes from recognizing the dramatic irony the second time around.

See IRONY.

dramatic monologue. A POEM in which a single CHARACTER, overheard speaking to a silent listener, reveals a dramatic situation. The poet best known for dramatic monologues is Robert Browning, who, in "My Last Duchess" and "Andrea del Sarto," created minor masterpieces of DRAMATIC IRONY. A number of FOLK BALLADS are dramatic monologues. Dramatic monologues also have been written by Edgar Lee Masters, Edwin A. Robinson,

Carl Sandburg, T. S. Eliot, Conrad Aiken, Robert Frost, Amy Lowell, and Robert Lowell, among others. Here is the beginning of one by Amy Lowell, entitled "Number 3 on the Docket":

> The lawyer, are you?
> Well! I ain't got nothin' t say.
> Nothin'!
> I told the perlice I hadn't nothin'.
> They know'd real well 'twas me.
> Ther warn't no supposin'.
> Ketchin' me in the woods as they did,
> An' me in my house dress.
> Folks don't walk miles an' miles
> In the drifted snow,
> With no hat nor wrap on 'em
> Ef everythin's all right, I guess.
> All right? Ha! Ha! Ha!
> Nothin' warn't right with me.
> Never was.
> Oh, Lord! Why did I do it?
> Why ain't it yesterday, and Ed here agin?

Dramatism. The system for analyzing LITERATURE proposed by Kenneth Burke, an American critic and author, based on his view that the active sentence provides the fundamental pattern of all literature:

Somebody	is always doing	something	to somebody else.
[subject]	[verb]	[object]	[indirect object]

Thus, according to Burke, all works of literature are made up of five elements (his "pentad"): Act (what happened), Scene (where it happened), Agent (who performed the act), Agency (how it was performed), and Purpose (why it was performed).

dramatis personae. The CHARACTERS in a PLAY; also the list of characters printed at the beginning of a published play or in the program for a live production, often with brief descriptions of the characters and their relationships. By extension, the term has also come to mean the characters that appear in poems and NOVELS.

dramaturgy.   The study of the composition and performance of DRAMA. Many theaters in Europe and an increasing number in the United States employ as a staff member a **dramaturge,** an expert on the performance history of drama.

dynamic character.   A CHARACTER who changes significantly during the course of a story; the opposite of a STATIC CHARACTER. See CHARACTER, CHARACTERIZATION.

dystopia.   A term applied to undesirable imaginary societies, such as the world in George Orwell's *1984;* the opposite of UTOPIA. See UTOPIA.

E

eclogue. A short PASTORAL poem, usually in the form of a DIALOGUE or, sometimes, a SOLILOQUY. See PASTORAL.

Edwardian. Referring to the period in England between the death of Queen Victoria (1901) and the outbreak of World War I (1914). Named after the reign of King Edward VII (1901–1910), it was an age of prosperity—even opulence—and stability, marked by stylish elegance. The term *Edwardian* is often used to describe these characteristics. The writers of this period were noted for their criticism of authority in religion, morality, and literature. Prominent among them were George Bernard Shaw, H. G. Wells, Arnold Bennett, and John Galsworthy.

See MODERNISM, VICTORIAN.

effect. The impression made by a work of LITERATURE—either on its actual audience or, as its author imagines the effect, on an ideal audience. The importance of effect is an issue in LITERARY CRITICISM. Practitioners of RHETORICAL CRITICISM are interested in exploring the relationship between the work itself and its effect. The objectivist New Critics have been inclined to mistrust critical judgments based on a work's effect because such judgments are necessarily SUBJECTIVE: A poem strikes different readers differently. Reader-response critics celebrate such subjectivity, even insisting that the real existence of a poem or a story lies in the reader's reporting of its effect.

See AFFECTIVE FALLACY, LITERARY CRITICISM, NEW CRITICISM, READER-RESPONSE CRITICISM, RHETORICAL CRITICISM.

elegiac stanza. A STANZA of four lines in IAMBIC PENTAMETER, rhyming *abab;* also called the **heroic quatrain.** See QUATRAIN.

elegy. A poem of sorrow or mourning for the dead; also a reflective poem in a solemn or sorrowful MOOD. The adjective *elegiac* is used to describe POETRY that exhibits the characteristics of an elegy.

Well-known elegies lamenting the death of a particular person include John Milton's *Lycidas* (Edward King), Percy Shelley's *Adonais* (John Keats), Alfred, Lord Tennyson's *In Memoriam* (Arthur H. Hallam), and Walt Whitman's *When Lilacs Last in the Dooryard Bloom'd* (Abraham Lincoln). Perhaps the most famous elegy, Thomas Gray's *Elegy Written in a Country Churchyard,* is a solemn, meditative poem mourning not the death of a person, but the passing of a way of life. Closely related terms are **monody, threnody,** and **dirge.**

See EULOGY.

Elizabethan. Referring to the period of the reign of Elizabeth I of England (1558–1603). An era of nationalism, colonial expansion, and commercial growth, as well as religious controversy, the Elizabethan period was also the culmination of the RENAISSANCE and the Golden Age of English LITERATURE, during which Christopher Marlowe, Philip Sidney, Edmund Spenser, William Shakespeare, Walter Raleigh, Ben Jonson, and John Donne brought DRAMA and LYRIC POETRY to their highest level.

emphasis. The stress placed on words or passages by highlighting their importance in some manner. There are many methods for securing emphasis: placement (first or last); repetition; length; use of contrast; arrangement in order of increasing importance; inversion; use of mechanical devices like spacing, boldface, italics, capitalization, and punctuation. In POETRY, emphasis is

achieved through the manipulation of METER, RHYME, line
length and arrangement, and FIGURATIVE LANGUAGE.

encomium.　A warm, enthusiastic expression of praise for a person
or thing. See EULOGY.

end rhyme.　RHYME at the ends of lines of VERSE, distinguished
from rhyme within a line (INTERNAL RHYME) and rhyme at the
beginning of a line (initial rhyme). End rhyme is the most common form of rhyme.

See INTERNAL RHYME, RHYME.

end-stopped lines.　Lines of POETRY in which the grammatical
structure, the sense, and the METER are completed at the end of
each line. The completion may be signaled by a pause or by a
complete stop. In Anne Bradstreet's poem "To My Dear and
Loving Husband," most of the twelve lines are end-stopped:

> If ever two were one, then surely we;
> If ever man were loved by wife, then thee;
> If ever wife was happy in a man,
> Compare with me, ye women, if you can.
> I prize thy love more than whole mines of gold,
> Or all the riches that the East doth hold.
> My love is such that rivers cannot quench,
> Nor ought but love from thee give recompense.
> Thy love is such I can no way repay,
> The heavens reward thee manifold, I pray.
> Then while we live in love let's so persevere,
> That when we live no more we may live ever.

See ENJAMBMENT, RUN-ON LINES.

English sonnet.　Another term for the **Shakespearean sonnet,** a
SONNET arranged into three QUATRAINS, rhyming *abab, cdcd, efef,*
followed by a concluding COUPLET, rhyming *gg.* The couplet is
often an EPIGRAM, summing up the problem or concern developed in the quatrains. See SONNET.

enjambment.　The carrying of sense and grammatical structure in a
poem beyond the end of one line, COUPLET, or STANZA and into

the next. Enjambment occurs with the use of RUN-ON LINES, as these opening lines from *The Explorer* by Gwendolyn Brooks illustrate:

> Somehow to find a still spot in the noise
> Was the frayed inner want, the winding, the frayed hope
> Whose tatters he kept hunting through the din.

See END-STOPPED LINES, RUN-ON LINES.

envoy (envoi). A concluding STANZA of a poem, shorter than the other stanzas, that serves as a postscript, dedicating the poem to a patron, summarizing the poem, or repeating the REFRAIN. The envoy has been used by Geoffrey Chaucer, Sir Walter Scott, Algernon Swinburne, and Oscar Wilde.

epic. A long NARRATIVE POEM in lofty STYLE, set in a remote time and place, and dealing with heroic CHARACTERS and deeds important in the LEGENDS and history of a nation or race. The epic HERO (for example, Achilles in Homer's *Iliad*) is larger than life, having superhuman strength, character, or intellect. The action is simple, presenting a central incident or series of incidents of historical or legendary significance (for example, the siege of Troy). Supernatural forces (gods, demons, angels) influence and participate in the action. In John Milton's *Paradise Lost* all the characters except Adam and Eve are supernatural beings. The SETTING may be national, worldwide, or cosmic; the time, a distant past that seems greater than the present, a heroic or golden age. The style is objective, elevated, and dignified.

The epic form is highly traditional and employs many CONVENTIONS. For example, the epic conventionally opens with a statement of the THEME (for example, the wrath of Achilles) and an appeal to the Muses for inspiration (an INVOCATION). The story begins IN MEDIAS RES, in the middle of things. There are CATALOGS, long lists, of warriors, armies, armor, and such. The *Iliad* has a catalog of ships; *Paradise Lost,* a catalog of fallen angels. There are long formal speeches by main characters and often a journey to the underworld. STOCK EPITHETS, like Homer's "rosy-fingered dawn," appear repeatedly throughout the poem, as do EPIC SIMILES, extended comparisons so long that the reader often forgets what is being compared.

Although there is general agreement that epics are an out-growth of traditional storytelling, there is some debate about the specific details of their development. As a result, epics are often divided into two types: the **folk epic,** also called the "primary epic" or "primitive epic," and the **literary epic,** also called the "secondary epic" or "art epic." Folk epics are of unknown or uncertain authorship, were recited before an audience, and were passed along as part of an oral tradition. Literary epics are written by a poet employing the epic conventions and are meant to be read. Examples of the folk epic are the *Iliad* and the *Odyssey* (Greek), *Beowulf* (Old English), *Song of Roland* (French), *Poem of the Cid* (Spanish), and *Mahabharata* (East Indian). Virgil's *Aeneid,* Dante's *Divine Comedy,* and John Milton's *Paradise Lost* are famous literary epics.

See CATALOG, EPITHET, MOCK EPIC, SIMILE.

epic simile. A lengthy, extensively elaborated SIMILE, often beginning with "as" or "as when"; also called **Homeric simile.** See SIMILE.

epic theater. Episodic, NARRATIVE theater; an approach to writing and presenting PLAYS initiated in Germany in the 1920s by theater director Erwin Piscator and developed by dramatist Bertolt Brecht. A Marxist, Brecht's goal as a playwright was didactic. Without writing overt PROPAGANDA, he nevertheless wished to stimulate the audience to think about and take action against the social evils they saw on the stage. He found the realistic theater of his day inadequate for his purpose because it so successfully created the illusion of reality that the audience could easily identify with the CHARACTERS and lose themselves in the DRAMA. They came out of the theater emotionally drained, rather than intellectually stimulated.

Brecht believed that the audience would remain more intellectually alert if a way could be found to prevent or at least interrupt their emotional identification with the play's action—some kind of *alienation effect,* as he put it. He decided to write plays with a large number of very short, often unconnected SCENES introduced by a NARRATOR, who would present the action as events in the past in order to DISTANCE the audience from the characters. Looking back to the way EPICS, such as the *Iliad* and the *Odyssey,* were narrated in the past tense to their audiences, Brecht called his narrative theater *epic theater.* In Piscator's dramatizations of Leo Tolstoy's *War and Peace* and of Jaroslav Hašek's *The Good Soldier Schweik,* as well as in Brecht's own *Threepenny Opera, A Man's a Man, Saint Joan of the Stockyards, Mother Courage, The Good Person of Setzuan,* and *The Caucasian Chalk Circle,* the distancing devices include not only short narrated scenes but also projected photographs, titles, and slogans; onstage musicians; a CHORUS that interrupts and comments on the action; and bright, nonatmospheric lights. The actors often break character to comment on the action or even to play another part.

The atmosphere in Brecht's plays is not unlike that of a courtroom in which a prosecuting attorney has called in a group of actors to dramatize a crime but frequently interrupts the action to keep the jury alert to the prosecution's POINT OF VIEW.

See DIDACTIC LITERATURE, DISTANCE, DRAMA, EPIC, REALISM.

epigram. In POETRY and PROSE, any terse, witty, pointed saying. Epigrams often pair opposing or contradictory ideas, for example, the anonymous "She knows the cost of everything but the value of nothing" or Oscar Wilde's "I can resist everything except temptation." Samuel Taylor Coleridge defined *epigram* as he wrote one:

> What is an epigram? A dwarfish whole;
> Its body brevity and wit its soul.

Originally an epigram meant an inscription, or epitaph, usually in verse, on a tomb. Later it came to mean a short poem that compressed meaning and expression in the manner of an inscription. Today *epigram* refers to a saying, a COUPLET, or a QUATRAIN that either stands alone or is part of a larger work. For instance, this couplet from a poem by Lady Mary Wortley Montague is an epigram:

> Satire should, like a polished razor keen,
> Wound with a touch that's scarcely felt or seen.

Epigrams differ from APHORISMS in that aphorisms express truths, offer morals, or give advice and are not barbed or satiric.
See APHORISM.

epigraph.   A quotation or motto at the beginning of a book or chapter. An epigraph relates to the content of the work in which it is quoted. Sometimes, the title of the work is taken from it. Lorraine Hansberry used a line from a Langston Hughes poem as the title of her PLAY *Raisin in the Sun* and quoted the complete poem as an epigraph at the beginning of the play.

epilogue.   A concluding section added to a NOVEL, PLAY, or long poem. In DRAMA, the epilogue is usually a plea by one of the actors for the goodwill of the audience and the indulgence of the critics. In a FABLE, the epilogue is a statement of practical application, the point or moral. An epilogue may also be the final section of a formal speech, the peroration. Commonly employed in plays of the seventeenth and eighteenth centuries, the epilogue is rarely used today.

See PROLOGUE.

epiphany.   A moment of revelation or profound insight. In Greek mythology, an epiphany was the sudden revelation to a human being of the hidden or disguised divinity of a god or goddess. The Christian feast of Epiphany commemorates the revelation of Christ's divinity to the three wise men. The modern literary use of the term *epiphany* originates with James Joyce, who discussed it in his novel *Stephen Hero.* According to Joyce, any event, however trivial, may have a "sudden spiritual manifestation" when "its soul, its whatness, leaps to us." It might be a bird flying by, a clock striking, a smile, or a street noise. Stephen Hero "believed that it was for the man of letters to record these epiphanies with extreme care, seeing that they themselves are the most delicate and evanescent of moments." Because such an epiphany lies at the heart of many of Joyce's stories, the stories themselves have been called epiphanies.

episode.   An INCIDENT or event that is presented as a single, unified action but that is also part of a longer NARRATIVE. Occasionally a DIGRESSION used to illuminate CHARACTER or provide background, an episode usually works with other episodes to forward the action of the main PLOT.

Also, the installments into which a serialized work is divided are sometimes called episodes.

A narrative is said to have **episodic structure** if it consists merely of a series of incidents loosely strung together with no solid interrelationship except, perhaps, chronological order. Any of the episodes in such a narrative may be removed without serious damage to the whole. In this sense, CHIVALRIC ROMANCES and PICARESQUE NOVELS have episodic structure.

epistolary novel. From *epistle,* or "letter." A NOVEL written in the FORM of a correspondence between CHARACTERS. In the eighteenth century, when the novel was still new and authors felt it important to offer a novel as a true account, the epistolary novel was a popular alternative to first-person FICTION. Using more than one letter writer allowed the author to present different POINTS OF VIEW. Although the form enjoyed only a forty-year heyday (1740–1780), several of the most successful eighteenth-century novels were epistolary: In England there were SENTIMENTAL NOVELS by Samuel Richardson, including *Pamela, or Virtue Rewarded,* and *Clarissa Harlowe* (in which the correspondence goes on for seven psychologically revealing volumes), and comic novels such as Tobias Smollett's *Humphrey Clinker* and Fanny Burney's *Evelina.* In France, Jean-Jacques Rousseau's *La Nouvelle Héloïse* and Pierre Laclos's *Les Liasons Dangereuses* were popular epistolary novels.

Epistolary novels continue to be written from time to time. A recent example is Alice Walker's *The Color Purple.*

See NOVEL, SENTIMENTAL NOVEL.

epithet. An adjective or adjective phrase applied to a person or thing to emphasize a characteristic quality or attribute, such as "*lily-livered* coward" or "*murmuring* brook"; also an appellation, such as William *the Conqueror* or Richard *Lion-Heart.*

An epithet consisting of a compound adjective, like "*ox-eyed* Hera," "*swift-footed* Achilles," or "*rosy-fingered* dawn," is called a **Homeric epithet** after Homer, who used the form extensively in his EPICS. When an epithet is used repeatedly, it is called a **stock epithet.** A **transferred epithet** is an adjective shifted from a noun it would normally modify to one that is closely related in experience if not in sense. For example, in "*boiling* kettle" *boiling,* which normally modifies *water,* is shifted to *kettle* for figurative effect.

equivoque. A type of PUN in which a word is used so that it means two different things at the same time. See PUN.

essay. A composition on a particular THEME or topic. So flexible and adaptable is the essay FORM that it cannot be defined with any precision. Essays are nearly always written in PROSE, but there have been a few in VERSE (notably, those by Alexander Pope), and there have even been some wordless essays—photo essays, for example: a series of photos on a theme. Most essays are short—some only a few hundred words, such as Francis Bacon's pithy, highly quotable essays of moral and practical advice, but some are book length (John Locke's *Essay Concerning Human Understanding;* John Stuart Mill's *On Liberty*).

   Essays have been written for all the purposes for which anyone writes—to express an opinion, to inform, to persuade, to entertain. The great majority of essays are exploratory—thoughtful personal interpretations of their subjects, modeled after the essays of the sixteenth-century French writer Michel de Montaigne, the first modern essayist. It was Montaigne who first called such writings *essays*—from the French word meaning "attempt." Their name suggests that essays are tentative explorations of a topic rather than authoritative and comprehensive dissertations.

   Nevertheless, a useful distinction can be made between **formal essays** and **informal essays.** Formal essays offer a serious, conclusive, logically organized treatment of their subject, expressed in relatively impersonal, but not overly technical, language. Informal essays, also called *familiar essays* or *personal essays,* are deliberately tentative in treatment; familiar, whimsical, or humorous in tone and style; and rambling and digressive in organization, with ideas flowing along the lines of random association, the way ideas pop up and connect in people's minds.

   Both informal and formal essays have proliferated with the development of magazines, newspapers, and other periodicals. Among the greatest of the periodical essayists were Joseph Addison, whose essays for the eighteenth-century *Tatler* and *Spectator* are models of keenly observed, gently amused social satire, and, in the romantic period, Thomas De Quincey, whose "impassioned prose," as he called it, laid bare the human subconscious before the birth of Sigmund Freud. The VICTORIAN essayists—

such as Thomas Carlyle, John Ruskin, Matthew Arnold, Thomas B. MacCauley, John Cardinal Newman, and Walter Pater—addressed the social, political, and AESTHETIC issues of their day, with the high seriousness and sometimes the rage of Old Testament prophets. Outstanding eighteenth- and nineteenth-century American essayists include Washington Irving, Oliver Wendell Holmes, Ralph Waldo Emerson, and Mark Twain. In the twentieth century, the range of interesting essayists is great: from Virginia Woolf, Max Beerbohm, Aldous Huxley, and George Orwell in England to H. L. Mencken, E. B. White, Gore Vidal, and Joan Didion in the United States.

eulogy. A formal composition or speech in high praise of someone (living or dead) or something. At the end of William Shakespeare's *Julius Caesar,* Mark Antony, speaking in praise of Brutus, delivers one of the most famous eulogies in literature:

> This was the noblest Roman of them all:
> All the conspirators, save only he,
> Did that they did in envy of great Caesar;
> He only, in a general honest thought
> And common good to all, made one of them.
> His life was gentle, and the elements
> So mix'd in him that Nature might stand up
> And say to all the world "This was a man!"

Closely related terms are **encomium** and **panegyric.**
See ELEGY.

euphony. A succession of sweetly melodious sounds; the opposite of CACOPHONY. The term is applied to smoothly flowing POETRY or PROSE.

Lingering vowels and liquid consonants, other consonants to move the lines along but none that beat or blast, and perhaps the meaning of the words all combine to create euphony in these lines from John Keats's "The Eve of St. Agnes":

> And still she slept an azure-lidded sleep,
> In blanched linen, smooth, and lavendered.

See CACOPHONY.

euphuism. An affected, excessive, artificial STYLE of writing and speech in vogue during the sixteenth century in England. Its name derives from John Lyly's *Euphues,* then considered a model of the elegance and polish that could be attained by English PROSE, which was struggling to become established as a reputable literary FORM. Its chief characteristics are balanced construction; excessive use of rhetorical questions, ANTITHESES with ALLITERATION, and elaborate SIMILES; ALLUSIONS to mythological and historical personages; and illustrations from natural history. These passages from *Euphues* are typical of the style:

> Achilles's spear could as well heal as hurt; the Scorpion, though he sting, yet he stints the pain; though the herb Nerius poison the sheep, yet is it a remedy to man against poison; though I have infected some by example, yet I hope I shall comfort many by repentance.

> Do we not commonly see that in painted pots is hidden the deadliest poison? that in the greenest grass is the greatest serpent? in the clearest water the ugliest toad? How frantic are those lovers which are carried away with the gay glistening of the fine face?

Today, affected or overly elaborated language used in the pursuit of elegance is called **euphuistic.**

exact rhyme. Also called **true rhyme,** RHYME in which the accented syllables and all succeeding sounds are identical between two words (*feature/creature*). Rhyme that is not exact is called SLANT RHYME. See RHYME.

exaggeration. Overstatement or stretching of the truth, as in a TALL TALE or fish story or in common expressions, such as "I cried my eyes out" or "I laughed my head off." People usually exaggerate to give emphasis to something, sometimes for humorous effect. The deliberate use of exaggeration as a literary device is called HYPERBOLE.

See HYPERBOLE.

exegesis. Originally, the detailed analysis, explanation, and INTERPRETATION of passages in the Bible, or, by extension, of any literary or intellectual text. The term carries with it a sense of digging out the meaning of a difficult passage.

See EXPLICATION DE TEXTE, HERMENEUTICS, INTERPRETATION.

exemplum.   A brief tale or ANECDOTE told to illustrate a biblical text or to teach a lesson or moral, especially common in sermons during the MIDDLE AGES. Collections of these moralized tales, or *exempla,* often classified by subject for the use of preachers, took their stories from folklore, legend, and history. Because of their human interest and concreteness, exempla were adapted by lay writers and had a great influence on MEDIEVAL literature. For example, in "The Pardoner's Tale," Geoffrey Chaucer uses the exemplum of Death overtaking three rioters to point up the moral that the love of money is the root of all evil. Exempla also appear in several of the other *Canterbury Tales.*

See FABLE, PARABLE.

existential criticism.   A modern school of LITERARY CRITICISM, identified especially with Jean-Paul Sartre, that rejects traditional critical questions and concerns and instead examines LITERATURE in the light of EXISTENTIALISM, a philosophical theory that emphasizes existence over essence, free will and the attendant responsibility for making choices, and anxiety in the face of a meaningless world.

See EXISTENTIALISM, LITERARY CRITICISM.

existentialism.   A philosophy that focuses on the individual human being's experience of, recognition of, and triumph over the meaninglessness of existence. Rooted in the thought of nineteenth- and early twentieth-century figures as diverse as Søren Kierkegaard, Friedrich Nietzsche, Fyodor Dostoevsky, and Franz Kafka, existentialism became widely influential in the 1940s, especially after the horrors of World War II, through the NOVELS, PLAYS, and philosophical writings of Jean-Paul Sartre.

According to Sartre, human beings are born into a moral and metaphysical void. There is no plan for their lives, no definition of their essential being. They simply exist. People can passively remain in that condition, hardly aware of anything, taking the path of least resistance. Or they can face themselves and the awful absurdity of their predicament, recognizing that they are alone, that there are no rules and no one to tell them what to do. It is important from the existentialist viewpoint that human awareness of this situation go beyond mere intellectual comprehension. People have to feel the horror of the meaninglessness. The anxiety (angst) produced by this awareness may lead to despair, but it can also make people recognize that they are responsible for shaping their own essential being, for creating their own authentic character. Angst can lead people to exercise their wills in acts of *engagement* that will give meaning to their lives. An act of engagement can be a commitment to social and political action (as in the case of Sartre), or it can be a leap to faith (as in the Christian existentialism of Kierkegaard and, more recently, Gabriel Marcel and Paul Tillich).

Anchored as it is in individual human dilemma, existentialism has been as much a literary movement as a philosophical development. The works of Albert Camus, Simone de Beauvoir, Samuel Beckett, Eugène Ionesco, Jean Genet, and Harold Pinter, as well as the novels and plays of Sartre himself, are proof of its pervasiveness. Camus's retelling of the MYTH of Sisyphus is considered a classic statement of existentialist affirmation:

> The gods had condemned Sisyphus to ceaselessly rolling a rock to the top of a mountain, whence the stone would fall back of its own weight. They had thought with some reason that there is no more dreadful punishment than futile and hopeless labour. . . . You have already grasped that Sisyphus is the absurd hero. He *is*, as much through his passions as through his torture. His scorn of the gods, his hatred of death, and his passion for life won him that unspeakable penalty in which the whole being is exerted toward accomplishing nothing. This is the price that must be paid for the passions of this earth.
>
> At the very end of his long effort measured by skyless space and time without depth the purpose is achieved. Then Sisyphus watches the stone rush down in a few moments toward that lower world whence he will have to push it up again toward the summit. He goes back down to the plain.
>
> It is during that return, that pause, that Sisyphus interests me. A face that toils so close to stones is already stone itself! I

see that man going back down with a heavy yet measured step toward the torment of which he will never know the end. That hour like a breathing space which returns as surely as his suffering, that is the hour of consciousness. At each of those moments when he leaves the heights and gradually sinks toward the lairs of the gods, he is superior to his fate. He is stronger than his rock. I leave Sisyphus at the foot of the mountain! One always finds one's burden again. But Sisyphus teaches the higher fidelity that negates the gods and raises rocks. He too concludes that all is well. This universe henceforth without a master seems to him neither sterile nor futile. Each atom of that stone, each mineral flake of that night-filled mountain, in itself forms a world. The struggle itself toward the heights is enough to fill a man's heart. One must imagine Sisyphus happy.

See ABSURD, THEATER OF THE; EXISTENTIALIST CRITICISM.

explication de texte. The detailed analysis, or "close reading," of a passage of VERSE or PROSE, derived from a method of teaching LITERATURE in French secondary schools. Such explication seeks to make meaning clear through a painstaking examination and explanation of STYLE, language, relationship of part to whole, and use of SYMBOLISM. It is an important method in NEW CRITICISM. By enhancing understanding, it improves appreciation and judgment.

exposition. 1. In DRAMA or other FICTION, the immediate or gradual revelation to the audience of the SETTING, relationship between CHARACTERS, and other background information needed for understanding the PLOT. Traditionally, the exposition occurs at the beginning of the PLAY, either in the speech of one character—the nurse in Euripides' *Medea,* the Chorus in *Romeo and Juliet*—or in conversation between two characters. In Sophocles' *Antigone,* a few swift exchanges between Antigone and her sister inform the audience that their two brothers are dead and that the king has buried one brother with a military funeral but refused burial to the other. In some plays with elaborate plots, particularly the "well-made plays" of the nineteenth century, the exposition is mechanical and unrealistic. For example, a maid and a butler might come onstage to gossip about the main characters, and end up telling each other things that logically they both would already know.

Beginning with the plays of Henrik Ibsen, who rebelled against such artificiality and is known for his gradual exposition, most modern drama and fiction present background information a little at a time, as it is needed, or through a FLASHBACK. In some contemporary drama, notably that of the THEATER OF THE ABSURD, exposition is minimal, which is one way the dramatist can suggest a meaningless world in which nothing is explained.

2. Explanation. One of the modes of written or spoken DISCOURSE, or as classified by Aristotle, one of three modes of ARGUMENT, the others being DESCRIPTION and NARRATION.

See DISCOURSE; FLASHBACK; PLOT.

expressionism. A movement influencing painting, DRAMA, POETRY, and FICTION, which attempts to express emotions, moods, and other aspects of inner experience by externalizing them through the use of nonrealistic devices. In painting, for example, objects are not represented realistically but are distorted or exaggerated, and colors are intensified to express emotion. In drama, expressionism involves dreamlike distortions; clipped, staccato DIALOGUE; abrupt, fantastic, and many-leveled action; and nonrealistic stage SETTINGS. For instance, the setting for a SCENE involving a mentally disturbed character might be a room with multicolored walls that veer off at crazy angles and furniture three times larger than life-size. Such a setting would express symbolically the character's confusion and disequilibrium. August Strindberg's *A Dream Play,* Bertolt Brecht's *The Threepenny Opera,* Elmer Rice's *The Adding Machine,* and Eugene O'Neill's *Emperor Jones* and *The Hairy Ape* are examples of expressionistic drama.

In poetry and fiction, expressionism is evident in works that present life not as it appears on the surface to a disinterested and objective observer, but as it is passionately *felt* to be by an author or a character. This requires a symbolic or abstract representation of reality, which often involves distorting real-world objects and dislocating time and space. T. S. Eliot's *The Waste Land* is an expressionistic CLASSIC in poetry, while James Joyce's *Finnegans*

Wake and *Ulysses* and the stories of Franz Kafka notably represent expressionism in fiction.

Actually, *expressionism* is a blanket term. Originating in painting and adopted by LITERATURE, it was most strongly established in drama, especially in Germany after World War I. Today, expressionism survives as a set of techniques and tendencies rather than as an organized or coherent movement.

See IMPRESSIONISM, REALISM, SYMBOLISM.

expressive criticism. An approach to LITERARY CRITICISM that focuses on a literary work as an expression of the individuality of the writer, rather than focusing on the work as an art object or on its EFFECT on a reader. M. H. Abrams coined the term to characterize the approach of the romantic critics Samuel Taylor Coleridge and William Wordsworth. Abrams described expressive criticism in almost their words: "It defines poetry as an expression, or overflow, or utterance of feelings, or as the product of the poet's imagination operating on his or her perceptions, thoughts, and feelings; it tends to judge the work by its sincerity, or genuineness, or adequacy to the poet's individual vision or state of mind; and it often looks in the work for evidences of the particular temperament and experiences of the author, who, consciously or unconsciously, has revealed himself in it." As Abrams also pointed out, expressive criticism is currently practiced by psychoanalytic critics and by critics of consciousness.

See LITERARY CRITICISM, PHENOMENOLOGY, PSYCHOANALYTIC CRITICISM, ROMANTICISM.

extended metaphor. A METAPHOR, or implied comparison, that is sustained for several lines or that becomes the controlling IMAGE of an entire poem. In "Sale Today" Phyllis McGinley indirectly compares the lure of bargains for shoppers to that of sweet syrup for flies, extending the metaphor and then stating the comparison in the SIMILE in the next to the last line:

> What syrup, what unusual sweet,
>   Sticky and sharp and strong,
> Wafting its poison through the street,
>   Has lured this buzzing throng
> That swarms along the counters there

> Where bargain bait is dangled—
> Clustered like flies in honey snare,
>   Shrill, cross, and well entangled?

See IMAGE, METAPHOR.

external conflict. A CHARACTER's struggle against nature or against another character. See CONFLICT.

eye rhyme. RHYME based on spelling rather than sound; for example, *bough* and *though, have* and *grave, watch* and *catch*. Note the words *move* and *love* in the following lines:

> If these delights thy mind may move,
> Come live with me and be my love.

Common in English poetry, eye rhyme may sometimes be the result of a change in pronunciation since the time the poem was written. Such is the case with *far* and *war, Cathay* and *tea*.

See RHYME, SLANT RHYME.

F

fable. Usually a short and fairly simple story designed to illustrate a moral lesson. The CHARACTERS are often animals who exhibit human frailties. The fables attributed to the Greek slave Aesop are the most familiar, having been passed down, translated, and reshaped by other Greeks, by Plautus, by Marie de France, and, in what is regarded as the best version, by the seventeenth-century French writer Jean de la Fontaine. La Fontaine's *Fables,* in turn, have been faithfully and excellently translated into English by Marianne Moore. Fables from the ORAL LITERATURE of West Africa featured a trickster character, either a snake or a spider or a hare. The trickster hare is an ancestor of Brer Rabbit in Joel Chandler Harris's Uncle Remus stories. Other collections of fables include *The Bidpai,* traditional fables from India; the *Just-So Stories* by Rudyard Kipling; and in a more satirical vein, James Thurber's original fables, *Fables for Our Time* and *More Fables for Our Time.* George Orwell's SATIRE, *Animal Farm,* has also been called a fable (although a complicated one) because of its animal characters.

fabliau. A MEDIEVAL tale in eight-syllable VERSE. Humorous, often bawdy, fabliaux frequently satirized women and the clergy. Adaptations of the fabliau appear in several of Geoffrey Chaucer's tales, including those of the Miller, the Reeve, the Friar, the Summoner, and the Merchant. See SATIRE.

falling action. That part of a dramatic PLOT that follows the CLIMAX, or point of highest interest, and leads (in TRAGEDY) to the CATASTROPHE. In the falling action, the CONFLICT is finally resolved, all questions are answered, loose ends are tied up, and an accounting is given of what happens to the main CHARACTERS. In an ELIZABETHAN tragedy of five acts, the climax occurs in the third act; the falling action, in acts four and five. The terms RESOLUTION and (sometimes) DENOUEMENT are used as synonyms for *falling action*.

See FREYTAG'S PYRAMID, RISING ACTION.

falling meter. In poetry, METER or RHYTHM that begins with a strong accent or stress, like TROCHEES and DACTYLS. See FOOT.

familiar essay. An ESSAY characterized by an intimate or familiar TONE and dealing with personal subjects such as impressions, opinions, and prejudices. See INFORMAL ESSAY.

fancy. In general, an aspect of IMAGINATION that often involves wishful thinking or whim. Up until the nineteenth century, fancy and imagination were used interchangeably. The romantic critics Samuel Taylor Coleridge and William Wordsworth considered fancy a limited form of imagination. They viewed fancy as the part of the mind that was able to associate remembered IMAGES in new ways, cutting across time and space, but was not able to change the individual images. By contrast, imagination was the ability to change images and to create new images. These lines from John Keats's poem "Fancy" describe how fancy associates images:

> Then let winged Fancy wander
> Through the thought still spread beyond her:
> Open wide the mind's cage-door,
> She'll dart forth, and cloudward soar.
>
> . . .
>
> She will bring, in spite of frost,
> Beauties that the earth hath lost;

She will bring thee, all together,
All delights of summer weather;
All the buds and bells of May,
From dewy sward or thorny spray;
All the heaped Autumn's wealth,
With a still, mysterious stealth:
She will mix these pleasures up
Like three fit wines in a cup,
And thou shalt quaff it—

See IMAGINATION, ROMANTICISM.

fantasy. In LITERATURE, a work that is set in an imaginary, unreal, or utopian world (such as Lilliput in *Gulliver's Travels*); that involves fantastic characters (such as the Cheshire Cat and the Mad Hatter in *Alice's Adventures in Wonderland*); or that employs principles of science and physics as yet unknown (such as the SCIENCE FICTION of Ursula LeGuin and Isaac Asimov). Fantasy may be written for pure enjoyment or as serious or satirical commentary on human affairs and institutions. Perhaps the most popular fantasy in recent literature is J. R. R. Tolkien's *The Lord of the Rings.* Fantasy is also alive in films (*2001: A Space Odyssey* and *Labyrinth*) and on television (*Star Trek* and *Beauty and the Beast*).

See SCIENCE FICTION, UTOPIA.

farce. A type of COMEDY, primarily visual, that depends for laughs on outlandish situations, stereotyped CHARACTERS, and exaggerated, often abusive, physical action. Farce is often just an element in a comedy. The complicated, fast-moving PLOTS of farces seem designed to prove Murphy's Law: Whatever can go wrong will go wrong. The silent-movie comedies of Charlie Chaplin, Buster Keaton, and Harold Lloyd, the films of the Marx Brothers, and many Saturday morning cartoons are pure farce, collections of perfectly timed disasters. In the theater, pure farce—comedy that refuses to be either witty or sentimental—is hard to find.

A few times in the history of the theater there have been great outpourings of farce: (1) the Italian RENAISSANCE commedia del l'arte, which exaggerated and streamlined the STOCK

CHARACTERS of the old Greek and Roman comedy and placed them in outrageous situations; (2) the French farces of the nineteenth century, especially those of Georges Feydeau, known for elaborate and surprise-laden plots; (3) silent-movie farce in America; and (4) the THEATER OF THE ABSURD, which emphasizes the meaninglessness of farcical situations, even offering farce as the modern world's substitute for TRAGEDY.

See ABSURD, THEATER OF THE; CHARACTER; COMEDY; PLOT; TRAGEDY.

feminine rhyme. RHYME in which accented syllables in two words are followed by identical unaccented syllables; also called **double rhyme.** Some examples are *turtle/fertile, sitter/hit her,* and *drifting/lifting.* Another sort of feminine rhyme is called **triple rhyme,** in which identical accented vowel sounds are followed by two identical unaccented syllables; for example, *hammering/stammering, tenderly/slenderly, ingratiate/I'll say she ate.* Triple rhyme is a device often employed in humorous verse and popular song lyrics.

See MASCULINE RHYME, RHYME.

feminist criticism. Scholarly and critical literary studies growing out of the 1970s feminist movement. Such studies are aimed at recovering and reassessing works by women authors, evaluating the female image as portrayed by male authors, analyzing sexism and gender privilege in language, evaluating critical methods devised by males, and developing a body of literary criticism from the point of view of feminine consciousness. Feminist critics agree that women's thinking, including creative work, "has tended to be received as if it appeared from nowhere . . . has been made to seem sporadic, erratic, orphaned of any tradition of its own" (Adrienne Rich, *On Lies, Secrets, and Silence,* 1979). The immediate goal of feminist criticism is thus to establish a tradition of literature and literary criticism by women to counterbalance the male tradition. Major accomplishments toward this end include the *Norton Anthology of Literature by Women: The Tradition in English* (1985), edited by Sandra M. Gilbert and Susan Gubar.

See LITERARY CRITICISM.

fiction. NARRATIVE writing that is the product of the author's IMAGINATION, an invention rather than actual history or fact. Its principal goal is entertainment or diversion, but it may also instruct, uplift, or persuade. Although DRAMA, EPICS, NARRATIVE POEMS, FABLES, PARABLES, fairy tales, and FOLKLORE all contain elements of fiction, the term is usually applied today to prose NOVELS and SHORT STORIES.

Even so, *fiction* has a rather broad reference. **Historical fiction** is generally a novel based on an actual person or period but fleshed out by the author's creative imagination; famous historical figures often play only minor roles in the story. **Fictionalized biography** uses the devices of the novel (invented DIALOGUE, illuminating incidents, revelations of a CHARACTER's thoughts and feelings) in an attempt to paint a compelling inner portrait of a real person. **Autobiographical fiction** presents actual events from the author's life, recreated, embellished, and transformed through the filter of his or her imagination. **Documentary fiction** builds imaginative stories around current news events, such as sensational trials, heroic rescues or survivals, disasters, serial murders, and the like.

See BILDUNGSROMAN, HISTORICAL NOVEL, NOVEL, ROMAN À CLEF, SHORT STORY.

figurative language. Language that contains **figures of speech,** such as METAPHOR, SIMILE, PERSONIFICATION, and HYPERBOLE, expressions that make comparisons or associations meant to be interpreted imaginatively rather than literally:

> Yet all experience is an arch wherethrough
> Gleams that untraveled world whose margin fades
> Forever and forever when I move.

In these lines from Alfred, Lord Tennyson's "Ulysses," "experience" is not literally an "arch"; it is being imaginatively compared to one. Nor does the "untraveled world" literally "gleam." But the use of *gleam* wonderfully suggests that world's allure. Although figures of speech occur in all vivid speech and writing, figurative language is essentially the language of POETRY. Poetry is more densely figurative than ordinary conversation or than most PROSE writing, and its figures, especially metaphors, are more evocative and compelling.

See HYPERBOLE, METAPHOR, PERSONIFICATION, SIMILE.

figure of speech. Expressions, such as METAPHORS, SIMILES, PER-SONIFICATIONS, that make comparisons or associations meant to be taken imaginatively rather than literally. See FIGURATIVE LAN-GUAGE.

first-person point of view. The vantage point assumed by a writer from which an "I" NARRATOR experiences (sees, hears, and un-derstands) the story he or she is telling: "I remember the first time I saw Emily, standing in the rain at my bus stop." The first-person point of view may be that of a major CHARACTER who is participating in the action (such as Jane Eyre), or it may be that of a minor character observing the action from the sidelines and reporting it (such as Nick in F. Scott Fitzgerald's *The Great Gatsby*).

See NARRATOR, POINT OF VIEW, THIRD-PERSON POINT OF VIEW.

flashback. In FICTION and film, a way of presenting SCENES or INCI-DENTS that took place before the opening scene. The flashback can be introduced in a number of ways. A CHARACTER may tell another character about past events, have a dream about them, or simply think back to the events. In Anne Tyler's *Breathing Les-sons,* Maggie, who is trying to get her son and his ex-wife back together, recalls events from the early days of their marriage, giv-ing the reader an opportunity to find out what went wrong. In film, there is usually no introduction to the flashback. The cam-era simply cuts back to the earlier event, and the viewer relates it to the story.

The advantage of using a flashback is that a story can start in the middle or near the end, get the reader involved, and then fill in what led up to that point. In Thornton Wilder's *The Bridge of San Luis Rey,* several people are on a bridge when it collapses. The rest of the story consists of flashbacks narrating the events in each character's life that destined him or her to be at that bridge at that moment. The practice of beginning a story IN MEDIAS RES (in the middle of things) derives from the Homeric EPICS the *Iliad* and the *Odyssey.*

See IN MEDIAS RES.

flat character. In FICTION, a two-dimensional character lacking the depth or complexity of a real person, one who is built around a single dominant trait or quality and who represents a TYPE; the opposite of a ROUND CHARACTER. See CHARACTER, CHARACTERIZATION.

fly-on-the-wall technique. An objective method of NARRATION, sometimes called the SCENIC METHOD. Presumably, the NARRATOR is like a fly on the wall, reporting events as they are observed. See POINT OF VIEW.

foil. Usually, a CHARACTER who, by contrast, points up the qualities or characteristics of another character. For example, a foolish character sets a wise character's wisdom in a stronger light. In William Shakespeare's *Henry IV, Part 1,* Hotspur, with his fiery determination, serves as a foil to Prince Hal, who is reluctant to leave off sowing his wild oats and to take up his princely responsibilities.
See CHARACTER, CHARACTERIZATION.

folk ballad. NARRATIVE POETRY, usually composed anonymously and arising out of an oral tradition, that tells a story of common people, often through the use of DIALOGUE. Important elements of folk ballads include action rather than CHARACTERIZATION or DESCRIPTION, a pronounced RHYTHM, simple language, REFRAINS, and INCREMENTAL REPETITION. See BALLAD.

folk epic. An EPIC of communal, unknown, or uncertain origin. See EPIC.

folklore. The traditional songs, LEGENDS, beliefs, crafts, and customs of a people that are passed from one generation to the next by word of mouth and usually not written down until they are collected by scholars. Folklore is often a pre-literature, in the sense that written LITERATURE absorbs the FORMS of folklore—BALLAD, work song, FABLE, riddle, TALL TALE, and so on—and makes continuing use of its situations, CHARACTERS, and THEMES. An example common to many countries is the legend of someone striking a bargain with the devil; the legend has been transformed into works as various as Johann Wolfgang von Goethe's *Faust,* Washington Irving's "The Devil and Tom

Walker," Guy de Maupassant's "The Devil," and Leo Tolstoy's "How Much Land Does a Man Need?"

See BALLAD, FABLE, LEGEND, MYTH, ORAL LITERATURE.

foot.   The basic unit of rhythmic measurement in a line of POETRY. In traditional English VERSE, a foot consists most often of at least one accented (stressed) syllable and one or more unaccented (unstressed) syllables. The number and type of feet in a line of a poem determine its METER.

The five most commonly used feet are illustrated below. Accented syllables are indicated by the mark (´); unaccented syllables by (˘).

The **iambus (iambic foot)** consists of one unaccented syllable followed by one accented syllable:

    reply   today   disturb

The **trochee (trochaic foot)** consists of one accented syllable followed by one unaccented syllable:

    nonsense   playful   final

The **anapest (anapestic foot)** consists of two unaccented syllables followed by one accented syllable:

    understand   serenade   in a flash

The **dactyl (dactylic foot)** consists of one accented syllable followed by two unaccented syllables:

    sympathy   bountiful   cover me

The **spondee (spondaic foot)** consists of two accented syllables:

    widespread   blue-green   Don't move!

Because the iambus (or iamb) and the anapest move toward stress, they are called **rising meters.** The trochee and the dactyl, which move away from stress, are called **falling meters.**

Of the five kinds of feet illustrated here, the iambus is by far the most often used in English verse; the spondee is the rarest. Other feet (such as the amphibrach, amphimacer, antibacchius, bacchius, and dibrach) appear so infrequently that they have not been considered.

See METER, RHYTHM, SCANSION.

foregrounding. Calling attention to something—a word, a RHYTHM, a CHARACTER, an idea, a viewpoint—by placing it in the foreground against a background. Taken from painting and the study of visual perspective, the term is used more broadly to mean setting anything off from its CONTEXT or creating something that stands out from the ordinary, the traditional, the routine. Interpreting a NOVEL as if it were being read by a woman foregrounds the woman's viewpoint.

This broad concept of foregrounding grows out of the theory of formalist critics in Prague before World War I, who, as LINGUISTICS experts, were particularly interested in foregrounding in POETRY. For example, a METAPHOR is foregrounded in an otherwise literal statement, and change of METER is foregrounded against the regular meter.

See FORMAL CRITICISM, LITERARY CRITICISM.

foreshadowing. In literature, the technique of giving hints or clues that suggest or prepare for events that occur later in a work. A somber, forbidding ATMOSPHERE can foreshadow impending tragedy, as it does in Thomas Hardy's description of menacing Egdon Heath in *The Return of the Native*. Seemingly incidental occurrences can prefigure a climactic event. In F. Scott Fitzgerald's *The Great Gatsby*, for example, two minor automobile accidents foreshadow the violent death of Myrtle Wilson, who is run down by Gatsby's car. Foreshadowing creates suspense, prepares the reader for what happens next, and makes final outcomes seem inevitable.

form. The organizing principle that shapes a work of LITERATURE. The nineteenth-century romantic poet and critic Samuel Taylor Coleridge distinguished two ways of thinking about form, a distinction that continues to be useful: (1) Form may be viewed as a preexisting STRUCTURE imposed on and restricting the content of an individual work; (2) Form may be viewed as the unique way content takes shape in a particular work.

In the second view, form and content develop simultaneously, modifying each other, as a work is written. The form is thus organic. There is no such thing as the same form with different content; a change in one results in a change in the other.

To determine what is unique about the form of a particular work, it is often necessary to combine these two ideas of form, to see the work against the form of the GENRE—for example, DETECTIVE STORY, MELODRAMA, BALLAD—that restricts it and is transformed by it, and also to analyze the unique way content is shaped in the particular work.

See GENRE, STRUCTURE.

formal criticism. An approach to LITERARY CRITICISM that attempts to explain or evaluate the way in which the content of a work is structured, or given FORM, but does not evaluate the content of the work against standards of truth or morality. Critical attitudes and methodologies as various as AESTHETICISM, Russian FORMALISM, NEW CRITICISM, NEOCLASSICISM, STRUCTURALISM, and SEMIOTICS can all be classified as formal criticism.

See AESTHETICISM, FORMALISM, LITERARY CRITICISM, NEW CRITICISM, SEMIOTICS, STRUCTURALISM.

formal essay. An objective, serious, carefully organized, and logically developed PROSE composition written to inform or to persuade. Today, formal essays appear in a variety of styles, lengths, and subject matter, most often as articles in magazines, newspapers, professional publications, and academic journals.

See ESSAY, INFORMAL ESSAY.

formalism. A school of LITERARY CRITICISM originating in Russia during the 1920s. To the formalist critic, art is STYLE, technique, and craftsmanship, and the primary function of criticism is the objective and "scientific" analysis of literary style. According to Viktor Shklovsky, a well-known formalist critic, "Art is a way of experiencing the artfulness of an object; the object is not important," and "A work of art is equal to the sum of processes used in it."

In the United States, the formalist emphasis on form rather than content became evident in the works of Edgar Allan Poe, Henry James, and T. S. Eliot, and in NEW CRITICISM. A later critical movement called STRUCTURALISM was greatly influenced by a linguistically oriented group of formalists known as the

Moscow Linguistic Circle, one of whose members was Roman Jakobson.

See NEW CRITICISM, STRUCTURALISM.

formal satire. The type of SATIRE, sometimes called **direct satire,** in which the author, or a NARRATOR created by the author, speaks in the first person directly to the reader or, sometimes, to a CHARACTER within the work. For example, Alexander Pope addresses the reader directly in *Moral Essays.* See SATIRE.

free verse. A type of POETRY that differs from traditional VERSE FORMS in that it is "free" of the regular beat of METER, depending instead on the individual poet's sensitivity to the music of natural speech RHYTHMS. Also, free verse usually lacks RHYME and often has irregular line lengths and fragmentary SYNTAX. The modern free-verse movement began in the nineteenth century with Walt Whitman's *Leaves of Grass* and the poetry of French SYMBOLISTS Charles Baudelaire and Paul Verlaine and of the English poet Gerard Manley Hopkins. Forerunners of free verse range from the alliterative verse of the MIDDLE AGES to the Psalms of the King James Bible to the BLANK VERSE of John Milton and a number of poems by William Blake and Emily Dickinson.

Although twentieth-century poetry is predominantly free verse, some poets are more comfortable working with traditional rhyme and meter. For them, writing free verse seems, as Robert Frost put it, "like playing tennis with the net down." For other poets, writing free verse is an opportunity to create their own rhythmic and visual form. Some free-verse poets invent a new form for each poem. Others establish a pattern that they use from poem to poem, such as William Carlos Williams' variable FOOT or Whitman's pause for breath at the end of each line:

When I heard the learn'd astronomer,
When the proofs, the figures, were ranged in columns before me,
When I was shown the charts and diagrams, to add, divide, and measure them,
When I sitting heard the astronomer where he lectured with much applause in the lecture-room,

How soon unaccountable I became tired and sick,
Till rising and gliding out I wander'd off by myself,
In the mystical moist night-air, and from time to time,
Look'd up in perfect silence at the stars.

See BLANK VERSE, METER, RHYTHM, SYMBOLIST MOVEMENT.

Freytag's pyramid.   A diagram representing the structure of a well-made play, especially a TRAGEDY in five acts. First proposed in 1863 by Gustav Freytag, a German novelist and critic, the pyramid has been widely adapted to illustrate the PLOT structure of NOVELS and SHORT STORIES as well as DRAMA.

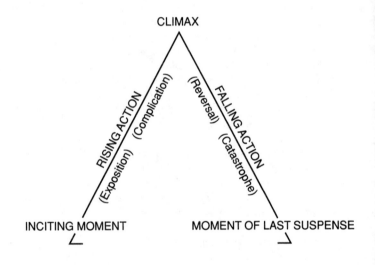

See CATASTROPHE, CLIMAX, DENOUEMENT, FALLING ACTION, PLOT, RISING ACTION.

G

generative poetics. A theory of LITERATURE that seeks to describe and explain the "literary competence" that experienced readers apply in order to understand how literary texts are constructed and what they mean. See POETICS.

genre. A type of literary work. The NOVEL, the SHORT STORY, and the LYRIC poem are all genres, with their own sets of characteristics, or CONVENTIONS. The EPISTOLARY NOVEL, HAIKU, the DETECTIVE STORY, and EPIC THEATER are examples of subgenres within the larger genres. Aristotle established the concept of genre in the *Poetics,* characterizing TRAGEDY, COMEDY, and EPIC among the genres of his day. The study of how an individual literary work both represents and transforms the genre to which it belongs is known as **genre criticism.**

See CONVENTION, LITERARY CRITICISM.

Georgian. An adjective applied to two different periods in English history. Although one period extends through the reigns of the four Georges (1714–1830), the term is most often used in reference to the reign of George V and the period between World War I and World War II, roughly 1914 to 1940. Sometimes called the Georgian Age, this was an especially rich era in English LIT-

ERATURE. Sir Edward Marsh edited five volumes of VERSE from 1912 to 1922 entitled *Georgian Poetry,* which included works by Thomas Hardy, John Masefield, Walter de la Mare, and W. B. Yeats, among others. During the 1920s, Dorothy Richardson, Virginia Woolf, and James Joyce stimulated tremendous interest in experimental FICTION, while Yeats and T. S. Eliot were the dominant voices in POETRY. During the 1930s, the prominent names in DRAMA were George Bernard Shaw, Somerset Maugham, and Noël Coward; in fiction, D. H. Lawrence, Aldous Huxley, Evelyn Waugh, and Graham Greene.

gestalt. A unified whole that is greater than the sum of its parts. According to the gestalt theory of LITERATURE, a poem, for example, must be experienced as a unified whole; it cannot be accounted for by the analysis of its elements. Gestalt psychology views human actions as gestalts (wholes) rather than breaking them down into elements such as stimuli, reflexes, and sensations.

gloss. An explanation, definition, or interpretation of a difficult, foreign, or technical word or passage. Glosses take the form of notes that appear between lines, in margins, or at the foot of a page. They are found most frequently in textbooks and in scientific and technical works, works in which a specialized vocabulary is used. Collected into an alphabetical list at the back of a book, glosses form a **glossary.** The word *gloss* can have a negative meaning, as in "to gloss over," to excuse or explain away.

Gothic. Barbaric; from the MIDDLE AGES. Originally referring to the Goths, barbarian tribes who sacked Rome in A.D. 410, the term *Gothic* was mistakenly applied by eighteenth-century critics to everything MEDIEVAL, including the kind of cathedral still known as Gothic—with its vaulted arches, flying buttresses, and gargoyles. Used in reference to LITERATURE, as when Carson McCullers's story "The Ballad of the Sad Cafe" is labeled Southern Gothic, the term calls to mind gloom, grotesqueness, mystery, and DECADENCE, the ATMOSPHERE also of earlier GOTHIC NOVELS, such as Victor Hugo's *The Hunchback of Notre Dame.*

See GOTHIC NOVEL.

Gothic novel.   A type of NOVEL characterized by mystery, horror, and the supernatural, often with haunted castles, secret passageways, grisly visions, all the paraphernalia of the tale of terror. Horace Walpole is credited with the original Gothic novel, his *Castle of Otranto* (1764). Other early examples of the type are Clara Reeve's *The Old English Baron,* Ann Radcliffe's *The Mysteries of Udolpho,* and Mary Shelley's *Frankenstein.* More recent practitioners of the form include Iris Murdoch, Shirley Jackson, Mary Stewart, Phyllis Whitney, and Victoria Holt. Present-day Gothic novels, like Daphne du Maurier's *Rebecca,* while lacking MEDIEVAL SETTINGS, still take place in terrifying and mysterious surroundings, create brooding ATMOSPHERES, and involve love stories in true GOTHIC style. Among the more prolific and popular writers of Gothic novels today is Stephen King, whose *Carrie, Pet Sematary, Salem's Lot,* and *The Shining* attest to the continuing popularity of the GENRE.

See GOTHIC.

graveyard school.   A group of preromantic English poets of the mid-eighteenth century who wrote meditative poems on death and immortality, partly in rebellion against a tendency in their time to avoid mentioning the subject of death. The best known of these poems, which were full of the ATMOSPHERE and IMAGERY of graveyards at night, is Thomas Gray's "Elegy Written in a Country Churchyard."

See ROMANTICISM.

grotesque.   Generally, anything distorted, ugly, abnormal, fantastic, or bizarre to the point of being ludicrous or absurd. Applied to decorative art, the term denotes a STYLE in which fantastic representations of human and animal forms are combined and interwoven to form a bizarre composite.

When applied to LITERATURE, the term *grotesque* refers to a type of writing, to a kind of CHARACTER, and to a kind of subject matter, all characterized by exaggeration and distortion of the natural or the expected. A work of FICTION may be called grotesque if it involves physically or psychologically deformed characters whose actions are abnormal, incongruous, or comically absurd. The grotesque can be found in the NOVELS and SHORT STORIES of such American writers as Frank Norris, Nathanael

West, Eudora Welty, William Faulkner, and Flannery O'Connor. Sherwood Anderson called *Winesburg, Ohio,* a collection of stories about people who do not fit into the ordinary pattern of life in the community, "The Book of the Grotesque."

See CARICATURE.

H

haiku. A LYRIC poem, originating in Japan, that captures the essence of a moment in a simple IMAGE:

> The cold winter wind
> writes its message in shivers
> on the drifting snow.

—Georgian Tashjian

Invariably written in the present tense, a haiku often makes some reference to a season or a time of day. In Japanese the haiku consists of seventeen symbol sounds and is unrhymed. The seventeen syllables of English-language haikus are usually arranged in three lines of five, seven, and five syllables, respectively.

See IMAGISTS, TANKA.

half rhyme. Another term for SLANT RHYME, an approximate RHYME. See RHYME, SLANT RHYME.

hamartia. The error, misstep, frailty, or flaw that causes the downfall of a tragic HERO. Sometimes called the TRAGIC FLAW, hamartia may be, but need not be, a flaw in character. It may instead be bad judgment, ignorance, accident, inherited weakness, or plain bad luck. In the *Poetics,* Aristotle describes the hero of

TRAGEDY as "a man, not preeminently virtuous and just, whose misfortune, however, is brought upon him not by vice and depravity but by some error." Whatever the error or defect, it results in action (or inaction) that leads to disaster. It could be said that the hamartia of Macbeth is ambition; of Othello, jealousy.

See TRAGEDY.

Harlem Renaissance. The flourishing of black creativity in New York City's Harlem in the 1920s. Led by writers James Weldon Johnson and Langston Hughes, the movement also included artists and musicians and is popularly known as the era of Duke Ellington's jazz at the Cotton Club. Important literary works produced during the Harlem Renaissance include *Color* and *Copper Sun,* collections of poems by Countee Cullen; Langston Hughes' *The Weary Blues; Caroling Dusk: An Anthology of Verse by Negro Poets,* edited by Cullen; a successful play, *Harlem,* by Wallace Thurman and William Jordan Rapp; and Arno Bontemps' first novel *God Sends Sunday.* The movement came to an end with the onset of the Depression.

hedonism. The pursuit of pleasure above all else. In Greek philosophy, hedonism emerged in the teachings of Aristippus (435–366 B.C.) and the Cyrenaics as a belief in the importance of sensual gratification. The highest virtue was the capacity to enjoy. The concept was refined by Epicurus (341–270 B.C.) and his followers. For Epicureans, the goal was intellectual pleasure, or serenity, achieved by controlling physical desires and thus avoiding the pain their indulgence invariably brings.

See CARPE DIEM.

heptameter. A line of POETRY consisting of seven metrical feet. These lines from Thomas Babington Macaulay's poem *Virginia* are in heptameter:

And none | will grieve | when I | go forth, |
  or smile | when I | return,
Or sit | beside | the old | man's bed, | or weep
  upon | his urn.

See FOOT, METER, RHYTHM, SCANSION.

hermeneutics.   The theory and practice of interpreting sacred and literary texts. Early Christian interpreters of the CLASSICS and the Bible found several levels of meaning in texts—grammatical, ethical, allegorical, and mystical. In the nineteenth century, Friedrich Schleiermacher originated the idea of the hermeneutic circle: Each part of a text must be interpreted with reference to the whole; yet the meaning of the whole cannot be grasped without considering the parts. In the twentieth century, Martin Heidegger shifted the concept of the hermeneutic circle to that of an open-ended dialogue between each new interpreter and the tradition of interpretation surrounding the text. More recent theories divide the interpretation of texts into **hermeneutics of belief,** which approaches a text as containing truths to be illuminated, and **hermeneutics of suspicion**—as practiced by Friedrich Nietzsche, Karl Marx, and Sigmund Freud—which approaches a text not so much to clarify it as to demystify or unmask its MYTHS and contradictions. DECONSTRUCTION is an application of the hermeneutics of suspicion.

See DECONSTRUCTION, EXEGESIS, LITERARY CRITICISM.

hero/heroine.   Usually the central CHARACTER in a literary work, a figure directly involved in the main action, one who commands the most interest and sympathy of the reader or audience. When the central character is a woman, she is often called a heroine.

The classical hero was a mythological or legendary personage possessing great strength, courage, or sagacity, aided by the gods and often believed to be of divine descent. In modern times, the hero is generally a person admired for noble qualities and actions, one who is considered a model or ideal.

See ANTIHERO, PROTAGONIST.

heroic couplet.   A pair of rhyming IAMBIC PENTAMETER lines; the favored VERSE FORM of eighteenth-century neoclassical poets. Although it was introduced by Geoffrey Chaucer, this couplet takes its name from its use in the heroic DRAMA of John Dryden and the MOCK EPICS of Alexander Pope. In the hands of these and other neoclassical writers, the closed form of the heroic couplet (each couplet syntactically complete) proved to be an appropriate instrument (one might almost say *weapon*) for their aphoristic

WIT. A few lines from Pope's *Essay on Criticism* will show the typical pattern of a complete thought every two lines:

> Whatever Nature has in worth denied,
> She gives in large recruits of needful pride;
> For as in bodies, thus in souls, we find
> What wants in blood and spirits, swelled with wind:
> Pride, where wit fails, steps in to our defense,
> And fills up all the mighty void of sense.
> If once right reason drives that cloud away,
> Truth breaks upon us with resistless day.
> Trust not yourself; but your defects to know,
> Make use of every friend—and every foe.

heroic quatrain. A four-line STANZA in IAMBIC PENTAMETER, rhyming *abab;* also called the **heroic stanza** or **elegaic stanza**. See QUATRAIN.

hexameter. A line of POETRY consisting of six metrical feet. A strictly patterned VERSE FORM in Greek and Latin poetry, true hexameters are not often found in English poetry because the dominant FOOT in the classical form, the SPONDEE, is rare in English. However, poets, notably Henry Wadsworth Longfellow in *Evangeline,* have modified classical hexameter to fit the language. These lines from "When I Was Young and Fair," a poem by Queen Elizabeth I, illustrate one such adaptation:

How mań | y weep | ing eyes | I made | to pine |
   with woe,
How mań | y sigh | ing hearts, | I have | no skill |
   to show.

See ALEXANDRINE, FOOT, METER, RHYTHM, SCANSION.

high comedy. COMEDY characterized by grace, elegance, and WIT, more intellectual than physical, the comedy of manners; the opposite of LOW COMEDY. See COMEDY.

historical criticism. An approach to LITERARY CRITICISM that views a work in the context of the time period in which it was written. Historical critics attempt to reconstruct the climate of ideas, beliefs, and social and literary CONVENTIONS within which writers work. For example, in Ignazio Silone's story "The Trap," knowledge of the Mediterranean tradition of hospitality to strangers aids understanding of the presence of a suspicious stranger—in fact, an enemy—as a guest in the HERO's house. Historical critics also study literary works as historical artifacts that offer insight into the periods in which they were produced.

See LITERARY CRITICISM.

historical fiction.   FICTION that attempts to re-create past events, events that occurred before the author's time. See FICTION.

historical novel.   A NOVEL that attempts to re-create an historically significant personage or series of events. Historical novels are usually set in times of great conflict and social change, periods in which one culture must fall so that another may be born. The PROTAGONIST may be an actual figure from history or a fictional CHARACTER whose destiny is determined by his or her involvement in actual events or with real people. Details of dress, manners, and other aspects of everyday life should be truthful to the age being re-created and should not function as mere window dressing, as is the case with so-called costume romances.

Although writers have combined FICTION and history since the beginning, it was Sir Walter Scott who established the historical novel as a distinctive FORM with his Waverley Novels, among them *Rob Roy, Ivanhoe,* and *Kenilworth.* Prominent examples by other authors include Alexander Dumas's *The Three Musketeers,* Victor Hugo's *Les Miserables,* Leo Tolstoy's *War and Peace,* James Fenimore Cooper's *The Last of the Mohicans,* Margaret Mitchell's *Gone with the Wind,* Kenneth Roberts' *Northwest Passage,* Boris Pasternak's *Doctor Zhivago,* and James Michener's *Alaska.*

See NOVEL.

history play.   A PLAY centered on historical events; the name often given the ten plays in William Shakespeare's *First Folio* that are labeled as *histories* rather than as COMEDIES or TRAGEDIES. See CHRONICLE PLAY.

Homeric epithet.   A hyphenated adjective used repeatedly in conjunction with the same noun, so as to form a unit of expression, for example, Homer's "wine-dark sea" and "all-seeing Jove." See EPITHET.

Homeric simile.   Another term for EPIC SIMILE, a lengthy, very elaborate SIMILE. See SIMILE.

Horatian satire.   SATIRE that is gentle, amused, witty, and mildly corrective; a direct contrast to JUVENALIAN SATIRE. See SATIRE.

hubris.   The Greek word for pride or insolence. In his discussion of TRAGEDY in the *Poetics,* Aristotle identifies hubris as the defect of character that leads the tragic HERO to disregard all warnings of impending disaster and thereby hasten the CATASTROPHE. William Shakespeare's Richard III's hubris causes him to have any who warn him put to death, which leaves him isolated, his last allies fled, in his final battle.

See TRAGEDY.

humanism.   In the broadest sense, any system of thought or action devoted to human interests (especially to the elevation of human values and dignity) rather than to religious ideals or to the animal world. In a stricter sense, *humanism* refers to the involvement in those studies that deal with the language, life, LITERATURE, or thought of ancient Greece and Rome.

Historically, the term *humanism* is used to designate the "rebirth" of classical literature and thought that began in Italy during the fourteenth century and that lay at the heart of the RENAISSANCE. Renaissance humanists rediscovered Greek and Roman poets, philosophers, and historians and embraced their beliefs in the essential dignity, worth, and potential of humankind and in the importance of the present life. These views sharply opposed the MEDIEVAL conception of humankind as essentially wicked, worthless, and doomed to perdition, a conception that emphasized the importance of the life hereafter.

Some Renaissance humanists, in their zeal to break away from medieval attitudes (especially spiritual subservience to the Church), stressed the secular to the detriment of the religious. Others, notably Erasmus and John Milton, seeing the rational wisdom of antiquity as a complement to revelation, fused humanism with Christianity.

Renaissance humanism exerted a powerful influence on literature. It resurrected important ideas from classical criticism and in doing so, stimulated the reexamination of the principles and practices of art. By advocating imitation of the CLASSICS, it nurtured grace, restraint, and form in vernacular literature and introduced writers to the INCIDENTS and CHARACTERS of classical mythology, leading directly to NEOCLASSICISM.

See NEW HUMANISM.

humor.   Anything that causes laughter or amusement. Deriving from the ancient theory of the four humors, humor originally had nothing to do with laughter. A humorous CHARACTER was a person whose temperament or disposition was out of balance: "The Duke is humourous," Le Beau warns Orlando in William Shakespeare's *As You Like It,* meaning that the Duke's mood is dangerously unpredictable. Because extremes of temperament are easily comic, in ELIZABETHAN DRAMA, humorous characters were often presented as laughable, and the word *humor* became synonymous with the laughable, not only in human character, but also in situation and INCIDENT.

See COMEDY; HUMORS, THEORY OF; WIT.

humors, theory of.   According to ancient and MEDIEVAL medicine, the four basic fluids of the body: blood, phlegm, yellow bile (choler), and black bile (melancholy).

It was believed that these four fluids directly affect a person's physical condition and disposition. When the humors are in balance, the result is a perfect temperament. If blood dominates, the person is *sanguine:* generous, happy, amorous. A preponderance of phlegm makes the person *phlegmatic:* apathetic, cowardly, pale. Too much yellow bile causes the person to be *choleric:* hottempered, impatient, vindictive. The dominance of black bile results in the person's being *melancholic:* pensive, sentimental, gluttonous, lethargic.

This conception of the humors exerted an important influence on ELIZABETHAN LITERATURE, especially on the development of CHARACTERS. In his comedy *Every Man Out of His Humour,* Ben Jonson writes that a humor may "so possess a man that it doth draw/All his effects, his spirits, and his powers,/In their confluxions, all to run one way." The old sense of *humor* still survives in the expression "She is in a bad humor."

See COMEDY.

hyperbole. Obvious, extravagant EXAGGERATION or overstatement, not intended to be taken literally, but used figuratively to create HUMOR or emphasis. The most extreme examples of hyperbole occur, not surprisingly, in love POETRY, a CONTEXT, moreover, in which hyperbole seems psychologically believable. In Andrew Marvell's "To His Coy Mistress," for example, the SPEAKER declares:

> My vegetable love should grow
> Vaster than empires, and more slow,
> An hundred years should go to praise
> Thine eyes, and on thy forehead gaze:
> Two hundred to adore each breast:
> But thirty thousand to the rest;
> An age at least to every part,
> And the last age should show your heart.
> For, lady, you deserve this state,
> Nor would I love at lower rate.

See FIGURATIVE LANGUAGE.

I

iamb (iambus). A metrical FOOT consisting of two syllables, an unaccented syllable followed by an accented syllable, as in the word
ĭnváde. The iamb, or iambus, is the most common foot in English
VERSE. This line from a poem by Sara Teasdale contains five
iambs, or iambic feet:

Ĭ múst | hăve pássed | thĕ crést | ă while | ăgó

See FOOT, METER, SCANSION.

iambic meter. METER composed of iambic feet, or IAMBS. The iamb
consists of an unaccented syllable followed by an accented syllable. The opening lines of this poem by William Wordsworth are
written in iambic meter. The first line is in iambic TETRAMETER
(four feet to the line) and the second in iambic TRIMETER (three
feet to the line):

Mў héart | leăps úp | whĕn Í | bĕhóld
Ă raín | bŏw ín | thĕ ský.

See FOOT, METER, SCANSION.

iambic pentameter.   A poetic line of five iambic feet. Iambic pentameter is a common METER in English poetry; it is the meter of BLANK VERSE, the SONNET, and the HEROIC COUPLET. These lines from "The Lost Symbols" by Elizabeth Jennings are written in iambic pentameter:

> And minds │ were gut │ted too. │ Men learned │ to act
> As though │ there were │ no mean │ing in │ the town.

See FOOT, IAMBIC METER, METER, RHYTHM, SCANSION.

identical rhyme.   RHYME in which the same word or a homonym of the word (a word that sounds the same but is spelled differently) is repeated, such as *bear/bare, blue/blew.* See RHYME.

idyll.   A short descriptive and NARRATIVE piece, usually a poem, about picturesque country life, an idealized story of happy innocence. The idyll originated with Theocritus, a Greek bucolic poet of the third century B.C., who described the simple, rustic life of Sicily for his patrician readers. The term has also been applied to PROSE tales of rural life and to longer descriptive and narrative poems with EPIC, romantic, or tragic themes, such as Alfred, Lord Tennyson's *Idylls of the King* and Robert Browning's *Dramatic Idylls.* Thus *idyll* is a descriptive term rather than a specific poetic GENRE. *Maude Muller,* by John G. Whittier, is perhaps the best-known American idyll.

See PASTORAL.

image.   Language referring to something that can be perceived through one or more of the senses—sight, hearing, smell, taste, touch, the sense of motion, or the sense of heat or cold. The following lines from John Masefield's "Sea Fever" contain images referring to sight, touch, hearing, and motion:

> And the wheel's kick and the wind's song and the white
>   sail's shaking,
> And a gray mist on the sea's face and a gray dawn breaking.

An image may simply name something; it may describe it literally; or it may invoke it figuratively, as in a METAPHOR, SIMILE, or PERSONIFICATION. An image can also be a SYMBOL.

See IMAGERY, METAPHOR, PERSONIFICATION, SIMILE, SYMBOL.

imagery. The making of "pictures in words," the pictorial quality of a literary work achieved through a collection of IMAGES. In a broader sense, *imagery* is often used as synonymous with FIGURE OF SPEECH or FIGURATIVE LANGUAGE (SIMILE, METAPHOR, or SYMBOL). Imagery appeals to the senses of taste, smell, hearing, and touch, and to internal feelings, as well as to the sense of sight. It evokes a complex of emotional suggestions and communicates MOOD, TONE, and meaning. It can be both figurative and literal, as these lines from Elinor Wylie's "Puritan Sonnet" demonstrate:

> I love those skies, thin blue or snowy gray,
> Those fields sparse-planted, rendering meager sheaves;
> That spring, briefer than apple-blossom's breath,
> Summer, so much too beautiful to stay,
> Swift autumn, like a bonfire of leaves,
> And sleepy winter, like the sleep of death.

See IMAGE.

imagination. The IMAGE-making and synthesizing power of the human mind; the source of creative thinking. Valued in artists and poets, but feared in the insane, *imagination* was traditionally used interchangeably with FANCY as a term for the faculty of the human mind that recombines remembered images. Imagination was distinguished from—even opposed to—reason and judgment. Eighteenth-century rationalists went so far as to insist that the products of the imagination be tested by reason and judgment. However, the romantic poets raised imagination above both reason and fancy. In *Biographia Literaria,* Samuel Taylor Coleridge distinguished fancy (the capacity simply to reassemble remembered images) from imagination (which "dissolves, diffuses, dissipates" images "in order to re-create"). John Keats wrote that "what the imagination seizes as beauty must be truth—whether it existed before or not."

See FANCY, ROMANTICISM.

Imagists. A group of early twentieth-century English and American poets who, in revolting against the excesses of ROMANTICISM,
sought to restore the precise use of visual IMAGES to POETRY.
Prominent Imagists were T. E. Hulme, Ezra Pound, H. D.
(Hilda Doolittle), John Gould Fletcher, Richard Aldington,
Harriet Monroe, Amy Lowell, and William Carlos Williams.
Their objectives were to use the language of common speech; to
use only the exact word and "absolutely no word that does not
contribute to the presentation"; to create new RHYTHMS "in the
sequence of the musical phrase, not in the sequence of a metronome"; to allow complete freedom of subject matter; to create
concrete, hard-edged, sharply delineated images. Influenced by
Oriental poetry, especially the Japanese HAIKU, the Imagists believed that concentration is the very essence of poetry. They usually wrote in FREE VERSE. "Oread" by H. D. is representative:

> Whirl up, sea—
> whirl your pointed pines,
> splash your great pines
> on our rocks,
> hurl your green over us,
> cover us with your pools of fir.

imitation. In general, a copy, facsimile, or representation. The idea
that LITERATURE is an imitation of life originated with the
Greeks and is often referred to by the Greek word for imitation,
MIMESIS. According to Aristotle, literature is an imitation of
things "as they are, as they are thought to be, as they ought to
be."

Imitation has been viewed as the goal of literature in another
sense. Neoclassical writers and critics believed that imitating
classical writers was the same or better than directly imitating
nature because—as Alexander Pope characterized the achieve-
ment of classical writers—they presented "nature methodized."

See LITERARY CRITICISM.

implied author. Not the author directly, but a PERSONA created by
the author to present a literary work to the reader, an assumed
voice through which the author speaks. According to Wayne C.
Booth (*The Rhetoric of Fiction*), to whom the term is attributed, ev-

ery work has an implied author who is consciously created and
who is an idealized version of the actual author.

See NARRATOR.

impressionism.   The theory and practice of emphasizing the subjective impression a writer or character has of reality, rather than attempting to re-create reality objectively. The term was originally
applied to the work of a group of nineteenth-century French
painters, including Claude Monet, Édouard Manet, Edgar De-
gas, and Jean Renoir, whose paintings are studies in the relationship between subjective perception and reality. Monet, for
example, was particularly interested in the effect of changing
light on the impression a viewer has of a scene. In literature, the
term *impressionism* has been applied to the technique used by
modern novelists such as James Joyce, Virginia Woolf, Dorothy
Richardson, and John Dos Passos, of focusing on the inner life of
the main CHARACTER and on the impression that character has
of reality. The term is even more aptly applied to the subjective
DESCRIPTION found in the poetry of the French and English SYM-
BOLISTS and the American IMAGISTS. Oscar Wilde's impressionistic description of a harbor reduces the real scene to a "Symphony
in Yellow":

> Big barges full of yellow hay
>   Are moored against the shadowy wharf,
>   And, like a yellow silken scarf,
> The thick fog hangs along the quay.

See STREAM OF CONSCIOUSNESS.

impressionistic criticism.   A type of LITERARY CRITICISM that centers on the personal sensitivities of the critic, "a sensitive soul
among masterpieces," who attempts to communicate how he or
she is affected by a work of art. The English critic, essayist, and
novelist Walter Pater has said that "the function of the aesthetic
critic is to distinguish, analyse, and separate from its adjuncts,
the virtue by which a picture, a landscape, a fair personality in
life or in a book, produces this special impression of beauty or
pleasure, to indicate what the source of that impression is, and
under what conditions it is experienced."

See LITERARY CRITICISM.

incident. An event or EPISODE in a work of FICTION that moves the PLOT forward or reveals CHARACTER. An incident need not be long. According to Henry James, writing in *The Art of Fiction,* "It is an incident for a woman to stand up with her hand resting on a table and look at you in a certain way."

See PLOT.

inciting moment. A term used to describe the INCIDENT or impetus that sets the RISING ACTION of a PLAY or other work of FICTION into motion. See FREYTAG'S PYRAMID, RISING ACTION.

incongruity. The quality of being incongruous, in any of a number of ways: of being inharmonious or incompatible or inconsistent; of lacking agreement or suitability. COMEDY is said to derive from the "juxtaposition of the incongruous," that is, the placing together of elements that do not belong together. What is funny in the PLAY (and later television series) *The Odd Couple,* for example, is the result of the juxtaposition of two incongruous CHARACTERS.

incremental repetition. In POETRY, the repetition of a previous line or lines, with a slight variation that adds to or advances the story by *increments,* or regular small additions; a device characteristic of the BALLAD. These two STANZAS from "The Wife of Usher's Well," a FOLK BALLAD, illustrate incremental repetition:

> They hadna been a week from her,
> A week but barely ane,
> Whan word came to the carline wife
> That her three sons were gane.
>
> They hadna been a week from her,
> A week but barely three,
> Whan word came to the carline wife
> That her sons she'd never see.

See BALLAD.

indirect satire. A type of SATIRE in which the author does not address the reader directly. Most often the author creates a fictional NARRATIVE peopled with CHARACTERS whose opinions, statements, motivations, and actions are the objects of ridicule. See SATIRE.

inference. A general conclusion drawn from particulars. For example, understanding literary CHARACTERS usually involves inferring what kind of people they are or what their moods are from the particular details of what they do and say and of what others say about them. When a writer says of a character that "he walked heavily, not looking where he put his feet," the reader is likely to infer that the man is tired.

influence. A term used by literary historians and critics to describe the effect of earlier writers and their works upon later writers. During the early part of the twentieth century, a good many critics occupied themselves with tracing obvious, subtle, and sometimes farfetched influences upon prominent writers. However, the method became strained and gradually fell into disrepute. More recently the theory of influence has undergone radical revision, due largely to the work of critic Harold Bloom and the theory he calls the **anxiety of influence.** Bloom feels that anxiety of influence (fear that the work of previous poets makes truly original POETRY impossible) forces a poet to read a precursor's work "defensively," distorting it beyond conscious recognition in order to protect his or her sense of autonomy and originality. Still, despite this defensive tactic, the poet unavoidably embodies the distorted earlier work into his or her own original poem. While Bloom originally applied his theory to both the writing and the reading of POETRY, other critics have applied his theory to FICTION as well.

informal essay. A PROSE composition, usually brief and without formal structure, written to amuse or to entertain; also called the **familiar essay** or the **personal essay.** Possible subject matter for the informal essay is unlimited and often reflects the whims and personality of the author. The style, while relaxed and conversational, is characteristically polished and sophisticated. According to John Fletcher, "the play of the mind in free associations around a given topic is what counts." Perhaps the best known American writer of informal essays is E. B. White.

See ESSAY, FORMAL ESSAY.

in medias res. From Latin, meaning "in the middle of things." The term describes the NARRATIVE practice of starting a story in the middle of the ACTION to involve the reader, and then using one or more FLASHBACKS to fill in what led up to that point. Although the technique is common in modern FICTION and, especially, in film, the term *in medias res* is usually reserved for EPIC POETRY, of which it is a CONVENTION. The *Iliad,* for example, begins near the end of the ten-year Trojan War; the *Odyssey,* near the end of Odysseus' ten-year journey home from that war.

See FLASHBACK.

In Memoriam **stanza.** A STANZA of four lines in iambic TETRAMETER, rhyming *abba.* The FORM was used by Alfred, Lord Tennyson in his long poem *In Memoriam.* See QUATRAIN, STANZA.

innuendo. An insinuation; the implication or hint of something derogatory; a device of SATIRE. See SATIRE.

intentional fallacy. A term used in modern criticism to describe what, according to the OBJECTIVE THEORY OF ART, is an error: using the author's stated or implied intention to evaluate or analyze a literary text. The objective theory holds that a literary work is separate, a thing in itself, and should not be judged by external evidence—by letters of the author, by introductions, by journal entries, by conversations. The theory holds that a literary work is AUTOTELIC; its meaning lies wholly within itself. Thus, Edgar Allan Poe's essay on POETRY, "The Philosophy of Composition," should not be used to evaluate or analyze Poe's own poems.

The term *intentional fallacy* was proposed by W. K. Wimsatt and M. C. Beardsley to describe a critical approach that they reject. Wimsatt and Beardsley do say, however, that what an author has to say about his or her work may be considered *after* a close analysis of the work has taken place.

The matter is not settled, and critics continue to debate how much weight should be given to biographical data, social and historical CONTEXTS, linguistic change, and author's statements in evaluating and analyzing literature.

See AFFECTIVE FALLACY, AUTOTELIC, NEW CRITICISM, OBJECTIVE THEORY OF ART.

interior monologue.   The presentation to the reader of the flow of a
CHARACTER's inner emotional experience, or STREAM OF CON-
SCIOUSNESS, at a particular moment. Masters of the technique—
notably James Joyce, Virginia Woolf, Dorothy Richardson, and
William Faulkner—have managed to capture the swirl of associations and IMAGES that characterizes human consciousness. In
Woolf's short story "The New Dress," Mabel Waring attends a
party in a new dress she feels is not right. Her thoughts flow like
this:

> We are all like flies trying to crawl over the edge of the saucer,
> Mabel thought, and repeated the phrase as if she were cross-
> ing herself, as if she were trying to find some spell to annul
> this pain, to make this agony endurable. Tags of Shake-
> speare, lines from books she had read ages ago, suddenly
> came to her when she was in agony, and she repeated them
> over and over again. "Flies trying to crawl," she repeated. If
> she could say that over often enough and make herself see the
> flies, she would become numb, chill, frozen, dumb. Now she
> could see flies crawling slowly out of a saucer of milk with
> their wings stuck together; and she strained and strained
> (standing in front of the looking glass, listening to Rose
> Shaw) to make herself see Rose Shaw and all the other people
> there as flies trying to hoist themselves out of something or
> into something, meager, insignificant, toiling flies. But she
> could not see them like that, not other people. She saw herself
> like that—she was a fly, but the others were dragonflies, but-
> terflies, beautiful insects, dancing, fluttering, skimming,
> while she alone dragged herself up out of the saucer.

See STREAM OF CONSCIOUSNESS.

internal conflict.   A CHARACTER's struggle against himself or herself. See CONFLICT.

internal rhyme.   The rhyming of two or more words in the same
line of POETRY, most often in the middle and at the end of the
line; also called **middle rhyme** and **leonine rhyme.** Internal
rhymes are indicated in the following lines from Percy Bysshe
Shelley's "The Cloud":

> I am the *daughter* of Earth and *Water,*
>   And nursling of the Sky;
> I pass through the *pores* of the ocean and *shores;*
>   I change, but I cannot die.

See RHYME.

interpretation. The attempt to understand both the verbal meaning of a literary work and the work's significance through an intuitive grasp of the work as a whole, balanced against and supported by analysis of the work's elements, structure, and effects.

See HERMENEUTICS.

intrusive narrator. A NARRATOR assuming the OMNISCIENT POINT OF VIEW who often interrupts the story to comment on the CHARACTERS and situation or to indulge in philosophical speculation. Though outside the story, the intrusive narrator often emerges as an enjoyable personality whose comments are important to the understanding of the book. Outstanding examples of the intrusive narrator are found in Henry Fielding's *Tom Jones,* William Thackeray's *Vanity Fair,* Leo Tolstoy's *War and Peace,* and George Eliot's *Adam Bede.*

See NARRATOR, OMNISCIENT POINT OF VIEW.

invective. Direct denunciation or name-calling; lacks the WIT of SATIRE. See SATIRE.

invention. In LITERATURE, originality in creating STYLE, PLOT, DICTION, or FORM. The meaning of the term and its application have changed over the centuries. In Latin oratory, *invention* referred to the finding of ARGUMENTS. Later, it came to mean the "discovery" of material already existing in nature. Still later, *invention* became synonymous with WIT and IMAGINATION. Today, *imagination* has replaced *invention* as the term used to identify the creation of an original or organizing principle.

inversion. Reversing the normal order of sentence parts. Inversion is commonly and effectively used to ask a question ("Is Mary going to the play?"); to impose a condition ("Had I known you were going, I would certainly have made an effort to go"); to place emphasis ("Never have I seen him in such a good mood"); or to create balance in an antithetical statement, a form of inversion known as CHIASMUS (Alexander Pope's "Destroying others, by himself destroyed"). Inversion used for what is mistakenly assumed to be poetic effect, for the sake of elegant variation, or obviously to achieve a RHYME sounds forced and is too artificial to be effective.

See ANASTROPHE, CHIASMUS.

invocation.   At the beginning of an EPIC, an appeal to a god or goddess for inspiration. See APOSTROPHE, EPIC.

irony.   In its broadest sense, the recognition of the incongruity, or difference, between reality (what is) and appearance (what seems to be).

Socratic irony—named after Socrates, who used the device in the Platonic DIALOGUES—is the feigned ignorance of another's POINT OF VIEW in order to draw that person out and refute his or her arguments. One who pretends a willingness to learn ("I am not sure I understand; would you please explain...") for the sake of exposing an opponent's errors is a Socratic ironist.

Verbal irony is a FIGURE OF SPEECH in which there is a contrast between what is said and what is actually meant. For example, when in *Julius Caesar* Antony repeatedly insists that "Brutus is an honourable man," he is being ironic. In speech, tone of voice makes ironic intent obvious: "That's just *wonderful!*" can clearly mean "That is terrible!" The writer has to convey irony more obliquely, and so it is sometimes more difficult for the reader to recognize. SARCASM is verbal irony that is harsh and heavy-handed rather than clever and incisive.

Situational irony refers to the contrast between what is intended or expected and what actually occurs. This passage from Anne Tyler's *The Accidental Tourist* presents an irony of situation:

> Seated in a stenographer's chair, tapping away at a typewriter that had served him through four years of college, he wrote a series of guidebooks for people forced to travel on business. Ridiculous, when you thought about it: Macon hated travel.

One form of situational irony, called DRAMATIC IRONY, involves the audience's being aware of a CHARACTER's real situation before the character is.

Irony of fate is a phrase used to identify the view that fate, destiny, or God, seeking diversion or amusement, manipulates human beings like puppets and thwarts their plans. Thus, it is an irony of fate that a pardon is delivered too late to stay an execution, or that the miserly Silas Marner recovers his long-lost gold after he ceases to have any desire for it.

Some of the devices through which irony is conveyed are HYPERBOLE (exaggeration), LITOTES (understatement), sarcasm, and SATIRE. Writers known for their masterful use of irony include Jonathan Swift, Alexander Pope, Voltaire, Jane Austen, Thomas Hardy, and Henry James.

See DRAMATIC IRONY, TRAGIC IRONY.

Italian sonnet. A SONNET that is organized into two parts—an OCTAVE, consisting of the first eight lines and rhyming *abba, abba;* and a SESTET, the remaining six lines, which usually rhyme *cde, cde.* The octave establishes a theme or poses a problem that is developed or resolved in the sestet. The Italian sonnet is also known as the **Petrarchan sonnet.** See SONNET.

J

Jacobean. From *Jacobus*, the Latin form of James, referring to the reign of King James I of England (1603–1625), an unpopular ruler who insisted on the divine right of kings and who contributed to the widening split between the CAVALIERS and the Puritans. It was a rich period in English LITERATURE, marked by a late flowering of ELIZABETHAN writing at its beginning and by the growth of cynicism and REALISM toward its end. During the Jacobean Age, William Shakespeare wrote his greatest TRAGEDIES; Ben Jonson, Francis Beaumont and John Fletcher, John Donne, and Francis Bacon were at the height of their creative powers; and in 1611 the King James Bible was published.

See ELIZABETHAN.

jeremiad. A prophecy that evildoing will bring on destruction; a lament. The term is an ALLUSION to the Old Testament prophet Jeremiah, who wrote both kinds of works. In Jeremiah, he prophesied the destruction of the people who turned away from God and worshiped other gods and the works of their own hands. In Lamentations, he grieved over the capture of Jerusalem.

jongleur. A wandering entertainer in France and Norman England during the MIDDLE AGES who sang and recited POEMS and stories and sometimes performed juggling and tumbling acts. The jongleur resembled the earlier Anglo-Saxon **gleeman** and the later **minstrel,** all of whom carried on the tradition of preserving and disseminating the BALLADS, EPICS, LYRICS, and folktales of the times.

journal. 1. A diary; a personal record of experiences, ideas, and reflections kept regularly. Although many people keep journals who do little other writing, poets and novelists often keep journals as a way of gathering ideas and impressions to use in their other writing or to maintain fluency between writing projects. Among the notable journal-keepers are Samuel Pepys, James Boswell, Dorothy Wordsworth, Ralph Waldo Emerson, Herman Melville, Virginia Woolf, Katherine Mansfield, and Anaïs Nin.
2. A scholarly periodical, such as the *English Journal.*

judicial criticism. A form of LITERARY CRITICISM that evaluates the content, organization, and STYLE of an individual NOVEL, PLAY, SHORT STORY, or POEM against some general standard of literary excellence. Samuel Johnson and the other eighteenth-century Neoclassical critics practiced judicial criticism. Their standard was the CLASSICAL heritage of Greece and Rome.
See LITERARY CRITICISM, NEOCLASSICISM.

Juvenalian satire. Harsh, biting SATIRE, full of moral indignation and bitter contempt; a direct contrast to HORATIAN SATIRE. See SATIRE.

K

kenning. A metaphoric compound word or phrase used as a synonym for a common noun. Kennings are characteristic of Old English POETRY. Some examples from *Beowulf* are "ring-bestower" (king), "whale-road" and "swan-road" (sea), "candle of heaven" (sun), "war-brand" and "leavings of the file" (sword), and "ring-stemmed sea-goer" (ship).

Künstlerroman. "Artist-novel," a type of BILDUNGSROMAN, or developmental NOVEL, that tells the story of an artist's development. An example is Margaret Atwood's novel *Cat's Eye.* See BILDUNGSROMAN.

L

lai. Broadly, a lai is a poem of adventure or ROMANCE intended to be sung. The oldest lais, written by Marie de France in the twelfth-century French court of Henry II, were based on the MINSTREL songs of Brittany. Written in VERSES of eight syllables, these lais were NARRATIVES about King Arthur and other Celtic heroes. LYRIC love songs of Provence were also known as lais.

In fourteenth-century England, poems similar to the lais of Marie de France were called **Breton lays** (Breton, from Brittany). The best known among these is Geoffrey Chaucer's *Franklin's Tale.* From the sixteenth century on, historical BALLADS were often called lays. Sir Walter Scott's *Lay of the Last Minstrel* is a familiar example.

See BALLAD.

Lake poets. The name applied to William Wordsworth, Samuel Taylor Coleridge, and Robert Southey, all of whom lived in the Lake District of Cumberland, and to their followers; also called the **Lake school** or the **Lakers.** The name "Lake poets" describes a shared locality, not a shared philosophy or unified "school." Lord Byron, who despised their poetry, referred to them as "the Lakers, who whine about nature because they live in Cumberland." Originally derisive, the name has since lost its negative connotations.

legend. A story, part fact and part fiction, about the life and deeds of a saint, folk hero, or historical figure, that is handed down from generation to generation and is popularly accepted as true. A legend differs from a MYTH in concerning itself less with the supernatural. EPICS and other literary works have often been based on legends. Beowulf, King Arthur, Faust, the Flying Dutchman, and Hamlet are notable examples of legendary figures. There are legends in the making about Casey Jones, Winston Churchill, Isadora Duncan, Ché Guevara, and others who capture the public imagination.

See MYTH.

leitmotif/leitmotiv. The repetition of a significant word, phrase, THEME, or IMAGE throughout a NOVEL or PLAY, which functions as a unifying element; from German, meaning "guiding motif." See MOTIF.

leonine rhyme. Another term for INTERNAL RHYME; the rhyming of two or more words in the same line of POETRY, usually in the middle and at the end of the line. See INTERNAL RHYME.

libretto. The text or words of the DIALOGUE and songs of an opera, oratorio, cantata, musical comedy, or other similar musical work; also called the **book.** The libretto (meaning "little book" in Italian) contains the story, tale, or PLOT of the work. The writer who produces the text for a musical work is called the **librettist.**

light verse. VERSE written to amuse. Witty, nonsensical, or playful, light verse is usually characterized by technical brilliance and grace. In form, light verse ranges from LIMERICKS to EPIGRAMS to PARODIES to various kinds of OCCASIONAL VERSE. Serious poets from John Milton to Johann Wolfgang von Goethe to T. S. Eliot have indulged in the writing of light verse. Poets known primarily for their light verse include Edward Lear, Lewis Carroll, W. S. Gilbert, Ogden Nash, and Dorothy Parker.

limerick. A type of NONSENSE VERSE with a definite pattern: a five-line STANZA rhyming *aabba* in which lines one, two, and five have three anapestic feet and lines three and four have two anapestic feet, as in this example:

There was a young lady of Wilts,	*a*
Who walked up to Scotland on stilts;	*a*
When they said it was shocking	*b*
To show so much stocking,	*b*
She answered, "Then what about kilts?"	*a*

The origin of the limerick is uncertain. Its name is said to come from the REFRAIN "Won't you come up, come up, won't you come up to Limerick?" Limericks first appeared in print with the publication of *Anecdotes and Adventures of Fifteen Young Ladies* and *History of Sixteen Wonderful Old Women* in 1820, but they were popularized by Edward Lear and his *Book of Nonsense* in 1846. During the early twentieth century, especially in America, the improvisation of limericks became a popular parlor game.

See ANAPEST, FOOT, LIGHT VERSE, NONSENSE VERSE, RHYME SCHEME.

limited omniscience. The POINT OF VIEW assumed by an author who reveals the thoughts of a single CHARACTER but presents all other characters only externally. See OMNISCIENT POINT OF VIEW, THIRD-PERSON POINT OF VIEW.

linguistics. The study of languages as systems. Branches of linguistics include **phonology,** the study of basic speech sounds; **morphology,** the study of the forms of words and word parts, such as prefixes and suffixes; **syntax,** the study of the organization of sequences of words—phrases, clauses, and sentences; and **semantics,** the study of meanings in language.

In the nineteenth century, language studies had focused on the similarities and differences of languages within language families and on the evolution of languages over long periods of time. Linguistics, with its emphasis on describing the operations of individual languages, is a twentieth-century development. Scholars who have made major contributions in linguistics include Ferdinand de Saussure, a Swiss who introduced the idea of language as a system; Edward Sapir and Leonard Bloomfield, who did systematic analyses of several American Indian languages; and Noam Chomsky, who introduced in his generative-transformational grammar the notion that the great variety of sentences produced by speakers of a language derives from a set of transformable kernel sentences that exist in the deep structure of a language. A number of important approaches to LITERARY CRITICISM—including STRUCTURALISM, FORMALISM, STYLISTICS, SEMIOTICS, speech-act theory, and DECONSTRUCTION—are indebted to discoveries made in linguistics.

literal translation. A TRANSLATION from one language to another that renders the text of a work word for word, without regard for differences in idiom and IMAGERY between the two languages. See TRANSLATION.

literary ballad. NARRATIVE POETRY written by known authors that imitates the general RHYTHM and STANZA patterns of FOLK BALLADS. Also called **art ballads,** literary ballads often contain more elevated language and poetic DICTION than are found in folk ballads. See BALLAD.

literary criticism. The practice of describing, interpreting, and evaluating LITERATURE. **Theoretical criticism** identifies general principles of literary excellence and establishes theories and methods for studying literature. **Practical criticism** (also called **applied criticism**) puts such insights, theories, and methods to use in the analysis and evaluation of individual works. Practical criticism ranges from the SUBJECTIVITY of **impressionistic criticism,** in which the critic attempts to communicate how he or she is affected by a work of art and views criticism itself as a form of literary art, to the OBJECTIVITY of **analytical criticism,** in which the critic performs a detailed analysis of the elements of a work and the relationship between them and views criticism as a branch of science. Somewhere along the subjectivity-objectivity continuum is found **judicial criticism,** which attempts to evaluate a literary work against general and, presumably but not necessarily, objective standards of literary excellence.

Among the methods of classifying the many types of critical theories and practices, the most basic and most illuminating is a four-part scheme proposed by M. H. Abrams, which distinguishes critical approaches "according to whether, in explaining and judging a work of literature, they refer the work primarily to the outer world, or to the reader, or to the author, or else look upon the work as an entity in itself":

1. Mimetic criticism judges the literary work in terms of the "truth" of its representation of the reality of the world and of human life and character.

2. Pragmatic criticism focuses on a literary work as something designed to produce emotional or moral responses in the reader, and on how those effects are produced.

3. Expressive criticism views a literary work as an expression of the individuality of its author.

4. Objective criticism focuses on the intrinsic qualities of the literary work, treating it as an object of art that can be studied and evaluated without reference to author or reader.

Abrams' classification provides a useful look at the history of literary criticism. Criticism began with Plato's charge that literature lacks value because it is not true (mimetic criticism) and because it harmfully excites people's emotions instead of appealing to their reason (pragmatic criticism). Aristotle defended literature against Plato's charge by pointing out that (1) literature imitates life by combining universal psychological truths with probable events rather than by being a literal account of actual events (mimetic criticism); (2) the beginning-middle-ending PLOT structure of a literary work engages and satisfies the mind (pragmatic criticism); (3) rather than exciting people's emotions, experiencing literature offers people a therapeutic release of emotion (pragmatic criticism). Aristotle's mimetic defense of literature reemerged in the nineteenth century as the basis of modern REALISM. His pragmatic defense was replaced by the idea, put forth by the Roman poet and critic Horace, that the function of literature is to instruct and delight. Variations of the Horatian pragmatic formula remained the dominant approach to criticism through the MIDDLE AGES, the RENAISSANCE, and in eighteenth century NEOCLASSICISM. (Pragmatic criticism has received fresh impetus in the latter part of the twentieth century under the name **rhetorical criticism.**)

In the late eighteenth and early nineteenth centuries, ROMANTICISM gave rise both to expressive criticism, as practiced by Samuel Taylor Coleridge, and to **historical criticism.** In viewing a literary work as expressive of its era, historical criticism can be considered a broadening of expressive criticism. Also rooted in the nineteenth century are several twentieth-century critical approaches that value literature for its expressivity: **Marxist criticism** looks into a literary work for what it reflects of the economic conflict between social classes. **Archetypal criticism,** also known as **mythic criticism,** concentrates on the expression in literature of universal situations, CHARACTER types, PLOT patterns, IMAGES, and THEMES known as ARCHETYPES. **Psychoanalytic criticism** views a literary work as the expression of the unconscious—of the individual psyche of its author or of the collective unconscious of a society. **Existential criticism** interprets a literary work in terms of aspects of the philosophy of EXISTENTIALISM—for example, the necessity of making choices in the context of a meaningless world.

Objective criticism, considered a twentieth-century phenomenon, rose out of the art-for-art's-sake attitude of AESTHETICISM, a movement that flourished in the 1890s. Variations of objective criticism include formalism, New Criticism, and structuralism. **Formalism,** a critical movement originating in Russia in the 1920s, focused on the scientific analysis of literary style; **New Criticism,** an American school of criticism prominent in the 1940s and 1950s, popularized the concept of close reading of literary works, especially LYRIC poetry, and detailed analysis of the relationships of words, images, and SYMBOLS. **Structuralism,** flourishing in Europe, primarily France, in the 1960s, has emphasized the structural patterns, both linguistic and narrative, that a large number of works have in common.

Because of its similarity to the sender-receiver-message-medium (code) scheme used to analyze the communication process, Abrams' classification can be adapted to describe the process-oriented approaches to literary criticism known collectively as **post-structuralism,** and including **reader-response criticism,** recent psychoanalytic criticism, **deconstructive criticism,** and some varieties of **feminist criticism.** Although post-structuralists refuse to treat a literary work as separable in its written form from the consciousness of the person who wrote it or from the consciousness of the person who reads it, they still tend to focus on one aspect of the process more than any other. Reader-response criticism, for example, attempts to analyze the process or activity that goes on in readers' minds. Post-structuralist developments in psychoanalytic criticism continue to focus on the subjectivity and consciousness of the author even while emphasizing the way the structure of language itself determines subjectivity or subverts authorial intention. Deconstructive criticism combines objective analysis of the language of a work with interpretation of the reader's response while ignoring authorial intention, denying the possibility of a determinate meaning or correct interpretation for any work, and, in the most extreme instances, denying that the work makes reference to or represents any reality outside itself.

During most of its history, literary criticism has developed as a succession of individual approaches, each viewed for a time as the only way to approach literature. In the second half of the twentieth century, however, the concept of pluralism in criticism, introduced earlier by R. S. Crane and the group of critics at the University of Chicago known as the Chicago critics, has become quite widespread. Pluralism implies that there are a number of valid approaches to studying literature. The approach one chooses depends largely upon the kind of question about the work one wishes to have answered.

See AFFECTIVE FALLACY, ANALYTICAL CRITICISM, ARCHE-TYPAL CRITICISM, ARISTOTELIAN CRITICISM, COMPUTATIONAL STYLISTICS, DECONSTRUCTION, DECONSTRUCTIVE CRITICISM, DRAMATISM, EXEGESIS, EXISTENTIAL CRITICISM, EXPRESSIVE CRITICISM, FEMINIST CRITICISM, FORMAL CRITICISM, HERMENEU-TICS, HISTORICAL CRITICISM, HUMANISM, IMPRESSIONISTIC CRITI-CISM, INFLUENCE, INTENTIONAL FALLACY, INTERPRETATION, JUDICIAL CRITICISM, MARXIST CRITICISM, MIMETIC CRITICISM, MORAL CRITICISM, MYTHIC CRITICISM, NEW CRITICISM, OBJEC-TIVE CORRELATIVE, OBJECTIVE CRITICISM, PHENOMENOLOGY, PLATONIC CRITICISM, POST-STRUCTURALISM, PRACTICAL CRITI-CISM, PRAGMATIC CRITICISM, PSYCHOANALYTIC CRITICISM, READER-RESPONSE CRITICISM, RHETORICAL CRITICISM, SEMIOT-ICS, SOCIOLOGY OF LITERATURE, STRUCTURALISM, STYLISTICS, TEXTUAL CRITICISM, THEORETICAL CRITICISM.

literary epic. An EPIC written by a known author employing the THEMES and CONVENTIONS of the FOLK EPIC. See EPIC.

literature. Writings in POETRY and PROSE of recognized excellence, valued for their intense, personal, and imaginative expression of life. Stopford A. Brook asserts that "writing is not literature unless it gives to the reader a pleasure which arises not only from the things said, but from the way in which they are said." In a general sense, the term refers to written works as a collective body, the whole sum of writings belonging to a particular era, language, or people, as in *Spanish literature.*

litotes. A FIGURE OF SPEECH, a form of ironical understatement that affirms something by stating the negative of its opposite. For example, to say "She is no fool" instead of "She is shrewd" is to use litotes. **Meiosis,** a near synonym, employs understatement to give the idea that something is less important or smaller than it really is: "That was a pretty good movie." HYPERBOLE, the use of exaggeration, is an antonym of *litotes*.

See HYPERBOLE.

local color. The use in writing of the physical SETTING, DIALECT, customs, and attitudes that typify a particular region. The NOVELS of Thomas Hardy, for example, provide so detailed and colorful a picture of "Wessex" (Dorsetshire) that that portion of England has become known as Thomas Hardy country. From 1870 to 1890, post–Civil War sectionalism gave rise in American LITERATURE to a local-color movement, involving such writers as Sara Orne Jewett (New England), Bret Harte (California), Joel Chandler Harris (the Old South), Mary E. Wilkins Freeman (Massachusetts and Vermont), Hamlin Garland (the Middle Border). The term *regional writer* is often applied to local-color writers, especially to writers of FICTION that is enhanced rather than overshadowed by its feeling of locale. Hardy, Mark Twain, and William Faulkner are among the great regional writers.

See REGIONALISM.

logical positivism. A philosophical movement, at its height from the 1920s to about 1940, that emphasized applying scientific empiricism (observation and experiment) to philosophy. See POSITIVISM.

loose translation. A TRANSLATION from one language to another that attempts to preserve the TONE, spirit, and effect of a work, rather than to produce an exact or precisely parallel version of the original. See TRANSLATION.

lost generation. A phrase used by Gertrude Stein to describe the generation that came to maturity in the 1920s, between World War I and the Depression. The phrase refers especially to the American expatriate writers, including Ernest Hemingway, who turned up in Paris during the 1920s, spiritually and morally shaken in the aftermath of the war. Stein reportedly told Hemingway, "You are all a lost generation." Hemingway used the comment as an EPIGRAPH for his NOVEL *The Sun Also Rises.*

low comedy. Crude, boisterous COMEDY characterized by slapstick HUMOR and crude jokes, more physical than intellectual; the opposite of HIGH COMEDY. See COMEDY.

lyric. A usually short, personal poem expressing the poet's emotions and thoughts rather than telling a story. The lyric, a broadly inclusive type of POETRY, is represented by such forms as the ELEGY, ODE, BALLAD, and SONNET. A strict definition of *lyric* is not possible. However, its distinguishing characteristics are emotion, SUBJECTIVITY, melodiousness, IMAGINATION, DESCRIPTION, and (sometimes) meditation. In ancient Greece, a lyric was a poem to be sung with the accompaniment of a lyre. The following poem by Alice Walker is a modern lyric:

New Face

I have learned not to worry about love;
but to honor its coming
with all my heart.
To examine the dark mysteries
of the blood
with headless heed and
swirl,
to know the rush of feelings
swift and flowing
as water.
The source appears to be

some inexhaustible
spring
within our twin and triple
selves;
The new face I turn up
to you
no one else on earth
has ever
seen.

M

macaronic.　A term applied to VERSE in which foreign words and phrases are inserted, usually for humorous effect. Macaronic verse that mixed Italian, French, German, or English with Latin was common during the MIDDLE AGES and the RENAISSANCE. The term derives from an Italian writer's description of mixed-language verse as the literary equivalent of macaroni ("a gross, rude, and rustic mixture of flour, butter, and cheese"). The Germans called macaronic verse *Nudelverse* ("noodle verse").

　　The writer of the following bit of macaronic verse has even given Latin endings to some of the English words:

> Qui nunc dancere vult modo,
> Wants to dance in the fashion, oh!
> Discere debet ought to know,
> Kickere floor cum heel and toe.
> 　One, two, three,
> 　Hop with me,
> Whirligig, twirligig, rapidee.

—G. A. à Beckett

malapropism.　The comic substitution of one word for another similar in sound but quite different in meaning. Although the technique was used well before the eighteenth century (William Shakespeare used it to great effect in creating the CHARACTER of Dogberry in *Much Ado About Nothing*), the term derives from Mrs. Malaprop, a character in Richard Brinsley Sheridan's COMEDY OF MANNERS *The Rivals*. Mrs. Malaprop's speech is riddled with such remarks as "I would have her instructed in geometry that she might know of contagious countries" and "If I reprehend anything in this world, it is the use of my oracular tongue, and a nice derangement of epitaphs."

Marxist criticism. A type of HISTORICAL CRITICISM of LITERATURE, based on the economic theory of Karl Marx, that interprets a literary work as both a reflection and a product of economic conflict between social classes. The basic assumption of Marxist criticism is that those who control a society's economics also control or largely influence the society's cultural and intellectual products. Traditional Marxist critics, such as György Lukács and Lucien Goldmann, study the relationship between historical epochs and the rise and fall of certain literary FORMS—for example, nineteenth-century REALISM or seventeenth-century TRAGEDY. Contemporary Marxists see literature, along with history, as something that must be constantly rewritten to serve current policy.

See LITERARY CRITICISM.

masculine rhyme. The rhyming of single accented syllables, as in *park/dark* or *define/align,* the most common rhyme in English. These lines by Phyllis McGinley end in masculine rhyme:

> Beyond the Alps, as histories *note,*
> Lies Italy and in her *throat.*

See FEMININE RHYME, RHYME.

masque. An elaborate form of entertainment popular with the royal courts in Italy, England, and France during the RENAISSANCE. Light on PLOT and lavish in costumes, stage sets, music, dance, and other elements of spectacle, masques were pageants of allegorical and mythological figures. The figures were sometimes played by professional actors and sometimes by members of the court, who disguised themselves with masks and unmasked for the final dance, in which they chose their partners from the audience.

Through the collaboration of playwright Ben Jonson and court architect Inigo Jones, who designed expensive stage sets with ingenious machinery, the splendor of the English masques during the reigns of James I and Charles I was unsurpassed. Dramatists incorporated elements of the masque into their plays. William Shakespeare's *As You Like It,* for example, is masquelike in its arrangement of SCENES. *The Tempest* includes a masque to celebrate the engagement of Ferdinand and Miranda. The most famous masque, John Milton's *Comus,* is atypical in its moral seriousness. Henry Purcell's *The Fairy Queen,* better known to opera audiences than to students of literature, captures the lightness and charm of the masque at its best.

medieval. Of or relating to the MIDDLE AGES, a period in European history lasting from roughly A.D. 500 to 1500. The adjective is also used in a general sense to refer to anything antiquated or outmoded. See MIDDLE AGES.

meiosis. A type of understatement used for ironic effect. See LITOTES.

melodrama. A type of DRAMA, popular since the nineteenth century, that pits unbelievably good CHARACTERS (the HERO and HEROINE) against a despicably, incorrigibly evil character (the VILLAIN). The PLOT moves in a thrilling downward spiral of dire events and near disasters (the mortgage is foreclosed, the heroine is tied to the railroad tracks) that is halted by the most improbable of happy accidents and resolved into an ending in which good is rewarded and evil punished. Well-known melodramas from the nineteenth-century stage include *Lady Audley's Secret, Ten Nights in a Barroom,* and *Sweeney Todd, The Demon Barber of Fleet Street.* In the twentieth century, melodrama left the stage for the movie screen. Silent movies capitalized on last-minute railroad-track rescues, accompanied by galloping music on the theater pipe organ. Some of the later movie melodramas, such as *Gaslight,* and a number of modern melodramatic plays—for example, Lillian Hellman's *The Children's Hour*—have been somewhat more probable and psychologically satisfying. Nevertheless, the adjective *melodramatic* is applied to any literary work containing sensational, unmotivated, and improbable action.

memoir. An account of a single period in a writer's life, often a period that coincides with important historical events. See AUTOBIOGRAPHY.

Menippean satire. A form of INDIRECT SATIRE that ridicules such things as pretentious erudition, bigotry, and overweening professionalism. It originated with Menippus, a third-century Greek satirist. See SATIRE.

metaphor. A FIGURE OF SPEECH, an implied ANALOGY in which one thing is imaginatively compared to or identified with another, dissimilar thing. In a metaphor, the qualities of something are ascribed to something else, qualities that it ordinarily does not possess. For example, in *Song of Myself,* Walt Whitman's striking metaphor for *grass* is "the beautiful uncut hair of graves." In Beatrice Janosco's "The Garden Hose," her metaphor for the *hose* is "a long green serpent / With its tail in the dahlias." Eve Merriam in "Metaphor" writes that "morning is / a new sheet of paper / for you to write on." In Edwin A. Hoey's "Foul Shout," *hanging* is a metaphor in the line "And two seconds hanging on the clock."

I. A. Richards says this in *Practical Criticism:*

> A metaphor is a shift, a carrying over of a word from its normal use to a new one. In a sense metaphor, the shift of the word, is occasioned and justified by a similarity or analogy between the object it is usually applied to and the new object. In an emotive metaphor the shift occurs through some similarity between the feelings the new situation and the normal situation arouse. The same word may, in different contexts, be either a sense or an emotive metaphor. If you call a man a swine, for example, it may be because his features resemble those of a pig, but it may be you have towards him something of the feeling you conventionally have towards pigs, or because you propose, if possible, to excite those feelings. Both metaphorical shifts may be combined simultaneously, and they often are.

A metaphor may be a single, isolated comparison, or it may be an **extended metaphor** that is sustained throughout the work and functions as a controlling IMAGE. In Emily Dickinson's "Because I could not stop for Death" the journey in a carriage is an extended metaphor for our journey through life—childhood, maturity, death. An ALLEGORY could be considered an elaborate extended metaphor.

A **dead metaphor** is one that has been used so often it has ceased to be figurative and is taken literally: the *head* of the class, the *eye* of a needle, the *cornerstone* of her success.

A **mixed metaphor** combines two or more inconsistent metaphors in a single expression, often resulting in unintentional humor: "He'll have to take the bull by the horns to keep the business afloat" mixes an agricultural metaphor with a nautical one.

See ANALOGY, FIGURATIVE LANGUAGE, IMAGE, SIMILE.

metaphysical conceit. Highly ingenious and startling ANALOGIES used as controlling IMAGES in METAPHYSICAL POETRY. See CONCEIT, METAPHYSICAL POETRY.

metaphysical poetry. A term applied to the POETRY of John Donne and several other seventeenth-century poets, including Richard Crashaw, George Herbert, Henry Vaughan, and Andrew Marvell. Rebelling against the conventional love poetry of the Elizabethans, with its predictable CONCEITS, or comparisons (teeth to pearls, cheeks to roses), the metaphysical poets saw contradiction, doubt, and ambivalence in the attitudes of lovers and persons facing death or searching for God. Their poetry is, as D. J. Palmer has pointed out, "essentially the poetry of 'WIT,' in the seventeenth-century sense of wit as the capacity to recognize similarity in disparity and to combine playfulness with seriousness." The **metaphysical conceit** (the most famous being Donne's comparison of a pair of lovers to the two parts of a compass) "turns upon a surprising and ingenious ANALOGY between apparently unrelated areas of experience."

The term *metaphysical,* first used by John Dryden to criticize Donne's "excessive use of philosophy," was established by Samuel Johnson as a label for a "race of poets" who, as he said, wrote poetry to "show their learning." Dr. Johnson objected to the IMAGERY of metaphysical poetry in which, he said, "the most heterogeneous ideas are yoked by violence together; [and] nature and art are ransacked for illustrations, comparisons, and allusions." Johnson's critical view of metaphysical poetry persisted through the eighteenth and nineteenth centuries. In the twentieth century the metaphysical poets were rediscovered by T. S. Eliot and others.

See CONCEIT.

meter. The fixed (or nearly fixed) pattern of accented and unaccented syllables in the lines of a poem that produces its pervasive RHYTHM.

The basic unit of rhythm is the FOOT, consisting most often of an arrangement of at least one accented syllable (´) and one or more unaccented syllables (˘). Meter is determined by the type and the number of feet in a line. The most common types of feet in English POETRY are iambic (˘ ´), trochaic (´ ˘), anapestic (˘ ˘ ´), and dactylic (´ ˘ ˘). The number of feet in a line is described as monometer (one foot), **dimeter** (two feet), **trimeter** (three feet), **tetrameter** (four feet), **pentameter** (five feet), **hexameter** (six feet), or **heptameter** (seven feet).

Thus, the meter of a line of poetry having five iambic feet is called IAMBIC PENTAMETER:

If áll | would léad | their líves | in lóve | like mé.

The meter of a line having four trochaic feet is called trochaic tetrameter:

Dóuble, | dóuble, | tóil and | tróuble.

The meter of a line having three anapestic feet is called anapestic trimeter:

Oh wéll | for the físh | erman's bóy

The meter of a line having six dactylic feet is called dactylic hexameter:

Nóthing was | héard in the | róom but the |
  húrrying | pén of the | strípling.

Note that in some of the example lines, while not all feet are identical, there is a prevailing pattern of accented and unaccented syllables that identifies the meter. Poets occasionally vary the basic metrical pattern to avoid the monotonous rhythm of a metronome. Analysis of the meter of a poem is called SCANSION.

See FOOT, RHYTHM, SCANSION.

metonymy. A FIGURE OF SPEECH that substitutes the name of a related object, person, or idea for the subject at hand. *Crown* is often substituted for *monarchy, the White House* for *the President of the United States and the staff,* and *Shakespeare* for *the works of Shakespeare.* Metonymy should not be confused with SYNECDOCHE, a substitution of a part of something for the whole or the whole for a part.

See SYNECDOCHE.

Middle Ages. The period in European history, the early part of which is sometimes called the Dark Ages, lasting from roughly A.D. 500 to 1500. Some historians mark its beginning with the fall of the Western Roman Empire in 476 and its end with the arrival in America of Christopher Columbus in 1492.

One of the most important developments in the LITERATURE of the Middle Ages was the acceptance of works written in vernacular (native) languages, rather than in Latin. Dante's *Divine Comedy* and Geoffrey Chaucer's *Canterbury Tales* are two MEDIEVAL masterpieces written in the vernacular (in Tuscan Italian and Middle English, respectively).

Popular literary GENRES during the period included the LAI and the ROMANCE (both of which centered on the THEME of COURTLY LOVE), and the religious MIRACLE PLAYS and MORALITY PLAYS (such as *Everyman*).

middle rhyme. Another term for INTERNAL RHYME; the rhyming of two or more words in the same line of POETRY, usually in the middle and at the end of the line. See INTERNAL RHYME.

mimesis. The Greek word for IMITATION. In his *Poetics* Aristotle says that LITERATURE is an imitation of life, of things "as they are, as they are thought to be, as they ought to be." The term is often used in LITERARY CRITICISM to refer to Aristotle's theory of imitation. Mimesis is considered by some critics to be a basic principle in the creation of art.

See IMITATION.

mimetic criticism.   An approach to LITERARY CRITICISM that views an individual work in terms of the "truth" of its representation of reality—the reality of the world and of human life and character. Mimetic criticism began as an attack on LITERATURE by Plato, was adapted by Aristotle as a defense of literature, and is the basis of modern literary REALISM.

See LITERARY CRITICISM, MIMESIS, REALISM.

minimalism.   A term that came into use in the 1960s to describe a form of modern art that, avoiding any embellishment or dramatization, employs geometric shapes and primary colors to achieve extreme simplicity of FORM and impersonal OBJECTIVITY. The term was subsequently applied to a "less is more" approach to writing FICTION that emphasizes the essential through a radical economy of form and expression. John Barth, in his essay "A Few Words About Minimalism," describes literary minimalism in this way:

> Old or new, fiction can be minimalist in any or all of several ways. There are minimalisms of unit, form and scale: short words, short sentences and paragraphs, super-short stories, those three-eighth-inch thin novels.... There are minimalisms of style: a stripped-down vocabulary; a stripped-down syntax that avoids periodic sentences, serial predications and complex subordinating constructions; a stripped-down rhetoric that may eschew figurative language altogether; a stripped-down, nonemotive tone. And there may be minimalisms of material: minimal characters, minimal exposition ...minimal action, minimal plot.

Here, in its entirety, is a section of a minimalist series of fictions called *Counting* by Jayne Anne Phillips:

15. Aqua

He writes letters to an address in the Yucatan. He pretends it doesn't matter where she is.

If she returns, he tells her, she will find his messages in a post office box he has rented in her name. He describes their street and says he is leaving it. Though it is nearly summer, used furs are displayed on headless mannequins outside the second-hand stores. Cuban children melt crayons in matchbook fires. They dot the cracked sidewalks with aqua. Scarlet. Tangerine.

He puts her belongings in storage. Cleans out the desk and finds a pair of pale blue stockings rolled up in a drawer. He hangs them in the bathroom and doesn't touch them again.

minstrel. A professional musician of MEDIEVAL times, often attached to a particular court as the official entertainer. See JONGLEUR.

miracle play. A MEDIEVAL religious DRAMA based on a miraculous event in a saint's life or on a story from the Bible. (PLAYS based on Bible stories are sometimes called **mystery plays.**) The religious plays began in the church service as bits of DIALOGUE inserted into the Latin liturgy and acted out as well as chanted. A well-known example, based on part of the Easter story, is *Quem quaeritis* ("Whom do you seek?"). These dramatizations gradually evolved into full-scale plays. Later performed outside the church and in the vernacular (native language) rather than in Latin, their production became the responsibility of the local trade guilds of artisans and merchants. Over the years secular lines—bits of humorous CHARACTERIZATION and even ribaldry—crept into the dialogue. Noah's wife emerged as a shrew. The shepherds in *The Second Shepherds' Play* arrived at the manger in Bethlehem only after a comic scene in which one shepherd tried to hide a sheep he had stolen from the others. Some plays—notably the Brome *Abraham and Isaac*—had SUSPENSE and depth of characterization.

From the thirteenth century on, the guilds presented the plays in great cycles ranging through the Old and New Testament, from the Creation to the Last Judgment. Each guild presented one play, which it mounted on a wagon bearing a curtained platform over a dressing area. Thirty or more of these pageant wagons paraded through the city, each pausing at designated points to present its play. In the English towns of Wakefield, York, Chester, and Coventry, especially, polished scripts, elaborate SETTINGS with trapdoors and pulleys, imaginative lighting effects, gorgeous costumes, and the participation of hundreds of actors made these cycles major theatrical entertainments.

See MORALITY PLAY.

mixed metaphor. A METAPHOR that combines two incompatible IMAGES in a single expression, like "She must clear that hurdle if she is to keep her head above water." See METAPHOR.

mock epic. A literary work that comically or satirically imitates the FORM and STYLE of the EPIC, treating a trivial subject in a lofty manner; also called **mock heroic.** Mock epics usually ape the epic CONVENTIONS: formal statement of THEME, INVOCATION to the muses, CATALOGS of warriors and equipment, use of STOCK EPITHETS and HOMERIC SIMILES, grandiloquent speeches, and intervention of gods in human affairs.

Well-known examples of the mock epic are Samuel Butler's *Hudibras,* a long poem satirizing the Puritans' repression of popular sports and amusements; Alexander Pope's *Dunciad,* attacking two personal rivals characterized as monarchs of dullness; and Jonathan Swift's *Battle of the Books,* a PROSE SATIRE on the controversy surrounding the comparative value of ancient and modern authors.

Pope's *The Rape of the Lock,* which mocks the affectations of polite society in the eighteenth century, is considered the finest mock epic in English. Here are the opening lines:

What dire offense from am'rous causes springs,
What mighty contests rise from trivial things,
I sing—This verse to Caryl, Muse! is due:
This, e'en Belinda may vouchsafe to view:
Slight is the subject, but not so the praise,
If She inspire, and He approve my lays.

    Say what strange motive, Goddess! could compel
A well-bred Lord t'assault a gentle Belle?
O say what stranger cause, yet unexplored,
Could make a gentle Belle reject a Lord?
In tasks so bold, can little men engage,
And in soft bosoms dwells such mighty Rage?

See BURLESQUE, EPIC.

modernism. The term applied to a certain group of tendencies in LITERATURE and the arts since the late nineteenth century, including breaking away from established rules and traditional values, experimenting radically with FORM and STYLE—sometimes even denying the need for form—and focusing on the subjective, often alienated, consciousness of the individual. These trends have found varying and often conflicting expression in a sequence of movements, including the SYMBOLIST MOVEMENT, post-IMPRESSIONISM, EXISTENTIALISM, EXPRESSIONISM, futurism, imagism, vorticism, Dadaism, and SURREALISM. The principal modernist writers are novelists Henry James, Joseph Conrad, Marcel Proust, Thomas Mann, André Gide, Franz Kafka, James Joyce, Virginia Woolf, and William Faulkner; playwrights August Strindberg, Luigi Pirandello, and Bertolt Brecht; and poets Stéphane Mallarmé, William Butler Yeats, T. S. Eliot, Ezra Pound, Gertrude Stein, Rainer Maria Rilke, Guillaume Apollinaire, and Wallace Stevens.

See DADA, EXISTENTIALISM, EXPRESSIONISM, IMAGISTS, SYMBOLIST MOVEMENT, SURREALISM.

monody. A lament in which the mourner expresses grief for the death of a loved one, usually in a SOLILOQUY. A famous example is Matthew Arnold's *Thyrsis, a Monody*. See ELEGY.

monologue. A relatively extended speech in a DRAMA or a NARRATIVE that is presented by one CHARACTER. It may stand alone as an independent unit or be part of a larger work. Sometimes used as a synonym for SOLILOQUY, *monologue* more strictly describes a larger category of which the soliloquy (thoughts spoken aloud while the character is alone), the ASIDE (comments directed only to the audience), the DRAMATIC MONOLOGUE (speech revealing both a dramatic situation *and* the speaker to a silent listener), and the INTERIOR MONOLOGUE (a representation of a character's inner thoughts) are specific types.

See ASIDE, DRAMATIC MONOLOGUE, INTERIOR MONOLOGUE, SOLILOQUY, STREAM OF CONSCIOUSNESS.

mood. The prevailing emotional attitude in a literary work or in part of a work, for example, regret, hopefulness, bitterness. Mood is often used interchangeably with TONE, although the attempt has been made to define *mood* as the author's attitude toward the subject or THEME and *tone* as the author's attitude toward the reader. This distinction is most evident in works of SATIRE such as Jonathan Swift's *A Modest Proposal,* in which the author's mood is one of moral indignation and the tone of his PERSONA is blithe, self-important enthusiasm.

See ATMOSPHERE, TONE.

moral criticism. A type of LITERARY CRITICISM that evaluates a work on the basis of the moral elements it contains and their correspondence to the accepted moral standards of the time or to those ethical principles that the critic feels should govern human life. Ideally the moral critic, in judging a literary work, applies only those moral standards presented in the work itself or, failing that, makes his or her own beliefs clear to the reader.

See LITERARY CRITICISM.

morality play. A type of ALLEGORY in dramatic form, popular in the later MIDDLE AGES and early RENAISSANCE. The HERO, who represents all humankind, is surrounded by PERSONIFICATIONS of virtues, vices, angels, demons, and death—all the forces of good and evil, who battle for possession of the hero's soul. In *Everyman,* the best-known MEDIEVAL morality play, when the title CHARACTER is summoned by death, he finds that of all his companions—Fellowship, Goods, Kindred, Beauty, Strength, and Good Deeds—only Good Deeds, though weak from his neglect, will accompany him on his journey toward judgment. Other well-known morality plays include *The Castle of Perseverance* and *Mankind.*

See MIRACLE PLAY.

morphology. The study of the forms of words and word parts, such as prefixes and suffixes; a branch of LINGUISTICS. Also, one of the three components of grammar, along with SYNTAX and PHONOLOGY. See LINGUISTICS.

motif. In LITERATURE, a recurring IMAGE, word, phrase, action, idea, object, or situation that appears in various works or throughout the same work. When applied to several different works, *motif* refers to a recurrent THEME, such as the CARPE DIEM motif—the idea that life is short, time is fleeting, and one must make the most of the present moment. When applied to a single work, *motif* (sometimes LEITMOTIF) refers to any repetition that tends to unify the work by bringing to mind its earlier occurrences and the impressions that surround them. Some examples are the periodic striking of clocks in Virginia Woolf's novel *Mrs. Dalloway* and the repetition of patterns—of a garden, a dress, a fan, and of life itself—in Amy Lowell's poem "Patterns."

motivation.   The psychological and moral impulses and external circumstances that cause a literary CHARACTER to act, think, or feel a certain way. Showing what motivates the actions of characters helps make the characters believable and their actions satisfying, even inevitable. In "The Revolt of Mother" by Mary E. Wilkins Freeman, Mother moves her household to the barn that Father has just built, an unusual, yet satisfying action because the reader has been made aware (1) that forty years ago Father promised to build Mother a new house where the barn is, (2) that the house Mother presently has is wretched, not at all suitable as the site of her daughter's upcoming marriage, and (3) that when Mother tried to discuss the matter with Father, he had nothing to say in return. On the other hand, giving characters inadequate motivation makes them seem shallow, their actions contrived for the sake of the PLOT.

muckrakers.   The derisive name given by Theodore Roosevelt to a group of American writers and journalists who, during the early 1900s, wrote to expose corruption and exploitation in business and politics. Some of the leading muckrakers were Lincoln Steffens, Ida Tarbell, and Upton Sinclair. Sinclair's *The Jungle* is a famous muckraking NOVEL that paints a grim picture of the meat-packing industry and life in the Chicago stockyards. Steffens' works include such titles as *The Shame of the Cities* and *The Struggle for Self-Government.* Ida Tarbell is chiefly known for her exposés that appeared in *McClure's Magazine.* Today the term *muckraking* is used to describe the sometimes overzealous seeking out and exposing of real or alleged misconduct, corruption, or scandal in business, government, or public life.

muses. In Greek mythology, the nine daughters of Zeus and Mnemosyne (Memory), each of whom patronized a field of study or art: Calliope, EPIC POETRY; Clio, history; Erato, love poetry; Euterpe, music and LYRIC poetry; Melpomene, TRAGEDY; Polyhymnia, sacred poetry (hymns); Terpsichore, dancing; Thalia, COMEDY; and Urania, astronomy. Practitioners in these fields traditionally invoked the aid of the appropriate muse. Such an invocation became a CONVENTION of epic poetry. Art forms lacking one of the original nine muses—filmmaking, opera LIBRETTO writing—have laid claim to the "tenth muse."

mystery play. A MEDIEVAL religious DRAMA based on an event in the Bible; more commonly known as MIRACLE PLAY. See MIRACLE PLAY.

myth. **1.** An anonymous NARRATIVE, originating in the primitive FOLKLORE of a race or a nation, that explains the origin of life, religious beliefs, and the forces of nature as some kind of supernatural occurrence, or that recounts the deeds of traditional superheroes. Like LEGENDS and FABLES, myths are fictitious tales preserved largely through oral transmission. However, myths lack the historical framework of legends and the moral teaching of fables. The making of myths is called **mythopoeia,** and every culture and LITERATURE has its collection of myths, its **mythology**.

Literary critics value myths for their universality and timelessness. Numerous studies have revealed a surprising recurrence of MOTIFS, STOCK CHARACTERS, and INCIDENTS in the mythologies of widely separated and racially diverse peoples. Some critics assert that myths are not simply the products of creative IMAGINATION but are instead the unconscious memories of archetypal experiences of the race, such as birth, mating, and death. Jungian criticism, based on the psychology of Carl Jung, posits a "collective unconscious," a repressed racial memory, which explains the evocative power that myth exerts on the reader. LITERARY CRITICISM that emphasizes myth and ARCHETYPE is sometimes called **mythopoetics.**

2. Any unsubstantiated belief that is accepted uncritically, for example, the "myth" of socialism or the "myth" of racial superiority.

3. Any invented or imaginary person, place, thing, or idea.
See ARCHETYPAL CRITICISM, ARCHETYPE, MYTHIC CRITICISM.

mythic criticism.   An approach to literary criticism, also known as
ARCHETYPAL CRITICISM, that sees literary GENRES and PLOT patterns of individual literary works as recurrences of the archetypal patterns—life and death, the cycle of seasons, spiritual journeys, children rebelling against their elders—of MYTHS.
See ARCHETYPAL CRITICISM, ARCHETYPE, MYTH.

N

naive narrator. An uncomprehending CHARACTER in a work of FICTION (a child, a simpleminded adult) who narrates the story without realizing its true implications. The result is that the reader knows more about what is actually going on than the NARRATOR does; the effect is often a sense of IRONY or PATHOS. Some well-known examples of the type are Benjy, who narrates the first part of William Faulkner's *The Sound and the Fury,* the loquacious barber in Ring Lardner's "Haircut," and Huck in Mark Twain's *The Adventures of Huckleberry Finn.* Other short stories with naive narrators are Sherwood Anderson's "I'm a Fool" and "The Egg," Kay Boyle's "Major Alshuster," and Dorothy Parker's "Diary of a New York Lady."

See NARRATOR, POINT OF VIEW.

narration. The telling of a story; the recounting of an INCIDENT or a series of incidents. Narration is one of the four modes of DISCOURSE, or chief types of PROSE writing, the others being ARGUMENT (or ARGUMENTATION), EXPOSITION, and DESCRIPTION. While narration may appear by itself, it is most usually coupled with description in such NARRATIVE FORMS as the NOVEL and the SHORT STORY. Here is the paragraph of narration that opens Jessamyn West's short story "Breach of Promise":

> Every afternoon between two and four, depending upon the amount of business or conversation he had encountered on his route, the mail carrier came by in his ramshackle, mud-spattered car. He didn't drive up the lane to the house, a lane a quarter of a mile long and crossing at one point a brook, which after heavy rains was more than a brook, but put the mail in the wobbly tin box, set the flag, honked three times, and drove on.

See DISCOURSE.

narrative. A recounting of a series of actual or fictional events in which some connection between the events is established or implied. Among the varied types of narratives are SHORT STORIES, NOVELS, EPICS, BALLADS, histories, BIOGRAPHIES, travel books, accounts of scientific experiments, and do-it-yourself articles.

See AUTOBIOGRAPHY, BALLAD, BIOGRAPHY, EPIC, NARRATION, NOVEL, PICARESQUE, ROMANCE, SHORT STORY.

narrative perspective. The vantage point or stance from which a story is told; a synonym for POINT OF VIEW. See POINT OF VIEW.

narrative poem. A poem that tells a story. EPICS and BALLADS are two of the many types of narrative POETRY. Some examples of its wide variety are Geoffrey Chaucer's *Canterbury Tales,* Robert Frost's "The Death of the Hired Man," Henry W. Longfellow's *Evangeline,* Mona Van Duyn's "The Vision Test," Alfred, Lord Tennyson's "The Charge of the Light Brigade," and Amy Lowell's "Patterns."

See BALLAD, EPIC.

narrator. The teller of a story or other NARRATIVE. A narrator may be the author speaking in his or her own voice, or a CHARACTER or PERSONA created by the author to tell the story. A narrator may stand inside the story, narrating events from the **first-person point of view**, or outside the story, narrating events from the **third-person point of view.** A first-person narrator is an "I" who may be the main character or a minor character. A third-person narrator may narrate events from (1) an **omniscient point of view,** relating the thoughts and feelings of the story characters; (2) a point of view of **limited omniscience,** relating the thoughts and feelings of only the main character; or (3) an **objective point of view,** relating only what can be seen and heard by an observer.

Any of these different kinds of narrators may do more than simply tell the story. An **intrusive narrator** is a storyteller who keeps interrupting the narrative to address the reader directly, to make extended personal comments about the characters or about other matters, as the narrator of William M. Thackeray's NOVEL *Vanity Fair* does so engagingly. Another type of narrator who does more than simply tell the story is an **unreliable narrator.** Characters telling their stories in first person are often created as unreliable narrators by their authors. The author gives such narrators attitudes and emotions that distort the story they tell. In Henry James's *The Turn of the Screw,* the story is narrated by a governess who believes that the children in her charge are being influenced by evil ghosts. James makes her account of what happens to the children unreliable and open to interpretation.

See FIRST-PERSON POINT OF VIEW, INTRUSIVE NARRATOR, NA-IVE NARRATOR.

naturalism. A literary movement that emerged in France, America, and England during the late nineteenth and early twentieth centuries and that emphasizes biological and socioeconomic DETER-MINISM in FICTION and DRAMA. Naturalism portrays human beings as higher animals lacking free will, their lives determined by natural forces of heredity and environment and by basic drives over which they have no control and which they do not fully comprehend. It rejects idealized portrayals of life and attempts complete accuracy, disinterested OBJECTIVITY, and frankness in depicting life as a brutal struggle for survival.

Émile Zola, the chief proponent of naturalism in France, insisted that the novelist, like the scientist, should analyze his or her subject with dispassionate minuteness. Naturalistic authors strive to emulate the scientific observer in neither praising nor blaming CHARACTERS for actions they cannot control. Characters in naturalistic NOVELS and PLAYS are typically the middle-class and working-class people of everyday life, motivated largely by such animalistic drives as sex, hunger, and fear. They often play out their predetermined roles in an ATMOSPHERE of depravity, sordidness, and violence.

Naturalism is apparent in the works of such authors as Frank Norris (*McTeague, The Octopus*), Stephen Crane (*Maggie: A Girl of the Streets*), Jack London (*The Call of the Wild*), Theodore Dreiser (*Sister Carrie, An American Tragedy*), Eugene O'Neill (*Anna Christie, The Hairy Ape*), James T. Farrell (*Studs Lonigan*), Richard Wright (*Native Son*), Willard Motley (*Knock on Any Door*), and James Jones (*From Here to Eternity*).

From the start, naturalism has been attacked for its pessimistic picture of life as a downhill struggle to oblivion; its concentration on the sordid, the violent, the gloomy; its graphic depiction of language and situations previously considered unsuitable for print; its failure to uplift or inspire. While it is an outgrowth of REALISM and shares its devotion to accurate portrayal and VERISIMILITUDE, naturalism differs significantly from realism, especially because it is firmly grounded in a pervasive philosophy.

See DETERMINISM, IMITATION, REALISM, ROMANTICISM.

near rhyme.   Unlike END RHYME, which is based on repeated vowel *and* consonant sounds, near rhyme is based only on repeated middle vowel sounds between different consonant sounds. See ASSONANCE.

negative capability.   A term used by John Keats, in a letter to his brothers, to characterize a quality he admired in William Shakespeare and found lacking in Samuel Taylor Coleridge:

> at once it struck me what quality went to form a man of achievement, especially in literature, and which Shakespeare possessed so enormously—I mean negative capability, that is when a man is capable of being in uncertainties, mysteries, doubts, without any irritable reaching after fact and reason. Coleridge, for instance, would let go by a fine isolated verisimilitude caught from the penetralium of mystery, from being incapable of remaining content with half-knowledge. This pursued through volumes would perhaps take us no farther than this; that with a great poet the sense of beauty overcomes every other consideration, or rather obliterates all consideration.

What Keats meant by *negative capability* has not been clearly established. Most interpretations equate negative capability with OBJECTIVITY, AESTHETIC DISTANCE, and impersonality on the part of the writer who, as Keats wrote in another letter, "has as much delight in conceiving an Iago as an Imogen." For Keats, negative capability appears also to include the ability to tolerate and even exult in AMBIGUITY and PARADOX for the sake of the beauty to be intuited in such uncertainty.

neoclassicism.   The dominant literary movement in England during the late seventeenth century and the eighteenth century, which sought to revive the artistic ideals of classical Greece and Rome. Neoclassicism was characterized by emotional restraint, order, logic, technical precision, balance, elegance of DICTION, an emphasis of FORM over content, clarity, dignity, and DECORUM. Its appeals were to the intellect rather than to the emotions, and it prized WIT over IMAGINATION. As a result, SATIRE and DIDACTIC LITERATURE flourished, as did the ESSAY, the PARODY, and the BURLESQUE. In POETRY, the HEROIC COUPLET was the most popular VERSE form. Important neoclassic writers of the period include John Dryden, Alexander Pope, Jonathan Swift, Joseph Addison, and Samuel Johnson.

Neoclassicism survives in the twentieth century in works that exhibit the styles, forms, and attitudes of classical antiquity and that emphasize the importance of universality, OBJECTIVITY, impersonality, and careful craftsmanship. The writings of T. S. Eliot and the New Critics are notable examples.

See CLASSIC, NEW CRITICISM.

New Criticism.   An approach to LITERARY CRITICISM, dominant in the United States in the 1940s and 1950s, that focuses on a poem or other literary work as an artistic object possessing value in and of itself. The literary work is considered apart from any relationship the work may have to the life or intentions of its author (INTENTIONAL FALLACY), to social or cultural conditions at the time of its production, or to its effect on the reader (AFFECTIVE FALLACY). The method of New Criticism, which has been more successful with LYRIC POETRY than with PLAYS or NOVELS, is close reading of the text and detailed analysis of what New Critics consider the principal elements of a literary work: words, IM-

AGES, and SYMBOLS (rather than PLOT and CHARACTER). New Critics tend to assume that these elements have opposing meanings, which are reconciled or at least brought into equilibrium by the THEME of the work.

New Criticism derives, to a large extent, from the theory of I. A. Richards that poetry is a special language, a language radically different from the language of science. Its practitioners include Ezra Pound and T. S. Eliot, followed by William K. Wimsatt, Cleanth Brooks, Robert Penn Warren, John Crowe Ransom, Allen Tate, and R. P. Blackmur.

See AFFECTIVE FALLACY, INTENTIONAL FALLACY, LITERARY CRITICISM, OBJECTIVE CORRELATIVE.

New Humanism. A school of philosophy and LITERARY CRITICISM in America between 1910 and 1930. Reacting against NATURALISM and its overemphasis on scientific DETERMINISM and the animal qualities in human nature, New Humanism sought to reassert the moral qualities of LITERATURE and the importance of human reason and freedom of will. Led by Irving Babbitt and Paul Elmer More, the New Humanists strove to avoid the extremes of both science and religion and stressed the importance of enlightened human reason as an "inner check" on animalistic impulses. They valued humility, harmony, and restraint and believed that there is a dualism between human beings and nature, that experience is essentially ethical rather than natural, and that the human will is free. The movement, under attacks by MARXIST CRITICISM and NEW CRITICISM, lost favor after 1930.

See DETERMINISM, HUMANISM, NATURALISM.

No drama. The CLASSIC Japanese DRAMA, dating from the fourteenth century and believed to have evolved out of the dances of Shinto ritual. Unlike the popular Kabuki drama, the No dramas were performed exclusively for aristocratic audiences and have not varied in their content or STYLE of presentation since the seventeenth century. Presented at a religious festival, a No program lasts about seven hours and includes several works that do not have PLOTS. The actor-dancers, wearing masks and elaborate costumes, arrive on the square platform stage characteristic of the No theater by means of a long slanting walk, actually a bridge, at stage left. Three trees, symbolizing heaven, earth, and humankind, provide the only scenery. Introductory DIALOGUE, chanted to the accompaniment of onstage musicians, presents the THEME of each play—most often, praise of a god or of a warrior—and is followed by a number of stylized dances. William Butler Yeats, Bertolt Brecht, and Thornton Wilder are among the Western dramatists who have been influenced by the techniques of the No drama.

See EPIC THEATER.

nom de plume.   A fictitious name assumed by a writer who wishes to remain anonymous or who chooses not to use his or her real name professionally; a **pen name.** Mary Ann Evans used the pen name George Eliot. Amantine Lucile Aurore Dupin was better known as the French novelist George Sand. Stendhal was actually Marie Henri Beyle. Pearl Buck, who used her own name for books with Asian SETTINGS, used the name John Sedges when she wrote books with an American setting. To demonstrate that unknown writers are mostly ignored, Doris Lessing wrote two books under the name of Jane Somers and proved her point. Finally, Eleanor Burford Hibbert uses three pen names: Victoria Holt for romantic suspense NOVELS, Jean Plaidy for HISTORICAL NOVELS, and Philippa Carr for ROMANTIC NOVELS with historical backgrounds.

nonsense verse.   A type of VERSE in which meaning or sense is subordinate to sound. Nonsense verse ranges from nursery rhyme jingles to the syllable collages of the DADA movement. The spirit of nonsense can be playful, satirical, or nihilistic. The best-known writers of nonsense verse are Lewis Carroll, with his fantastic invented words ("brillig"; "frabjous"), and Edward Lear, with his absurd characters and situations:

> Far and few, far and few,
>   Are the lands where the Jumblies live;
> Their heads are green, and their hands are blue;
>   And they went to sea in a sieve.

novel.   A lengthy fictional NARRATIVE in PROSE dealing with CHARACTERS, INCIDENTS, and SETTINGS that imitate those found in real life. Usually the novel is concerned with the depiction of middle-class and working-class characters (rather than legendary heroes) engaged in such ordinary pursuits as falling in love; getting married; traveling; making money; contending with their environment, with other characters, or with their own limitations; and struggling for advancement in their society or profession. The author, while obviously inventing people and situations, attempts to give the impression that he or she is reporting the facts as they occurred. But these are merely general characteristics, not hard-and-fast requirements. Because of tremendous variety in type, FORM, and subject matter, the novel resists neat and tidy classification.

While the roots of the novel reach back into classical LITERATURE and can be found later in such forms as the EPIC, the Italian NOVELLA (from which the word *novel* derives), the PICARESQUE tale (Miguel de Cervantes' *Don Quixote*), and the MEDIEVAL and French ROMANCES, the English novel did not emerge as a clearly recognizable GENRE until the eighteenth century. Many critics and literary historians credit Samuel Richardson's *Pamela* (1740) with being the first work that can be called a fully realized novel. Other eighteenth-century writers important to the development of the novel are Daniel Defoe (*Moll Flanders*), Henry Fielding (*Tom Jones*), Tobias Smollett (*Roderick Random*), Laurence Sterne (*Tristram Shandy*), Fanny Burney (*Evelina*), and Ann Radcliffe (*The Mysteries of Udolpho*).

The first truly American novel, *The Power of Sympathy* by William Hill Brown, did not appear until 1789. Charles Brockden Brown, considered to be the first important American novelist, wrote in the GOTHIC tradition. His *Ormond* was published in 1799. Two decades later, James Fenimore Cooper wrote *The Spy, The Pioneers, The Pilot,* and his Leatherstocking series of novels, the best known of which is *The Last of the Mohicans.* Nathaniel Hawthorne's *The Scarlet Letter* appeared in 1850 and Herman Melville's CLASSIC *Moby-Dick* in 1851.

Since these beginnings in England and America, each successive era has found its mode of life, political and social philosophies, triumphs and failures, fads and fashions, fears and aspirations mirrored in the novels of the time. Today the novel remains the most popular and most widely read form of literature.

The extremely broad scope of subject matter embraced by the novel is evident in its many subtypes, most of which are discussed elsewhere in this book.

See BILDUNGSROMAN, DETECTIVE STORY, EPISTOLARY NOVEL, GOTHIC NOVEL, HISTORICAL NOVEL, NOVEL OF MANNERS, PICARESQUE, PROBLEM NOVEL, PSYCHOLOGICAL NOVEL, ROMAN À CLEF, ROMANTIC NOVEL, SCIENCE FICTION, SENTIMENTAL NOVEL, SOCIOLOGICAL NOVEL, STREAM-OF-CONSCIOUSNESS NOVEL.

novelette. PROSE FICTION that is built on one INCIDENT and is shorter than a NOVEL but has more development of CHARACTER and THEME than a SHORT STORY. Herman Melville's *Billy Budd,* Henry James's *The Turn of the Screw,* Ernest Hemingway's *The Old Man and the Sea,* and Virginia Woolf's *Between the Acts* are all novelettes.

See NOVELLA.

novella. A short PROSE NARRATIVE or tale, about the length of a long SHORT STORY, that usually presents a single major INCIDENT, rather than a series of events as in the NOVEL. The FORM originated in Italy with Giovanni Boccaccio's *Decameron,* a collection of one hundred tales.

The term is also applied to the short novel (in German, *Novelle*) and is sometimes used synonymously with NOVELETTE. Thomas Mann's *Tonio Kröger,* Kay Boyle's *The Crazy Hunter,* Katherine Anne Porter's *Noon Wine,* Henry James's *Madame de Mauves,* and Joseph Conrad's *Heart of Darkness* are modern novellas.

novel of manners. A term adapted from COMEDY OF MANNERS for a type of NOVEL, usually comical and satirical, whose CHARACTERS and PLOT emerge from, exemplify, and are limited by the social customs, values, habits, and other idiosyncrasies of a particular social class in a particular time and place—the upper middle class in New York City in 1900, for example. Among the great writers of novels of manners are Henry Fielding, Jane Austen, Henry James, Edith Wharton, and J. P. Marquand.

See NOVEL.

novel of sensibility. A NOVEL reflecting the cult of SENSIBILITY that was pervasive during the last half of the eighteenth century. See SENTIMENTAL NOVEL.

novel of the soil.   A type of SOCIOLOGICAL NOVEL that focuses on the hardships of those who struggle to wrest a living from the land. An example is Willa Cather's *O Pioneers!* See NOVEL, SOCIOLOGICAL NOVEL.

O

objective correlative. The IMAGE of an object, situation, or event that communicates an emotion without an explanation. This HAIKU by Kyoshi presents an image that indirectly communicates a feeling of terrified fascination and functions as an objective correlative:

> The snake is fleeing,
> but its eyes—glaring at me—
> remain in the grass.

Although the term *objective correlative* had been used as early as 1850, it was popularized by T. S. Eliot. In his 1919 essay on *Hamlet,* Eliot announced,

> The only way of expressing emotion in the form of art is by finding an "objective correlative"; in other words, a set of objectives, a situation, a chain of events which shall be the formula of that *particular* emotion; such as when the external facts, which must terminate in sensory experience, are given, the emotion is immediately evoked.

The term gained wide use among critics and proved useful in describing the kind of POETRY that is pure image. It is less useful as a description of a writer's creative process. Eliseo Vivas has pointed out that to assume that a writer deliberately creates an objective correlative for a given emotion is to overlook the creative process of the writer's unconscious mind. A writer often begins with images and discovers their emotional content in the process of writing.

See DISTANCE, NEGATIVE CAPABILITY, OBJECTIVITY.

objective criticism. An approach to LITERARY CRITICISM that focuses on the intrinsic qualities of a work, rather than on the work's relationship to the life of its author, to the time in which it was written, or to its EFFECT on a reader. NEW CRITICISM is a form of objective criticism.

See LITERARY CRITICISM, NEW CRITICISM.

objective point of view. A method of NARRATION in which a story is told in a completely objective manner, the author avoiding any expression of personal opinions, attitudes, or emotions.

See POINT OF VIEW.

objective theory of art. In LITERARY CRITICISM, a term applied to the idea that a work of LITERATURE is most significant as an *object* in itself, independent of any goal outside itself, such as its reference to some external truth, its author's stated or implied intention, its stature among similar works, or its effect upon the reader or audience. Thus judgment of a work should focus exclusively on the work itself.

See AUTOTELIC.

objectivity. In a literary work, the detached, impersonal presentation of situations and of CHARACTERS and their thoughts and feelings. The author does not personally intrude to comment on the characters. Robert Browning's DRAMATIC MONOLOGUE "My Last Duchess" is an objective poem in which a character is the SPEAKER. Ernest Hemingway's SHORT STORY "The Killers" is narrated by an objective third-person NARRATOR who stands outside the story and reports without comment.

See NEGATIVE CAPABILITY, OBJECTIVE CORRELATIVE, POINT OF VIEW, SUBJECTIVITY.

occasional verse. POETRY written for a particular occasion, usually in commemoration of a social, literary, or historical event. One of the responsibilities of the poet laureate is to write poetry for special occasions. Some well-known examples of occasional verse are John Milton's SONNET "On the Late Massacre in Piedmont," Anne Bradstreet's "On the Burning of Our House," Alfred, Lord Tennyson's "Ode on the Death of the Duke of Wellington," Walt Whitman's "When Lilacs Last in the Dooryard Bloom'd" (commemorating Abraham Lincoln's death), and W. H. Auden's "In Memory of W. B. Yeats." While these examples are memorable for their intrinsic literary value, many occasional poems are not. They are often considered LIGHT VERSE, or *vers de société.*

octameter. A poetic line containing eight metrical feet. A long line that tends to break into two four-foot lines, the octameter is rare in English POETRY. The bulkiness of the octameter line is demonstrated by the frequency with which the second of the following pair of octameter lines from Alfred, Lord Tennyson's *Locksley Hall* is misquoted in a shorter form:

> Ĭn thĕ | spríng ă | lívĕliĕr | íris | chángĕs | ŏn thĕ |
> búrnĭshĕd | dóve,
> Ĭn thĕ | spríng ă | yŏung mắn's | fáncў | líghtlў |
> túrns tŏ | thóughts ŏf | lóve.

See FOOT, METER, SCANSION.

octave. The first eight lines, or **octet,** of the ITALIAN (or PETRARCHAN) SONNET. Usually the octave asks a question or states a generalization that is answered or resolved in the last six lines, the SESTET, of the poem.

An octave is also a STANZA of eight lines. In this sense the term is often applied to **ottava rima,** an eight-line stanza of IAMBIC PENTAMETER rhyming *abababcc*. This stanza pattern was used with distinction by such English poets as Edmund Spenser, John Milton, John Keats, and Lord Byron. This last stanza from W. B. Yeats's "Sailing to Byzantium" is ottava rima:

Once out of nature I shall never take	*a*
My bodily form from any natural thing,	*b*
But such a form as Grecian goldsmiths make	*a*
Of hammered gold and gold enamelling	*b*
To keep a drowsy Emperor awake;	*a*
Or set upon a golden bough to sing	*b*
To lords and ladies of Byzantium	*c*
Of what is past, or passing, or to come.	*c*

See RHYME SCHEME, SONNET, STANZA.

ode.   A long and elaborate LYRIC poem, usually dignified or exalted in TONE and often written to praise someone or something or to mark an important occasion. The Greek poet Pindar developed the FORM of the ode from the varying STANZA pattern of the choral songs in Greek TRAGEDY. Pindar's odes were written in honor of the winners of the Olympic Games and for other public occasions. The Latin odes of Horace were private, personal expressions written in regular stanza form.

The seventeenth-century English poet Abraham Cowley developed the free, or irregular, ode, influencing John Dryden, who wrote the finest odes in English, among them "Song for St. Cecelia's Day" and "Alexander's Feast." Other well-known odes include John Milton's "On the Morning of Christ's Nativity," William Wordsworth's "Ode: Intimations of Immortality," Percy Bysshe Shelley's "Ode to the West Wind," and several great odes by John Keats: "On a Grecian Urn," "To a Nightingale," "To Autumn," and "On Melancholy." Among odes written in the twentieth century are two particularly fine ones: W. H. Auden's "In Memory of W. B. Yeats" and Allen Tate's "Ode to the Confederate Dead."

See LYRIC.

omniscient point of view.   In FICTION, the POINT OF VIEW from which a godlike author, who can see, hear, and know everything, tells the story. By assuming omniscience, the author is free to enter CHARACTERS' minds and reveal their thoughts, to comment on or interpret their actions, to report INCIDENTS the characters have not witnessed themselves, to move about in time and place without restriction, and to make clear the THEME of the story in whatever ways he or she desires. This brief passage from Flannery O'Connor's SHORT STORY "The Life You Save May Be Your Own" demonstrates the omniscient point of view:

> He was more depressed than ever as he drove on by himself. The late afternoon had grown hot and sultry and the country had flattened out. Deep in the sky a storm was preparing very slowly and without thunder as if it meant to drain every drop of air from the earth before it broke. There were times when Mr. Shiftlet preferred not to be alone. He felt too that a man with a car had a responsibility to others and he kept his eye out for a hitchhiker. Occasionally he saw a sign that warned: "Drive carefully. The life you save may be your own."

If a NARRATOR assumes **limited omniscience,** he or she reveals the thoughts of a single character and presents the other characters only externally.

See FIRST-PERSON POINT OF VIEW, NARRATOR, POINT OF VIEW, THIRD-PERSON POINT OF VIEW.

one-act play. A PLAY in one act, presenting a simple INCIDENT involving two or three CHARACTERS and running for fifteen to forty minutes. Comparable to a SHORT STORY in its dependence on UNITY of EFFECT, the one-act play came into its own in the late nineteenth century and has become popular with playwrights working in the noncommercial and experimental theater. Among the best-known one-act plays are Anton Chekhov's *The Proposal,* August Strindberg's *The Stronger,* John M. Synge's *Riders to the Sea,* Eugene O'Neill's *Hughie,* Samuel Beckett's *Krapp's Last Tape,* Eugène Ionesco's *The Bald Soprano,* and Harold Pinter's *The Dumb Waiter.* From time to time in the commercial theater, two or three one-act plays are grouped together as an evening's entertainment.

onomatopoeia. The use of words whose sound imitates the sound of the thing being named. For example, the pronunciation of words like *hum, buzz, clang, boom, hiss, crack,* and *twitter* suggests their meaning. The value of onomatopoeia as a poetic device becomes evident when sound echoes sense throughout an entire phrase or line:

> The murmurous haunt of flies on summer eves.

> And the silken, sad, uncertain rustling of each purple
>   curtain.

> The moan of doves in immemorial elms,
> And murmuring of innumerable bees.

> "Tis the night of doom," say the ding-dong doom-bells.

oral literature.   The BALLADS, folktales, and PROVERBS of preliterate
or nonliterate cultures that are sung or recited to audiences and
are passed with changes from generation to generation through
memory rather than by being written down. Common to all oral
literature are devices that aid memory, such as traditional
phrases, repetition, and metrical patterns. Among the works believed to have had a long life as oral literature before they were
written down are the earliest versions of the *Iliad* and the *Odyssey,*
MEDIEVAL BALLADS, and nearly all pre-twentieth-century African
literature.

   See BALLAD.

ottava rima.   An eight-line STANZA of IAMBIC PENTAMETER rhyming
abababcc. See OCTAVE.

oxymoron.   A figure of speech in which two contradictory words or
phrases are combined in a single expression, giving the effect of a
condensed PARADOX: "wise fool," "living death," "cruel kind-
ness," "eloquent silence." Still found in modern POETRY, the oxymoron was the primary rhetorical expression of the BAROQUE
era, especially in METAPHYSICAL POETRY. Romeo uses a series of
oxymora to describe his "loving hate" in these lines from
William Shakespeare's *Romeo and Juliet:*

> O heavy lightness! serious vanity!
> Mis-shapen chaos of well-seeming forms!
> Feather of lead, bright smoke, cold fire, sick health!

These lines describe the infant Jesus in Richard Crashaw's
poem "An Hymn of the Nativity":

Welcome, all wonders in one sight!
Eternity shut in a span,
Summer in winter, day in night,
Heaven in earth, and God in man!

See PARADOX.

P

panegyric.   Elaborate praise, often poetical in FORM. See EULOGY.

parable.   A short tale illustrating a moral lesson. A parable is often
an ALLEGORY that parallels the situation to which it is being applied, as are the best-known parables of Jesus. In the Prodigal
Son, for example, the loving response of the human father to the
son who returns after a period of wasteful living is an allegory of
the love of God for the repentant sinner.

See ALLEGORY, APOLOGUE, EXEMPLUM, FABLE.

paradox.   A statement that, while apparently self-contradictory, is
nonetheless essentially true. Paradox, a rhetorical device common in epigrammatic writing, appears often in the writing of
Oscar Wilde and of G. K. Chesterton, who has been called a
"paradox monger." Here are some examples of paradox:

> That I may rise and stand, o'erthrow me.
>
> —John Donne

> The amount of women in London who flirt with their own
> husbands is perfectly scandalous.
>
> —Oscar Wilde

Success is counted sweetest
By those who ne'er succeed.

—Emily Dickinson

The more unintelligent a man is, the less mysterious existence seems to him.

—Arthur Schopenhauer

I never found the companion that was so companionable as
solitude.

—Henry David Thoreau

See CONCEIT, EPIGRAM, OXYMORON.

parallelism. The technique of showing that words, phrases, clauses,
or larger structures are comparable in content and importance
by placing them side by side and making them similar in FORM.
Parallelism is a common unifying device in POETRY, especially in
ancient poetry growing out of the oral tradition—for example,
the Hebrew Psalms—and in modern FREE VERSE. It is the pervasiveness of Walt Whitman's parallelism that gives his poetry an
antique, sometimes even biblical, ring:

Halcyon Days

Not from successful love alone,
Nor wealth, nor honor'd middle age, nor victories of politics
    or war;
But as life wanes, and all the turbulent passions calm,
As gorgeous, vapory, silent hues cover the evening sky,
As softness, fulness, rest, suffuse the frame, like fresher,
    balmier air,
As the days take on a mellower light, and the apple at last
    hangs really finish'd and indolent-ripe on the tree,
Then for the teeming quietest, happiest days of all!
The brooding and blissful halcyon days!

paraphrase. A restatement of an expression or a passage that retains the meaning of the original but presents it in different
words and often in a different form; a rewording. A paraphrase
usually expands or amplifies the original as an aid to clarification
and understanding. For example, the paraphrase of a poem is a

PROSE restatement that explains difficult passages, obscure ALLU-SIONS, and poetic DICTION. Many modern critics, including Cleanth Brooks, object to what Brooks in *The Well Wrought Urn* calls "the heresy of paraphrase," maintaining that, since FORM and content are inseparable, paraphrase is not possible. They hold that LYRIC poetry especially, given its SUBJECTIVITY and its highly individualized expression of personal emotion, is in prac-tical terms unparaphrasable. Nevertheless, paraphrase remains one of the most important and universally applied tools of LITER-ARY CRITICISM.

parody. A composition that ridicules another composition by imi-tating and exaggerating aspects of its content, STRUCTURE, and STYLE, accomplishing in words what the caricature achieves in drawing. The following anonymous parody pokes fun both at the insistent trochaic METER of Henry W. Longfellow's poem *Hiawa-tha* and at its repetitious STYLE:

The Modern Hiawatha

He killed the noble Mudjokivis.
Of the skin he made him mittens,
Made them with the fur side inside,
Made them with the skin side outside.
He, to get the warm side inside,
Put the inside skin side outside;
He, to get the cold side outside,
Put the warm side fur side inside.
That's why he put the fur side inside,
Why he put the skin side outside,
Why he turned them inside outside.

See BURLESQUE, MOCK EPIC, SATIRE.

pastoral. A poem having to do with shepherds and rural life; from *pastor,* the Latin word for shepherd. Theocritus (third century B.C.) perfected three forms of the pastoral that became governed by CONVENTIONS and were widely imitated by poets in later cen-turies, among them Virgil, Edmund Spenser, and John Milton. The three forms are the singing match between two shepherds, sometimes called the **eclogue;** the **monologue** of a single lovesick shepherd lamenting his mistress's aloofness; and the **elegy,** or **dirge**, for a dead friend.

Rather than presenting a realistic picture of the hardships of rustic life, conventionalized pastorals feature lovelorn shepherds and cold-hearted shepherdesses leading idyllic artificial existences, singing and wooing, and moving about in idealized SETTINGS with a few ornamental flowers, a few sheep, and perhaps a bubbling brook. Pastorals in several forms were popular in England between 1550 and 1750. Some examples are Milton's *Lycidas,* Percy Bysshe Shelley's *Adonais,* Matthew Arnold's *Thyrsis,* Spenser's *The Shepheardes Calender,* Sir Philip Sidney's prose pastoral *Arcadia,* and John Fletcher's pastoral PLAY *The Faithfull Shepheardesse.* Over the years the meaning of *pastoral* broadened to include any composition concerning rustic people in a simple, charming, or serene rural setting. Thus, the term has become more descriptive of content than of FORM, so that there are pastoral LYRICS, pastoral DRAMA, pastoral elegies, and pastoral ROMANCES.

See IDYLL.

pathetic fallacy. A term coined by John Ruskin to criticize the use of PERSONIFICATION, in which human emotions are attributed to nature. Although many poets use this device, Ruskin found it a form of false emotionalism, as he made clear in the third volume of *Modern Painters:*

> They rowed her in across the rolling foam—
> The cruel, crawling foam.

> The foam is not cruel, neither does it crawl. The state of mind which attributes to it these characters of a living creature is one in which the reason is unhinged by grief. All violent feelings have the same effect. They produce in us a falseness in all our impressions of external things, which I would generally characterize as the "pathetic fallacy."

See PERSONIFICATION.

pathos. The quality in a work of art or LITERATURE that arouses feelings of sympathy, pity, or sorrow in the viewer or reader. Although pathos and TRAGEDY both evoke such feelings, a distinction is commonly made between the pathetic and the tragic. The suffering experienced by the weak, the passive, and the innocent is pathetic, while the suffering inflicted upon the strong, the aggressive, and the heroic (who are often in part responsible for their own suffering) is tragic. In these senses, Antigone's fate is tragic, Desdemona's pathetic.

See BATHOS.

pen name. A fictitious name assumed by an author to conceal his or her true identity. See NOM DE PLUME.

pentameter. A five-foot line of VERSE. The most common pentameter line, IAMBIC PENTAMETER, is the basis of BLANK VERSE, the SONNET, and the HEROIC COUPLET, and is the most widely used line in English verse. The following COUPLET, by Alexander Pope, is in iambic pentameter:

> Trŭe eáse │ ĭn wrít│ĭng comés │ from árt, │ nŏt chánce,
> Ăs thóse │ mŏve eás │ ĭest whó │ hăve leárned │
> tŏ dánce.

See FOOT, IAMBIC PENTAMETER, SCANSION.

peripeteia. In Greek DRAMA, the sudden and dramatic change of fortune for the PROTAGONIST; also called **peripety.** See REVERSAL.

persona. A term used in LITERARY CRITICISM to refer to the VOICE (or mask), created by the author, through which a story is told. The persona is not the author, the person who sits down to write, but a "second self," an artistic creation, through whom the author speaks. The persona may be the NARRATOR, the "I" in a first-person NARRATIVE, as is Holden Caulfield, the prep-school adolescent of J. D. Salinger's *The Catcher in the Rye.* However, the persona need not be a CHARACTER in the story but can be what Wayne C. Booth calls the "implied author," a teller realized by the reader not directly but in and through the words on the page.

See IMPLIED AUTHOR, NARRATOR.

personal essay. A brief PROSE composition expressing personal opinions, impressions, and biases in a familiar, whimsical, or humorous TONE. See ESSAY, INFORMAL ESSAY.

personification. A FIGURE OF SPEECH in which human characteristics and sensibilities are attributed to animals, plants, inanimate objects, natural forces, or abstract ideas. John Updike employs personification in this short poem:

Sunday Rain

The window screen
is trying to do
its crossword puzzle
but appears to know
only vertical words.

See FIGURATIVE LANGUAGE.

Petrarchan conceit. The type of CONCEIT, first employed by Petrarch in his love SONNETS and later imitated by ELIZABETHAN sonneteers, that consists of elaborate and exaggerated comparisons, or ANALOGIES, and, often, OXYMORA. See CONCEIT.

Petrarchan sonnet. A SONNET arranged into two parts—an OCTAVE, consisting of the first eight lines and rhyming *abba, abba;* and a SESTET, the remaining six lines, which usually rhyme *cde, cde.* Also called an **Italian sonnet**, the Petrarchan sonnet is named after Petrarch, the fourteenth-century Italian poet who perfected its form. See SONNET.

phenomenology. A philosophical viewpoint, influential in modern LITERARY CRITICISM, that sees the reality of any object only in a person's awareness or consciousness of the object. Phenomenological literary criticism thus focuses not on the literary work itself, but on the experience of reading, and attempts to describe the process by which a work enters, influences, and is influenced by a reader's consciousness.

See READER-RESPONSE CRITICISM.

phonology. The study of basic speech sounds; a branch of LINGUIS-TICS. Also, one of the three components of grammar, along with MORPHOLOGY and SYNTAX.

See LINGUISTICS.

picaresque. A term usually applied to a NOVEL whose principal CHARACTER is a low-born rogue who lives by his or her wits and who becomes involved in one predicament after another. The Spanish word for rogue is *picaro;* the English is *picaroon.*

The picaresque novel usually takes the form of a series of loosely connected EPISODES, frequently arranged as journeys, and is often but not always autobiographical. It treats its subject realistically, with vivid details and plain if not earthy language. Because the picaroon's many adventures involve people from all stations of life, the author is afforded the opportunity for social SATIRE and usually makes the most of it.

Picaresque tales originated in sixteenth-century Spain. The best-known Spanish tale is Miguel de Cervantes' *Don Quixote;* the best-known French story is Lesage's *Gil Blas.* In England Thomas Nash's *The Unfortunate Traveler,* Daniel Defoe's *Moll Flanders,* Henry Fielding's *Tom Jones,* and William M. Thackeray's *Barry Lyndon* represent the type. (Both *Tom Jones* and *Barry Lyndon* have been made into popular movies.) Mark Twain's *Huckleberry Finn* and Saul Bellow's *The Adventures of Augie March* are sometimes described as modern American picaresque novels.

See NOVEL.

plagiarism. Using another writer's ideas or words as one's own. Plagiarism, which comes from a Latin word meaning "to kidnap," ranges from deliberate literary theft to inept paraphrasing to unconscious borrowing. From a legal standpoint the term is defined as "demonstrable use of matter plainly taken from another without credit."

During the RENAISSANCE and earlier, much of what today would be considered plagiarism was tolerated and even admired—because of the emphasis on writing as IMITATION of earlier writers of distinction. The Roman writer Seneca maintained, "Whatever has been well said by anyone is mine." Writers were judged more for the comprehensiveness of their reading and their taste in imitating or borrowing than for originality. Since most of their readers could be expected to recognize writers' sources from their own voluminous reading, quotation marks doubtless seemed unnecessary. Copyrights did not exist, and ideas and words did not strike people as something owned, like property, by individuals. Today, the proliferation of ghostwriters and committee-generated writing threatens to raise new questions about ownership of the written word.

See IMITATION, PARAPHRASE.

Platonic criticism. A type of criticism (named for Plato) that stresses the extrinsic rather than the intrinsic values of a work of art. It centers not on the work itself but on the external purposes (moral, historic, religious) that the work may serve. Platonic criticism stands in opposition to ARISTOTELIAN CRITICISM, which focuses on values found within the work itself.

See ARISTOTELIAN CRITICISM, LITERARY CRITICISM.

play. A literary work written in DIALOGUE and intended for performance before an audience by actors on a stage or other performing area. See DRAMA.

plot. The careful arrangement by an author of INCIDENTS in a NARRATIVE to achieve a desired effect. Plot is more than simply the series of happenings in a literary work. It is the result of the writer's deliberate selection of interrelated actions (what happens) and choice of arrangement (the order of happening) in presenting and resolving a CONFLICT. In *Aspects of the Novel,* E. M. Forster explains the difference between *plot* and *story* in this way:

> We have defined a story as a narrative of events arranged in their time sequence. A plot is also a narrative of events, the emphasis falling on causality. "The king died and then the queen died," is a story. "The king died, and then the queen died of grief" is a plot. The time-sequence is preserved, but the sense of causality overshadows it.

Aristotle considered plot the most important element of DRAMA or EPIC. He defined plot as the "arrangement of incidents" and the "IMITATION of an action," which should have a beginning, a middle, and an ending, related as to cause and effect and unified in such a manner that removing or reordering any part would damage the whole.

Some critics dispute the centrality of plot, maintaining that CHARACTER and CHARACTERIZATION are more important. In their view plot simply provides the structured framework that serves to illuminate characters. Other critics feel that plot and character are inseparable, that action (what a character does) is largely determined by personality (what sort of person a character is), and that the writer's principal task in developing a plot is translating character into action.

Most plots involve conflict, a struggle between two opposing forces. The conflict may be external (one person against another) or internal (two elements at war within the same person). In a typical plot structure the action begins with EXPOSITION (presentation of important background information), rises through a COMPLICATION (building of tension between opposing forces) toward a CLIMAX (turning point), and falls to a final DENOUEMENT, or RESOLUTION of the conflict. Although some modern works are essentially "plotless," depending upon character, STYLE, or MOOD for their artistic unity, most NOVELS and plays are still built on coherent plots.

See CHARACTER, CHARACTERIZATION, FREYTAG'S PYRAMID, STRUCTURE.

poetic justice. Rewarding the good and punishing the bad. The term was first used by Thomas Rhymer in 1678 to express the idea that in LITERATURE, if not always in life, rewards and punishments should be carefully distributed so that readers may be inspired to goodness and discouraged from evil. Widely held in the seventeenth and eighteenth centuries, the concept of poetic justice led theater directors to perform rewritten versions of some of William Shakespeare's tragedies—*King Lear,* for example— with happy and poetically just endings. Although modified by the goals of REALISM, poetic justice persists in the RESOLUTIONS of popular ROMANCES, DETECTIVE STORIES, westerns, and movie MELODRAMAS of today.

See MELODRAMA.

poetic license. The liberty poets and other literary artists have to depart from normal word order, distort pronunciation or create

EYE RHYMES, use archaic words, or invent new words in order to achieve certain effects.

poetics. Traditionally, the technique, art, and theory of poetic composition; the study of the nature of POETRY. In modern usage, however, the term has broadened to refer to the general theory of LITERATURE, the identification of universal properties that constitute literature and make it possible. Poetics is concerned not with the criticism or interpretation of specific literary works but with the general laws that underlie them. In *A Dictionary of Modern Critical Terms,* edited by Roger Fowler, Michael O'Toole characterizes the poetician's stance in this manner: "One should study 'literariness' rather than existing works of 'literature.' " **Generative poetics,** which seeks to identify and describe the "literary competence" of experienced readers, has been greatly influenced by the generative LINGUISTICS of Noam Chomsky, which attempts to describe the "linguistic competence" of native speakers.

See FORMALISM, POST-STRUCTURALISM, STRUCTURALISM.

poetry. LITERATURE in its most intense, most imaginative, and most rhythmic FORMS. Poetry differs from PROSE most basically in being written in lines of arbitrary length instead of in paragraphs. In general, poetry's richness in IMAGERY, particularly in META-PHOR, results in a far greater concentration of meaning than is ordinarily found in prose. Although the term *poetry* is commonly used for all composition in VERSE, it is also used more restrictively to identify serious verse composition of high quality, in contrast to LIGHT VERSE. The poets of each generation and their interpreters have had their own definition of poetry, their own sense of what poetry is and what poetry does:

> Poetry is "a speaking picture—with this end, to teach and delight."
>
> —Sir Philip Sidney

> Poetry is "the spontaneous overflow of powerful feelings... recollected in tranquility."
>
> —William Wordsworth

Poetry is "a criticism of life."

—Matthew Arnold

"Poetry is not an assertion of truth, but the making of that truth more fully real to us."

—T. S. Eliot

Poetry consists of "imaginary gardens with real toads in them."

—Marianne Moore

"Poetry provides the one permissible way of saying one thing and meaning another."

—Robert Frost

point of view. The vantage point, or stance, from which a story is told, the eye and mind through which the action is perceived and filtered; sometimes called **narrative perspective.**

There are two general narrative points of view, **first person** (*I*) and **third person** (*he, she, they*), which depend on whether the NARRATOR stands inside the story or outside it. Each of these general viewpoints has several variations.

The "I" narrator may be the central CHARACTER, the first-person PROTAGONIST; a minor character, the first-person participant; or a character who is not directly involved in the action but who functions only as an observer and recorder, the first-person observer. All first-person NARRATION requires the author to create a PERSONA—a mask, or "second self"—through which the author tells the story. If this narrator does not fully understand the implications of his or her tale, the character is called a NAIVE NARRATOR. If the first-person narration presents only the unspoken thoughts of the protagonist, the result is an INTERIOR MONOLOGUE.

Employing a first-person point of view has several advantages. One of these is credibility. A strange or fantastic story is easier to believe if told by someone who is supposedly relating a firsthand experience. And it is far more natural for a character to reveal her own thoughts than it is for the author to tell us what she is thinking and feeling. Another advantage is intimacy. The "I" narrator seems to address the reader directly and from the heart, sharing his personal observations and insights with an interested listener. But first-person narration also has disadvantages. The reader can see, hear, and know only what the narrator sees, hears, and knows. The reader's perceptions of other characters are colored by the narrator's predispositions, prejudices, and personal limitations. Characterization of a first-person protagonist is difficult. For instance, an "I" narrator cannot tell the reader that he or she is an admirable person. The reader must form an opinion indirectly, evaluating what the narrator says, thinks, and does. Some of these difficulties are overcome, however, when the "I" narrator is a minor character, a participant who can describe the protagonist from the outside.

The most common third-person narrative perspective is called the **omniscient point of view.** Here the narrator, standing outside the story, assumes a godlike persona, moving about freely in time and space, revealing the thoughts and motives of all the characters, knowing the present, past, and future, and (sometimes) commenting on or interpreting the actions of the characters. The major advantage of this approach is its obvious freedom and unlimited scope. Its major disadvantage is a relative loss of vividness, involvement, and intimacy. This difficulty is overcome somewhat if the narrator assumes **limited omniscience,** focusing on the thoughts of a single character and presenting the other characters only externally. This more restricted approach surrenders the privileges of seeing and knowing everything and typically follows one character throughout the story, presenting only those incidents in which that character is involved.

The **objective point of view** is an even more restricted type of third-person limited omniscience that prohibits any subjective commentary by the author. In this case, by remaining unobtrusive, the author is called a **self-effacing author.** When this approach *also* abandons freedom of movement in time and space, examination of motives, and revelation of thoughts, and restricts the narrator to only those objective details that can be seen and heard by an invisible witness, it is called the **scenic method,** or the **fly-on-the-wall technique.** While SHORT STORIES are usually presented from a single point of view, longer works of FICTION frequently employ several.

See FIRST-PERSON POINT OF VIEW, INTERIOR MONOLOGUE, NARRATOR, STREAM OF CONSCIOUSNESS, THIRD-PERSON POINT OF VIEW.

popular romance.   Also known as the *love story,* one of the FORMS of the ROMANCE in today's FICTION; characterized by strange or exotic SETTINGS, mysterious INCIDENTS, and passionate love. See ROMANCE, ROMANTIC NOVEL.

pornography.   Writing that seems designed solely to arouse sexual excitement in the reader, that lacks any redeeming social value or literary quality. This definition owes its substance to Judge John Woolsey, who, in ruling favorably on James Joyce's *Ulysses,* which had been banned in the United States, based his opinion on the book as a whole, on the author's intention, and on the reaction of a normal reader. It is surely easier to define *pornography* than to decide whether a book should be labeled pornography. Such a decision is highly subjective and greatly influenced by the standards of the time in which one lives.

See CENSORSHIP.

portmanteau words.   Words coined by combining or "telescoping" two or more words in such a way that their meanings are also combined; sometimes called **blends.** Lewis Carroll originated the term to describe words he had invented. In *Through the Looking-Glass* he has Humpty Dumpty explain to Alice that *slithy* means both "lithe" and "slimy," and thus "it's like a portmanteau [suitcase]—there are two meanings packed up into one word." Other examples of Carroll's coinages are *chortle* (chuckle and snort), *frumious* (fuming and furious), and *mimsy* (flimsy and miserable). James Joyce makes frequent use of portmanteau words in *Finnegans Wake,* such as *amuckst* (amongst and amuck) and *rugaby* (rugby and rockabye). Some familiar examples in general use are *brunch, smog, motel, splurge,* and *camporee.*

positivism.   A system of philosophy developed in the nineteenth century, principally by Auguste Comte, that held that knowledge must be based on empirical (observed or experienced) evidence, that metaphysics and all speculation about ultimate causes is invalid, that the objective of knowledge is scientific description, not subjective explanation.

During the beginning of the twentieth century, a movement (an outgrowth of positivism) called **logical positivism,** led by Ludwig Wittgenstein, emerged in Vienna. Its proponents considered the goal of philosophy to be the logical clarification of thought, achieved by applying the methods of scientific empiricism found in mathematics and the physical sciences. Thus, philosophy is not a speculative pursuit, but an analytical one. Both of these philosophical movements have had indirect but powerful influences on twentieth-century LITERATURE and LITERARY CRITICISM.

post-structuralism. An umbrella term that came into use in the 1970s and covered several approaches to LITERARY CRITICISM, including DECONSTRUCTION, READER-RESPONSE CRITICISM, and some varieties of PSYCHOANALYTIC CRITICISM and FEMINIST CRITICISM. Each of these approaches has sought to compensate for the neglect by structuralist criticism of important elements of literary study, such as the roles of the reader and the author and the function of ideology.

    See DECONSTRUCTION, FEMINIST CRITICISM, LITERARY CRITICISM, PSYCHOANALYTIC CRITICISM, READER-RESPONSE CRITICISM, SEMIOTICS, STRUCTURALISM.

practical criticism. An objective approach to LITERARY CRITICISM that applies principles of art and theoretical insights when analyzing and evaluating particular works; sometimes called **applied criticism.** Practical criticism contrasts with THEORETICAL CRITICISM, which aims to identify and codify the general principles that underlie art and to formulate aesthetic and critical tenets. Theoretical critics supply the insights, methods, and tools put to use by the practical critic.

    See LITERARY CRITICISM, THEORETICAL CRITICISM.

pragmatic criticism. An approach to LITERARY CRITICISM that focuses on a work as something designed to produce certain emotional and moral responses in the reader and on how those effects are produced. The dominant approach to criticism up through the eighteenth century, pragmatic criticism, or **rhetorical criticism**, as it is also called, has received fresh impetus in the latter part of the twentieth century, notably in the work of critic Wayne Booth (*The Rhetoric of Fiction; The Company We Keep: An Ethics of Fiction*). In their insistence on seeking the source of the reader's reaction in the work itself rather than in the consciousness of the

reader, pragmatic critics differ sharply from reader-response critics.

See LITERARY CRITICISM, READER-RESPONSE CRITICISM.

primitivism.   The doctrine that primitive people—"noble savages"
living simple, unspoiled lives close to nature—are superior to
modern humankind, who have been corrupted by civilization.
Primitivism presupposes a natural goodness and nobility in humans from which modern humanity has fallen. One of its central
assumptions is that progress means decay. The movement flourished in England and France during the eighteenth century,
given impetus by such philosophers as the third Earl of Shaftesbury and Jean-Jacques Rousseau. Shaftesbury reasoned that
since God exists in nature and primitive peoples live "natural"
lives, they are closer to God and therefore better than civilized
peoples. Rousseau argued that human beings were essentially
good but had been corrupted by a society that stifled individual
freedom and thus eroded moral goodness.

Primitivism and its idealization of the noble savage greatly
influenced the romantic movement and, later, the rise of REAL-
ISM in America. Its effects can be seen in William Wordsworth's
emphases on nature, simple language, peasants, idiot boys, and
children; in James Fenimore Cooper's extolling of Native Amer-
icans in the five novels of his Leatherstocking series; and in Michel Crèvecoeur's depiction of primitive pioneer life in the
essay-letters of his *Letters from an American Farmer.*

Primitivism is commonly divided into **chronological primitivism** and **cultural primitivism,** but these categories are not
mutually exclusive. Chronological primitivism considers the past
as better than the present (the life of the feudal peasant better
than the life of the modern industrialist, the child better than the
adult) and blames culture and society for humankind's current
sad state. Cultural primitivism values the natural over the artificial, the childlike and untutored over the sophisticated and intellectual, the spontaneous and uninhibited over the consciously
crafted and controlled, nature over art.

See ROMANTICISM.

problem novel.   A type of realistic NOVEL that presents a social
problem as its central CONFLICT—for example, the injustice of

slavery presented in Harriet Beecher Stowe's *Uncle Tom's Cabin* or the plight of the migrant workers from Oklahoma in John Steinbeck's *The Grapes of Wrath*. If, in addition to presenting the problem, the novelist takes a political stand on the solution of the problem, a problem novel becomes PROPAGANDA LITERATURE.

See NOVEL, PROPAGANDA LITERATURE, SOCIOLOGICAL NOVEL.

proletarian novel.   A type of SOCIOLOGICAL NOVEL that concerns the problems of the working class. See NOVEL, SOCIOLOGICAL NOVEL.

prologue.   An introduction or preface, especially to a PLAY. In Greek and Roman DRAMA, a speaker gave the audience background information in a short speech before the CHORUS entered and the main action of the play began. This custom was continued in the homilies that preceded English MIRACLE PLAYS, and reached its peak in RESTORATION and eighteenth-century drama. Today the term is sometimes used to refer to the introductory part of a NOVEL or a long poem. The most famous prologue in English LITERATURE does not introduce a play; it is the Prologue to Geoffrey Chaucer's *Canterbury Tales*.

See EPILOGUE.

propaganda literature.   Literature designed to influence public opinion on a social or a political issue, often by appealing to people's fears and prejudices. During World War II, both Germany and the United States produced feature movies that functioned as propaganda literature.

prose.   In the broadest sense, all forms of ordinary writing and speech lacking the sustained and regular rhythmic patterns found in POETRY. Prose is characterized by the sort of plain, straightforward statement found in everyday speech. It is the language of ESSAYS, SHORT STORIES, and NOVELS. The distinction between poetry and prose is not always clear-cut. Perhaps the most obvious difference is simply that they look quite different on the printed page. While poetry is presented in lines of arbitrary length, often arranged in tightly structured STANZA patterns, prose appears in a more or less continuous flow, interrupted only occasionally by paragraph divisions. Reaching his own sudden understanding of the term, Monsieur Jourdain, a character in Molière's *The Bourgeois Gentleman,* exclaims, "Good Heavens! For more than forty years I have been speaking prose without knowing it."

See DISCOURSE, POETRY, VERSE.

prose poem. A short composition printed in PROSE paragraphs, yet containing the striking IMAGERY, calculated rhythmic EFFECTS, and other devices of POETRY. Aloysius Bertrand's *Gaspard of the Night* established the prose poem as a GENRE in 1836, influencing Charles Baudelaire to write *Little Poems in Prose.* Arthur Rimbaud, Oscar Wilde, Amy Lowell, and T. S. Eliot have all written prose poems.

See POETRY, PROSE.

protagonist. The principal and central CHARACTER of a NOVEL, SHORT STORY, PLAY, or other literary work. Ántonia Shimerda, a nineteenth-century immigrant girl, is the protagonist of Willa Cather's *My Ántonia;* Bigger Thomas, a victim of the Black Belt slums of Chicago, the protagonist of Richard Wright's *Native Son.* The term originated in Greek DRAMA, which was enacted by a CHORUS, its leader, and three additional actors: the protagonist, the first or chief actor; the deuteragonist, a second actor who usually played the rival, or ANTAGONIST; and the tritagonist, or third actor.

See ANTAGONIST, CHARACTER.

protest literature. POETRY, FICTION, or DRAMA written in protest of a social or political policy or action. The policy of apartheid in South Africa has stimulated a long TRADITION of protest literature, beginning early in the twentieth century with Solomon T. Plaatje's *Native Life in South Africa* and including the work of both white and black writers: NOVELS, PLAYS, and SHORT STORIES, such as Alan Paton's *Cry the Beloved Country,* Peter Abrahams' *A Night of Their Own,* Doris Lessing's *Children of Virtue,* Nadine Gordimer's *Something Out There,* Alex La Guma's *In the Fog of the Season's End,* Gibson Kente's *Too Late,* and Mthuli Shezi's *Shanti;* and poetry by Mongane Serote, Njabulo Ndebele, Mandlenkosi Langa, Mafika Gwala, James Matthews, and Don Mattera.

proverb. A short saying that expresses some commonplace truth or bit of folk wisdom concerning some aspect of practical life. A few examples are "A stitch in time saves nine," "He who laughs last laughs best," "A friend in need is a friend indeed," "A rolling stone gathers no moss," and "He who goes a borrowing goes a sorrowing." Proverbs remain memorable because of their uses of METAPHOR, RHYME, PARALLELISM, and ANTITHESIS. They treat a wide variety of subjects, including agriculture, medicine, health, efficiency, personal conduct, the weather, and superstitions. Collections can be found in Proverbs of the Old Testament, in Benjamin Franklin's *Poor Richard's Almanack,* and more recently in *The Oxford Dictionary of English Proverbs,* edited by W. G. Smith and F. P. Wilson.

See APHORISM, EPIGRAM.

psychic distance. Being aware that a work of art is art and not real life; standing apart from the work as a reader or viewer. See DISTANCE.

psychoanalytic criticism. An approach to LITERARY CRITICISM, influenced by Sigmund Freud and Carl Jung, that views a literary work as an expression of the unconscious—of the individual psyche of its author or of the collective unconscious of a society or of the whole human race. Recently, READER-RESPONSE CRITICISM and critics of consciousness have applied the techniques of psychoanalytic criticism to their analysis of the experience of reading a work. That is, they focus on the psyche of the reader.

See LITERARY CRITICISM.

psychological novel. A NOVEL that focuses on the "interior" lives of its CHARACTERS, their mental states and emotions, and that concentrates more on the psychological MOTIVATION of their actions than on the actions themselves.

Interest in the psychology of characters appears as early as Geoffrey Chaucer's *Troilus and Criseyde,* which is considered by some to be a psychological novel in VERSE. But the modern psychological novel did not begin to emerge until the nineteenth century in works by George Eliot, Elizabeth Gaskell, George Meredith, and Joseph Conrad. The acknowledged master of the type was Henry James, whose *The Portrait of a Lady, The Wings of the Dove, The Ambassadors,* and *The Golden Bowl* set the standards for later novelists.

In the twentieth century the psychological novel reached the peak of its development with the use of INTERIOR MONOLOGUE and STREAM OF CONSCIOUSNESS, techniques perfected in the novels of James Joyce (*A Portrait of the Artist as a Young Man, Ulysses*), Virginia Woolf (*Mrs. Dalloway, To the Lighthouse*), and William Faulkner (*The Sound and the Fury*).

See NOVEL.

pun. A form of WIT, not necessarily funny, involving a play on a word with two or more meanings. In William Shakespeare's *Merchant of Venice,* Portia puns on the meanings of *dear* (costly; cherished) when she says to Bassanio: "Since you are *dear* bought, I will love you *dear.*" The type of pun known as an **equivoque** involves a word being used so that it means two different things at once. In *Romeo and Juliet* Mercutio says as he dies, "Ask for me tomorrow and you will find me a *grave* man." The equivoque can aid a CHARACTER in making his or her meaning plain to the audience even as it is hidden from other characters in the PLAY. Shakespeare's Richard Gloucester says dutifully to his brother, the Duke of Clarence,

> Well, your imprisonment shall not be long;
> I will deliver you, or else *lie* for you.

He wants Clarence to believe that he will, if necessary, tell lies to help him, but he lets the audience know that he means he will lie in wait for Clarence, as he himself is planning to have Clarence killed.

See WIT.

Q

quantitative verse. VERSE based on the duration of the sound of a syllable (quantity) rather than on a pattern of accented and unaccented syllables. Ancient Hebrew, Greek, Latin, and Japanese poetry is quantitative, while English verse is largely accentual-syllabic. Some English poets—Sir Philip Sidney, Edmund Spenser, Samuel Taylor Coleridge, and Alfred, Lord Tennyson—have tried writing quantitative verse.

quatrain. A STANZA of four lines, rhymed or unrhymed; also a poem consisting of four lines only. The quatrain is the most common stanza FORM in English. It exists in a variety of RHYME SCHEMES and METERS, including IAMBIC PENTAMETER lines rhyming *abab*, called the **heroic quatrain;** iambic TETRAMETER lines rhyming *abba,* called the *In Memoriam* **stanza;** alternating tetrameter and TRIMETER lines rhyming *abcb,* called the **ballad stanza;** iambic pentameter lines rhyming *aaba,* called the *Rubáiyát* **stanza;** and lines rhyming *aabb.* This last pattern of rhyme is illustrated in the following quatrain from "Self-Analysis," a poem by Anna Wickham:

The tumult of my fretted mind	*a*
Gives me expression of a kind;	*a*
But it is faulty, harsh, not plain—	*b*
My work has the incompetence of pain.	*b*

See BALLAD STANZA, METER, RHYME SCHEME.

R

reader-response criticism. A collective term used to describe a number of critical theories that have emerged since the 1960s, all of which focus in some way on the responses of the reader rather than on the text itself as the source of meanings in a literary work. In reader-response criticism, a work of LITERATURE, rather than being considered a fixed and stable entity with a single "correct" meaning, is viewed instead as an activity or process that goes on in readers' minds. This process evolves as readers experience anticipation, frustration, retrospection, and reconstruction. In a sense, the literary work has its existence in the mind of the reader, not on the printed page, so that the reader participates in its "creation."

Regardless of their particular perspectives, all reader-response critics agree that since, in varying degrees, the individual reader creates or produces the meanings of a text, there is no one correct meaning for a text or for any of its linguistic parts. However, these critics offer differing opinions regarding how readers do in fact read, what the specific factors are that influence readers' responses, and what "controls," if any, the text exerts in shaping those responses. Some figures prominent in the different forms of reader-response theory are Wolfgang Iser, Jonathan Culler, Norman Holland, Harold Bloom, Stanley Fish, and Louise Rosenblatt.

See DECONSTRUCTION, INFLUENCE, LITERARY CRITICISM, POST-STRUCTURALISM.

realism. Generally, accuracy in the portrayal of life or reality, or VERISIMILITUDE; a recurring goal of LITERATURE, often seen in contrast to the aims of ROMANTICISM, IMPRESSIONISM, and EXPRESSIONISM. Realism is also the name of a literary movement in Europe—particularly France—America, and England in the nineteenth century that established the NOVEL as the GENRE uniquely capable of reflecting the ordinary life of the average person. The nineteenth-century realists included novelists as diverse in outlook and STYLE as Honoré de Balzac and Gustave Flaubert in France; George Eliot, George Meredith, Anthony Trollope, and Thomas Hardy in England; William Dean Howells, Mark Twain, and Henry James in the United States; and Ivan Turgenev, Fyodor Dostoyevsky, and Leo Tolstoy in Russia.

Influenced by a greatly expanding middle-class readership, these realists wrote about the problems and conflicts of CHARACTERS with whom they and their readers could easily identify. Their goal was to present characters and situations as if they were simply reporting them from life. There was, however, nothing the least bit haphazard about the craft of the realists. They took pains to select events, SETTINGS, and DIALOGUE that were representative, and their style was carefully calculated. Flaubert's *Madame Bovary* is famous for its transparent style, despite the fact that Flaubert described himself as rolling on the floor in the agony of searching for the exact word ("le mot juste"). The realists also wished to create the illusion that their stories were telling themselves. They placed less emphasis on PLOT and far more on psychological analysis of characters, a tendency which led through James and the PSYCHOLOGICAL NOVEL to the STREAM-OF-CONSCIOUSNESS NOVEL.

Realism is sometimes confused with NATURALISM, a movement that grew out of realism but did not supplant it. Naturalism, an expression of the philosophy of DETERMINISM, showed characters who were trapped by forces of heredity and environ-ment they could not control.

See NATURALISM, PSYCHOLOGICAL NOVEL, STREAM-OF-CONSCIOUSNESS NOVEL.

recognition. In TRAGEDY, the moment when a CHARACTER gains es-sential knowledge, insight, or understanding that he or she has previously lacked; also called **discovery.** In some instances rec-ognition occurs when the true identity of a character is revealed. In others it involves a sudden and profound insight, often self-knowledge, that changes the course of the action. The classic ex-ample is Oedipus's discovery that the man he is searching for is himself: that he has murdered his father and married his mother. The device is also used in COMEDY, in which the discovery is a happy one, for example, when a rich society matron discovers that the kitchen maid is really her long-lost daughter.

refrain. A phrase, line, or group of lines repeated at intervals during a poem, usually at the end of a STANZA. In a song, a refrain is of-ten called a CHORUS because it allows everyone to join in. Non-sense refrains, such as William Shakespeare's "With a hey and a ho and a hey nonny no," easily serve this purpose. Refrains are also used to reestablish an idea or a mood, as in this FOLK BALLAD:

Lord Randal

"O where hae ye been, Lord Randal, my son?
  Oh where hae ye been, my handsome young man?"
"I hae been to the wild wood; mother, make my bed soon,
  For I'm weary wi' hunting, and fain wald lie down."

"Where gat ye your dinner, Lord Randal, my son?
  Where gat ye your dinner, my handsome young man?"
"I din'd wi' my true-love; mother, make my bed soon,
  For I'm weary wi' hunting, and fain wald lie down."

"What gat ye to your dinner, Lord Randal, my son?
  What gat ye to your dinner, my handsome young man?"
"I gat eels boil'd in broth; mother, make my bed soon,
  For I'm weary wi' hunting, and fain wald lie down."

> "What became of your bloodhounds, Lord Randal, my son?
>> What became of your bloodhounds, my handsome
>>> young man?"
> "O they swell'd and they died; mother, make my bed soon,
>> For I'm weary wi' hunting, and fain wald lie down."
>
> "O I fear ye are poison'd, Lord Randal, my son!
>> O I fear ye are poison'd, my handsome young man!"
> "O yes! I am poison'd; mother, make my bed soon,
>> For I'm sick at the heart, and I fain wald lie down."

Sometimes a refrain changes its meaning in each new CON-
TEXT, as does Edgar Allan Poe's "Nevermore" in "The Raven."
The refrain itself may also be modified each time it is repeated, a
process known as INCREMENTAL REPETITION.

See INCREMENTAL REPETITION.

regionalism. The tendency in LITERATURE to focus on a specific
geographical region or locality, re-creating as accurately as possible its unique SETTING, speech, customs, manners, beliefs, and
history. While regionalism is an element in nearly all literature
that attempts the realistic portrayal of a locale, the term is usually
reserved for those writings in which the locale and its influences
assume major importance as subjects in themselves. Thomas
Hardy's novels, set in the countryside of Dorset ("Wessex"), are
examples of regional literature. In America, regionalism is most
often associated with the LOCAL COLOR movement of the late
nineteenth century, including such writers as Bret Harte, George
Washington Cable, Joel Chandler Harris, Sarah Orne Jewett,
Rose Terry Cooke, Kate Chopin, Mary Eleanor Wilkins Freeman, and Hamlin Garland. Strong elements of regionalism are
found in twentieth-century works by Willa Cather, Ellen Glas-
gow, Edith Wharton, Edward Arlington Robinson, Thomas
Wolfe, Ruth Suckow, William Faulkner, John Steinbeck, Eudora
Welty, and John Cheever, among many others.

See LOCAL COLOR.

Renaissance. The historical period following the MIDDLE AGES, beginning in Italy as early as the thirteenth century, arriving in England in the fifteenth century, and ending early in the
seventeenth century. The rediscovery of CLASSIC LITERATURE,

particularly that of Greece, renewed the idea that human existence was not just painful preparation for an afterlife but had interest and value in itself. This new HUMANISM was supported by and found expression in a burgeoning of creative activity in literature, science, and art and in geographical, commercial, and political expansion. The Renaissance saw many notable authors (Dante, Petrarch, Rabelais, Michel Montaigne, Miguel de Cervantes, Edmund Spenser, Christopher Marlowe, William Shakespeare, Ben Jonson, and John Donne); artists and musicians (Michelangelo, Raphael, Leonardo da Vinci, Claudio Monteverdi, Henry Purcell); scientists and thinkers (René Descartes, Francis Bacon, Nicolaus Copernicus, Niccolò Machiavelli, Erasmus, and Martin Luther). Although some of the most important scientific and philosophical ideas that began circulating during the Renaissance (the Copernican theory of the solar system, for example) did not take root until the Enlightenment in the late seventeenth and early eighteenth centuries, the Renaissance is given credit for ushering in the modern world.

See HUMANISM.

requiem. A chant, DIRGE, or poem for the dead; from the Roman Catholic mass for the dead, which begins *Requiem aeternam dona eis, Domine:* "Give them eternal rest, O Lord." Lines from Robert Louis Stevenson's poem "Requiem" are carved on his tombstone:

> Under the wide and starry sky,
> Dig the grave and let me lie.
> Glad did I live and gladly die,
>   And I laid me down with a will.
>
> This be the verse you grave for me:
> *Here he lies where he longed to be;*
> *Home is the sailor, home from the sea,*
>   *And the hunter home from the hill.*

See ELEGY.

resolution. The final unwinding, or resolving, of the CONFLICTS and complications in the PLOT of FICTION or DRAMA. A resolution may be elaborate, as in Charles Dickens' novels, when even the minor characters are accounted for; or swift, as when in Henrik Ibsen's *A Doll House,* Nora walks out of her husband's house.

See CATASTROPHE, DENOUEMENT, FALLING ACTION, PLOT.

Restoration.   In English LITERATURE, the period from 1661 to 1700, following the Puritan Interregnum (1649–1660). This period saw the return of Charles II to the throne and with him the restoration of the Stuart monarchy. The literature of the age—urbane, witty, and licentious—reflected a reaction against the repressive seriousness of Puritanism. The greatest poet of the time was John Dryden; the most prominent PROSE writers were John Bunyan, John Locke, Sir William Temple, and Samuel Pepys. However, the period's major contribution to English literature was Restoration DRAMA, especially the COMEDY OF MANNERS (also called RESTORATION COMEDY) developed by George Etherege, William Wycherley, Susanna Centlivre, and William Congreve. Theaters, freed from the Puritan ban of 1642, flourished. For the first time actresses assumed the roles previously played by boys.

See COMEDY, RESTORATION COMEDY.

Restoration comedy.   A FORM of COMEDY that flourished in England during the RESTORATION (1661–1700). Sometimes called the **comedy of manners,** Restoration DRAMA featured witty DIALOGUE with many ASIDES, and complicated PLOTS that involved incredible stage business (such as CHARACTERS in disguise or hiding behind screens). The SETTINGS were usually urban and the characters men and women of the world. Popular PLAYS of the period include Susanna Centlivre's *The Busie Body* and William Congreve's *The Way of the World.*

See COMEDY, RESTORATION.

revenge tragedy.   A sensational kind of TRAGEDY, popular during ELIZABETHAN times, that featured murder and revenge. See TRAGEDY.

reversal.   A sudden change of fortune for the PROTAGONIST in a PLAY or other work of FICTION; also called **peripety,** or in ancient Greek DRAMA **peripeteia.** If the play is a TRAGEDY, the reversal involves a fall or loss of power; if a COMEDY, a success or a change from bad luck to good. As part of the structure of the PLOT, the reversal occurs as an element in the FALLING ACTION at or immediately following the CLIMAX and preceding the CATASTROPHE, or DENOUEMENT.

See FREYTAG'S PYRAMID, PLOT.

rhetoric.   The art of persuasion, in speaking or writing. Rhetoric originated in ancient Greece as principles for orators (rhetors) to follow in "discovering all the possible means of persuading in any given case or situation." The rhetorical process included five stages—INVENTION (discovering the logical, ethical, and emotional arguments), arrangement (organizing the arguments), STYLE (choosing words and figures in which to express the arguments), memory, and delivery. Aristotle, who focused on invention in his *Rhetoric,* stressed that learning how to persuade other people required being a competent judge of virtue and character, having a thorough knowledge of human emotion, and possessing skill in reasoning. He also pointed out that the two excellences of style are CLARITY and propriety (appropriateness) and recommended a style that led to easy learning rather than one that was difficult or showy.

Some other early writers of rhetorical guides—known as Sophists—differed from Aristotle in focusing on stylistic devices and tricks of persuasion. Many of these devices are known today as logical and emotional fallacies. As a result of the abuse of its methods by the Sophists and their followers—including modern Madison Avenue advertisers—rhetoric has some negative CONNOTATIONS. People use the phrase "mere rhetoric" to describe speaking or writing that is showy but empty.

Nevertheless, the second half of the twentieth century has seen renewed interest in the principles of Aristotelian rhetoric—both for what they have to offer in the teaching of written composition and for insight into the elements of NOVELS and poems that "persuade" the reader to share the author's vision.

See PRAGMATIC CRITICISM, RHETORICAL CRITICISM.

rhetorical criticism.   An approach to LITERARY CRITICISM that emphasizes the author's use of language in communicating with the reader. RHETORIC, the art of persuasion, is concerned with the effectiveness and general appeal of communication and with methods for achieving them. Rhetorical criticism analyzes the author's rhetoric, especially those devices employed by the author for communicating the intended meaning of a work to the reader.

See LITERARY CRITICISM, PRAGMATIC CRITICISM, RHETORIC.

rhyme. The similarity of sound between two words (*old/cold; foam/ dome; dusky/husky*). When the sounds of their accented syllables and all succeeding sounds are identical, words rhyme (*rend/ befriend; order/recorder*). The most common form of rhyme, rhyme coming at the ends of lines of POETRY, is called **end rhyme,** as in Robert Herrick's "To Electra":

> I dare not ask a *kiss,*
>   I dare not beg a *smile,*
> Lest having that, or *this,*
>   I might grow proud the *while.*

> No, no, the utmost *share*
>   Of my desire shall *be*
> Only to kiss that *air*
>   That lately kissed *thee.*

Rhyme within the line is called **internal rhyme,** as in Edgar Allan Poe's "The Raven":

> Once upon a midnight *dreary,* while I pondered weak and
>   *weary,*
> Over many a quaint and curious volume of forgotten lore,
> While I nodded, nearly *napping,* suddenly there came a
>   *tapping,*
> As of someone gently *rapping, rapping* at my chamber door.

Rhyme of one syllable, as in the Herrick poem, is called **masculine rhyme.** Two-syllable rhyme, as in "The Raven," is called **feminine rhyme.** Rhyme of three syllables or more is more common in LIGHT VERSE than in serious poetry.

Rhyme may also be classified by sound. The rhymes in the preceding selections are **true rhymes,** sometimes called **exact rhymes. Identical rhymes** repeat the same word or a homonym of the word (a word that sounds the same but is spelled differently): *two/too; rain/reign.* **Slant rhymes** are approximate rhymes,

substituting either ASSONANCE (*comb/coat; rule/room*) or CONSO-
NANCE (*hope/heap; walk/weak*) in place of exact rhyme.

A traditional device of poetry, rhyme contributes to
RHYTHM, helps organize the language of poetry, makes poetry
easier to memorize, and is a source of pleasure in itself.

See ASSONANCE, CONSONANCE, END RHYME, FEMININE
RHYME, INTERNAL RHYME, MASCULINE RHYME, RHYME SCHEME,
SLANT RHYME.

rhyme royal. A STANZA pattern of seven lines of IAMBIC PENTAME-
TER, rhyming *ababbcc*. See STANZA.

rhyme scheme. The pattern of RHYMES in a STANZA or poem, usually indicated by letters of the alphabet. For instance, the most
common rhyme scheme for the QUATRAIN (a four-line stanza), in
which the first line rhymes with the third and the second line
rhymes with the fourth, is *abab.* This stanza from Elinor Wylie's
"Let No Charitable Hope" illustrates the pattern, *alone* rhyming
with *stone* (*a* rhymes) and *beset* rhyming with *get* (*b* rhymes):

I was, being human, born alone;	*a*
I am, being woman, hard beset;	*b*
I live by squeezing from a stone	*a*
The little nourishment I get.	*b*

Fixed VERSE forms, such as the SONNET, have prescribed
rhyme schemes. For example, the English (Shakespearean) sonnet has a rhyme scheme of *abab, cdcd, efef, gg.* Here is such a sonnet, "Well, I Have Lost You" by Edna St. Vincent Millay:

Well, I have lost you; and I lost you fairly:	*a*
In my own way, and with my full consent.	*b*
Say what you will, kings in a tumbrel rarely	*a*
Went to their deaths more proud than this one went.	*b*
Some nights of apprehension and hot weeping	*c*
I will confess; but that's permitted me;	*d*
Day dried my eyes; I was not one for keeping	*c*
Rubbed in a cage a wing that would be free.	*d*
If I had loved you less or played you slyly	*e*
I might have held you for a summer more,	*f*

But at the cost of words I value highly,	*e*
And no such summer as the one before.	*f*
Should I outlive this anguish—and men do—	*g*
I shall have only good to say of you.	*g*

See SCANSION.

rhythm. The patterned flow of sound in POETRY and PROSE. In traditional English poetry, rhythm is based on the combination of accent and numbers of syllables known as METER. Meter is only the basic pulse of rhythm, however. Other sound devices, such as RHYME, ALLITERATION, ASSONANCE, and ONOMATOPOEIA, contribute greatly to rhythm. Whether words are made up of harsh sounds or soft sounds also affects the rhythm of a line of poetry.

See METER.

rising action. That part of a dramatic PLOT that leads through a series of events of increasing interest and power to the CLIMAX, or TURNING POINT. The rising action begins with an INCITING MOMENT, an action or event that sets a CONFLICT of opposing forces into motion, and moves through COMPLICATION, an entangling of the affairs of the CHARACTERS in conflict, toward the climax, the major crisis that brings about a change in the fortunes of the PROTAGONIST. In an Elizabethan TRAGEDY of five acts, such as *Macbeth,* the rising action occurs largely in the first two acts and the climax in the third.

See FALLING ACTION, FREYTAG'S PYRAMID, PLOT.

rising meter. A METER that ends with a strong accent, or stress, like IAMBS and ANAPESTS. See FOOT.

roman à clef. A French term, meaning "novel with a key," referring to NOVELS in which actual persons are presented under fictitious names. The roman à clef began in France with novels by Madeleine de Scudéry and La Bruyère, who provided keys to the real names after their novels were published. Later examples of the GENRE include Thomas Love Peacock's *Nightmare Abbey,* Nathaniel Hawthorne's *Blithedale Romance,* Aldous Huxley's *Point Counter Point,* Somerset Maugham's *Cakes and Ale,* Robert Penn Warren's *All the King's Men,* and Saul Bellow's *Humboldt's Gift.*

See NOVEL.

romance.   In the broadest sense, any extended work of FICTION that
deals with adventure, extravagant CHARACTERS, strange or exotic
places, mysterious or supernatural INCIDENTS, heroic or marvelous achievements, or passionate love. The romance, with its emphasis on the purely imaginary, differs from the NOVEL, which
attempts a more or less realistic portrayal of ordinary people and
their experiences.

In the MIDDLE AGES, CHIVALRIC ROMANCES, such as *Sir Gawain and the Green Knight,* centered on the exciting adventures of
knights errant and their episodic encounters with monsters, giants, and beautiful damsels in distress. During the English RE-
NAISSANCE, the romance took such forms as Edmund Spenser's
Faerie Queene and John Bunyan's ALLEGORY of Christian life, *The
Pilgrim's Progress.* Later, GOTHIC elements were introduced, and
Sir Walter Scott added historical SETTINGS to PLOTS filled with
intrigue and mystery. Today the romance appears most often in
two popular FORMS: the **adventure story** (DETECTIVE STORIES
and espionage thrillers) and the love story, or **popular romance**
(typified by the widely read Harlequin Romances).

See CHIVALRIC ROMANCE, ROMANTIC NOVEL.

romanticism.   A movement in art and LITERATURE in the eighteenth
and nineteenth centuries in revolt against the NEOCLASSICISM of
the previous centuries. There is reason to believe that *romanticism*
may be either the most meaningful or the most confusing word
in any lexicon of literary terms. The English critic F. L. Lucas
unearthed and counted 11,396 definitions of *romanticism.*

The German poet Friedrich Schlegel, who is given credit for
first using the term *romantic* to describe literature, defined it as
"literature depicting emotional matter in an imaginative form."
This is as accurate a general definition as can be accomplished,
although Victor Hugo's phrase "liberalism in literature" is also
apt. IMAGINATION, emotion, and freedom are certainly the focal
points of romanticism. Any list of particular characteristics of the
literature of romanticism includes SUBJECTIVITY and an emphasis on individualism; spontaneity; freedom from rules; solitary
life rather than life in society; the beliefs that imagination is superior to reason and devotion to beauty; love of and worship of
nature; and fascination with the past, especially the MYTHS and
mysticism of the MIDDLE AGES. In the work of the great romantic

poets in England—William Wordsworth, Samuel Taylor Coleridge, Lord Byron, Percy Bysshe Shelley, and John Keats—romanticism found its most complete expression. The most important American Romantic writers were Ralph Waldo Emerson, Nathaniel Hawthorne, Edgar Allan Poe, Henry David Thoreau, Herman Melville, and Walt Whitman.

See IMAGINATION, SUBJECTIVITY.

romantic novel. A type of NOVEL emphasizing action rather than CHARACTER, often in the FORM of a series of EPISODES involving adventure, love, and combat; a term used interchangeably with ROMANCE. As it is used here with *novel,* the term *romantic* derives from *romance,* an extended fictional NARRATIVE of heroic deeds, exotic SETTINGS, and mysterious events, or a story of gallant love. Because the romantic novel depends on the fertile IMAGINATION of its author rather than on real life as the source of its action, setting, and characters, it most often appeals to the reader seeking escape from reality rather than VERISIMILITUDE.

See NOVEL, ROMANCE.

round character. A character in FICTION portrayed in detail as a complex, multifaceted personality; the opposite of a FLAT CHARACTER. See CHARACTER, CHARACTERIZATION.

***Rubáiyát* stanza.** A STANZA of four lines in IAMBIC PENTAMETER, rhyming *aaba.* The FORM was developed by Edward FitzGerald for his translation of Persian poet Omar Khayyám's *Rubáiyát.* See QUATRAIN.

run-on lines. VERSE in which the thought of one line runs into the next line with no punctuation or grammatical break; also called **enjambment**, and the opposite of END-STOPPED LINES. These lines from William Wordsworth's "Westminster Bridge" are run-on lines:

> This City now doth, like a garment, wear
> The beauty of the morning.

See END-STOPPED LINES, ENJAMBMENT.

S

saga. Specifically, a MEDIEVAL Icelandic or Scandinavian PROSE NAR-
RATIVE. Sagas were memorized and recited long before they
were written down during the twelfth and thirteenth centuries.
They deal with the EPIC adventures of noble HEROES and important families. Generally they fall into two groups, those based on
historical events and those recounting legendary stories, although many combine LEGEND and history. The STYLE of the
saga is straightforward, bald, matter-of-fact, without explanation or interpretation, and yet its terseness and conscious understatement succeed in creating suspense and emotional impact.
Well-known sagas include *The Saga of Grettir the Strong (The Grettis
Saga), The Volsung Saga (Völsunga Saga), The Heimskringla* (a collection used by Henry W. Longfellow as the source for his group of
poems called *The Saga of King Olaf*), and *The Story of Burnt Njal
(Njala Saga).*

Today the term *saga* is commonly used to refer to any traditional legend or tale involving heroic deeds or extraordinary or
marvelous adventures. It is also applied to stories covering the
fictional history of several generations of the same family, for example, John Galsworthy's *The Forsyte Saga.*

sarcasm. Harsh, cutting, personal remarks to or about someone, not necessarily ironic. In August Strindberg's play *The Dance of Death,* Alice accuses the Captain of teaching their daughter to lie. The Captain's response is sarcastic: "I had no need to—you had taught her already." If the Captain had said, for example, "I see that our daughter has already learned to lie. You have taught her well," his sarcasm would also be ironic. He would be saying the opposite of what he meant.

See IRONY.

satire. A term used to describe any form of LITERATURE that blends ironic HUMOR and WIT with criticism for the purpose of ridiculing folly, vice, stupidity—the whole range of human foibles and frailties—in individuals and institutions. Satire differs from COMEDY in that satire seeks to correct, improve, or reform through ridicule, while comedy aims simply to amuse. It differs from **invective,** direct denunciation or name-calling, and mere insult in the sharp wit of its presentation. If in *MacFlecknoe* John Dryden had called Thomas Shadwell "a dolt, a numskull," he would simply have been insulting. But when he wrote

> Some beams of wit on other souls may fall,
> Strike through, and make a lucid interval;
> But Sh—'s genuine night admits no ray,
> His rising fogs prevail upon the day

he was being satirical.

The tone of satire varies from light and witty chiding to passionate indignation to bitter denunciation. Its chief device is **irony**, the recognition of the incongruity that exists between appearance and reality. The satirist may, for example, praise a person for qualities he or she does not possess, present follies as highly desirable virtues, or use ironic **understatement,** as in Jonathan Swift's "Last week I saw a woman flayed, and you will hardly believe how much it altered her appearance." In the MOCK EPIC, trivial situations and CHARACTERS are satirized by being treated in a lofty or heroic manner. Alexander Pope's *Rape of the Lock* is the classic example. Other satiric devices include **sarcasm** (personal taunts), **innuendo** (derogatory insinuations), **burlesque** and **parody** (mimicking designed to ridicule), and **caricature** (ludicrous distortion of personal characteristics).

Satire is sometimes divided into formal satire and indirect satire. In **formal satire** the author, or a PERSONA created by the author, speaks in the first person directly to the reader or, sometimes, to a character who responds and leads the speaker on. In **indirect satire,** the satirist creates a story or PLAY peopled with characters who speak and act in such a manner that they themselves are the targets of satire. Most modern satire is indirect. One form of indirect satire is called **Menippean satire,** which according to Northrop Frye "deals less with people . . . than with mental attitudes." It mocks pretentious erudition, its characters serving as mouthpieces for ideas that are made absurd by the excess of their erudition. Short Menippean satires often take the form of DIALOGUES; longer ones are usually loosely plotted, rambling NARRATIVES (often NOVELS) that have unusual SETTINGS, long DIGRESSIONS, and large accumulations of facts organized according to some intellectual framework. Some examples are Robert Burton's *Anatomy of Melancholy,* Jonathan Swift's *Gulliver's Travels,* Lewis Carroll's *Alice's Adventures in Wonderland,* and more recently, John Barth's *Giles Goat-Boy.*

Satire may also be classified as **Horatian satire** (after Horace) or **Juvenalian satire** (after Juvenal). Horatian satire is gentle, amused, mildly corrective. In contrast, Juvenalian satire is harsh, biting, bitter, full of moral indignation and contempt.

Because satire is for the most part a literary manner or technique rather than a fixed GENRE, satire and satirists appear throughout literature. The Greeks had Aristophanes; the Romans, Juvenal and Horace. During the MIDDLE AGES satire emerged in beast epics and FABLIAUX, humorous, often bawdy, tales in eight-syllable verse satirizing women and the clergy. During the RENAISSANCE it persisted in the PICARESQUE novels of Miguel de Cervantes and François Rabelais. It flourished in the NEOCLASSICISM of seventeenth-century France (in the plays of Molière) and of eighteenth-century England (in the writing of John Dryden, Alexander Pope, Richard Steele, Joseph Addison, Jonathan Swift, and Henry Fielding). In the nineteenth century the most famous satirists were Lord Byron, William M. Thackeray, and W. S. Gilbert in England, Mark Twain and Oliver Wendell Holmes in America. During the present century satire finds effective expression in the diverse works of such writers as George Bernard Shaw, Noël Coward, Aldous Huxley, Evelyn

Waugh, Edith Wharton, Sinclair Lewis, Rose Macaulay, John P. Marquand, Philip Roth, Joseph Heller, and John Cheever.
See BURLESQUE, CARICATURE, IRONY, PARODY.

scansion. Analyzing the METER in lines of POETRY by counting and marking the accented and unaccented syllables, dividing the lines into metrical feet, and showing the major pauses, if any, within the line. The conventional system for scanning English poetry calls for marking accented syllables (´) and unaccented syllables (˘). Other symbols include a vertical line (|) to separate one FOOT from another, and a double line (||) to indicate a CAESURA, or major pause. The scansion of A. E. Housman's "When I Was One-and-Twenty" shows the standard way to indicate the meter of a poem:

> When I | was one- | and-twenty
> I heard | a wise | man say, |
> "Give crowns | and pounds | and guineas
> But not | your heart | away;
> Give pearls | away | and rubies
> But keep | your fan | cy free."
> But I | was one- | and-twenty,
> No use | to talk | to me.
>
> When I | was one- | and-twenty
> I heard | him say | again,
> "The heart | out of | the bosom
> Was ne | ver given | in vain;
> 'Tis paid | with sighs | a-plenty
> And sold | for end | less rue."
> And I | am two- | and-twenty,
> And oh, | 'tis true, | 'tis true.

Some methods of scansion also include refinements, such as symbols indicating secondary accents and long and short syllables.

See FOOT, METER, RHYME SCHEME.

scene. **1.** In DRAMA, a subdivision of an act that usually does not involve a change of locale or a shift in time. However, there seems to be no universal agreement about what constitutes a scene. Changes of scene may be signaled by CHARACTERS entering or leaving the stage or by a clearing of the stage, as in ELIZABETHAN drama, which made no clear division of scenes, and in RESTORATION drama, in which new scenes were numbered with each entrance or exit. Modern playwrights generally consider a scene to be a continuous EPISODE, a unit of action without interruption or break in continuity. The end of a scene is often marked by dimming the stage lights or by dropping the curtain.

2. A part of a drama featuring a single, specific INCIDENT or segment of DIALOGUE, for example, a death scene or a mad scene.

3. In NARRATIVE FICTION, the place in which the action is set.

4. In Kenneth D. Burke's system of analyzing LITERATURE, one of the five items in his "pentad," elements he considers essential to all literary works: Act (what happened), Scene (where), Agent (who did it), Agency (how), and Purpose (why). Burke's system, which centers on the idea that literature is a form of action, is called DRAMATISM.

scenic method. A method of NARRATION that presents a work of FICTION in SCENES, as if it were a PLAY. See POINT OF VIEW.

science fiction. NOVELS and SHORT STORIES set either in the future or on some imaginary world, their SETTINGS, PLOTS, CHARACTERS, and THEMES the result of scientific or technological speculation; often called **science fantasy.** Science fiction that portrays an imaginary ideal world is a form of utopian LITERATURE. Although there has been speculative FICTION since ancient times, science fiction as a GENRE originated with Jules Verne (*Around the World in Eighty Days, Twenty Thousand Leagues Under the Sea, Journey to the Center of the Earth*) and H. G. Wells (*The Time Machine, War of the Worlds*), both writing in the late nineteenth century. The vast output of science fiction in the twentieth century has resulted in many works of sophisticated technological plausibility and some of moral or philosophical import. Modern science fiction CLASSICS include Ray Bradbury's *Fahrenheit 451* and *The Illustrated Man;* Arthur C. Clarke's *2001: A Space Odyssey* and *Childhood's End;* Isaac Asimov's *I, Robot* and *Foundation;* Robert Heinlein's *Stranger in a Strange Land* and *The Unpleasant Profession of Jonathan Hoag;* Walter M. Miller's *A Canticle for Leibowitz;* Roger Zelazny's *A Rose for Ecclesiastes;* Ursula Le Guin's *The Left Hand of Darkness;* and J. G. Ballard's *The Terminal Beach.*

See UTOPIA.

scop. A court poet during Anglo-Saxon times. The scop, a sort of early poet laureate, was both composer and singer or reciter, while the gleeman, a wandering entertainer, most often sang or recited the compositions of others. Like the scop, the Celtic (Welsh) bard, the Gaelic (Irish) filidh, and the Scandinavian skald were professional poets attached to the courts of early kings and chieftains.

See JONGLEUR.

self-effacing author. A writer who presents the actions, thoughts, and DIALOGUE of CHARACTERS in a work of FICTION directly, without personal or subjective commentary; an author who has effectively removed any traces of himself or herself from the NARRATIVE. See POINT OF VIEW.

semantics. The study of meanings in language; a branch of LINGUISTICS. See LINGUISTICS.

semiotics. The study of signs, or signals of communication, including words, Morse code, music, traffic signals, gestures, facial expressions, clothing, or anything that can be said to communicate meaning. The most important developments in semiotics have taken place in LINGUISTICS (Ferdinand de Saussure's initial proposal of such a science), cultural anthropology (Claude Lévi-Strauss's study of kinship systems and other communication structures in primitive societies), and psychoanalysis (Jacques Lacan's interpretation of the subconscious as a system of signs).

In LITERARY CRITICISM, semiotics is the study of the ways literary CONVENTIONS and the conventions of human DISCOURSE affect meaning in a literary work.

See CONVENTION, LITERARY CRITICISM.

sensibility. The capacity for sensitive feeling and emotional response; a reliance on emotion rather than intellect as a guide to goodness and truth. The term refers to the pervasive attitude that arose during the eighteenth century as a reaction against seventeenth-century Stoicism, a philosophy emphasizing reason and emotional restraint, and against the theory—proposed by Thomas Hobbes and others—that humans are innately selfish and motivated mainly by ambitious self-interest. Those championing sensibility maintained that benevolence—sympathy for others, forgiving tenderness—is an innate human characteristic and that the intensity of one's sensitivity and responsiveness to the joys and sorrows of others is the measure of one's virtue and gentility. Popular morality held that shedding sympathetic tears was not only the hallmark of the well-bred but also, because they were shed for others, a pleasurable experience in itself. As a result, LITERATURE written during this time (such as the **novel of sensibility**) is to modern tastes excessively, if not ludicrously, sentimental, with tearful situations, middle-class CHARACTERS who prove their virtue by weeping or fainting at the sight of distress, and repentant and forgiven VILLAINS. The last fifty years of the eighteenth century are sometimes called the **Age of Sensibility.**

In twentieth-century criticism, the term *sensibility* is used to refer to the poet's sensitive response to the sensations, thoughts, and emotions of experience as made evident in his or her writing. T. S. Eliot's phrase "dissociation of sensibility" identifies his contention that in the seventeenth century thought and feeling became separated, resulting in inferior poetry that persists to the present day. Eliot argued that before John Milton and John Dryden thought and feeling were one, but that from about 1660 onward poets either thought rather than felt or felt rather than thought. He believed a unified sensibility of mind and emotion had to be reestablished before English poetry could regain its former power.

See PRIMITIVISM, ROMANTICISM, SENTIMENTALISM, SENTIMENTAL NOVEL.

sentimentalism. In LITERATURE, demonstrating or evoking an exaggerated emotional response or an emotional response disproportionate to the situation that prompted it. Sentimentalism is a principal trait of works commonly called tearjerkers, such as television soap operas or books like *Love Story* by Erich Segal, a NOVEL that countless readers enjoyed crying over. Although it is currently viewed negatively, sentimentalism was viewed positively in the second half of the eighteenth century, a period known as the AGE OF SENSIBILITY. It was believed that shedding copious sympathetic tears over the misfortunes of others signaled good breeding and lack of selfishness and, at the same time, provided a peculiar pleasure—one could luxuriate in the grief of others without experiencing personal pain.

See SENSIBILITY, SENTIMENTAL NOVEL.

sentimental novel. A NOVEL reflecting the cult of SENSIBILITY in vogue during the later eighteenth century; also called the **novel of sensibility.** Sentimental novels present CHARACTERS—usually benevolently virtuous and intensely sensitive HEROES and HEROINES of the middle class—involved in distresses of various sorts for the purpose of evoking pity and pleasurable tears from the reader. Samuel Richardson's *Pamela, or Virtue Rewarded,* Lawrence Sterne's *A Sentimental Journey,* Oliver Goldsmith's *The Vicar of Wakefield,* and Henry MacKenzie's *The Man of Feeling* are examples of the type. The decline of the sentimental novel is marked by Jane Austen's *Sense and Sensibility,* published in 1811, although its influence is apparent later in such tearjerkers as Charles Dickens' *The Old Curiosity Shop* and Harriet Beecher Stowe's *Uncle Tom's Cabin.*

See NOVEL, SENSIBILITY, SENTIMENTALISM.

sestet. A six-line poem or STANZA. The term is most commonly used to designate the second part of an ITALIAN (or PETRARCHAN) SONNET, which is organized into two sections of eight lines (the OCTAVE) and six lines (the sestet) respectively.

See OCTAVE, SONNET.

setting. 1. The general locale, time in history, or social milieu in which the action of a work of LITERATURE takes place. In this general sense, the setting of Willa Cather's NOVEL *My Ántonia* is the

Nebraska prairie of nineteenth-century America. Setting is often important in establishing the MOOD or ATMOSPHERE of a work. When setting functions as the dominant influence on the lives of CHARACTERS, or when the purpose of a piece of FICTION is to present the manners and customs of a unique or picturesque locale, the writing is called LOCAL COLOR writing, or REGIONALISM.

2. The particular physical surroundings in which a SCENE or EPISODE that is part of a larger work occurs. In this more restricted sense, the setting in *Julius Caesar* of Antony's speech over the corpse of Caesar is the steps of the Forum in Rome.

3. In DRAMA, the backdrop scenery and the movable furniture, or props, on stage.

seven deadly sins. According to MEDIEVAL theology, those sins that lead to spiritual death, namely pride, envy, wrath, sloth, avarice, gluttony, and lust. Pride was held to be the worst sin because it led to Satan's treacherous rebellion against God. The theme of the seven deadly sins figured importantly in the literature of the MIDDLE AGES and the RENAISSANCE, notably in Dante's *Divine Comedy;* Geoffrey Chaucer's *Canterbury Tales,* especially the "Parson's Tale"; William Langland's *Piers the Plowman;* and Edmund Spenser's *Faerie Queene.*

Shakespearean sonnet. A SONNET that is arranged into three QUATRAINS, rhyming *abab, cdcd, efef,* followed by a concluding COUPLET, rhyming *gg.* The couplet is often an EPIGRAM, summing up the problem or concern developed in the quatrains. Named for William Shakespeare, this sonnet FORM is also called an **English sonnet.** See SONNET.

short story. A fictional NARRATIVE in PROSE, ranging in length from about 500 words (a "short short story") to about 15,000 words, often, though certainly not always, limited to a very few CHARACTERS, a single SETTING, and a single INCIDENT. Edgar Allan Poe's description was "a short prose narrative, requiring from a half-hour to one or two hours in its perusal." Due, at least in part, to its relative brevity and compression, the short story has as its chief quality a consciously crafted UNITY (of EFFECT, TONE, MOOD, impression). Like the much longer NOVEL, the short story may be tragic, comic, or satiric. It may represent a work of REALISM, NATURALISM, or FANTASY. The novel and the short story share most of the same elements and techniques of FICTION, but the short story *reveals* CHARACTER, usually by means of a single central and representative incident, whereas the novel *traces the development* of character through a series of incidents stretching over a span of time. But these are simply broad, general characteristics that are very often not evident in specific works. The tremendous diversity of the short story prevents a strict, universally applicable description of the GENRE.

The roots of the short story reach back into antiquity. A collection of Egyptian stories survives from about 4000 B.C. Other early collections of short prose narratives come to us from the Greeks and the Romans, the Chinese and Japanese, the Hindus, the Hebrews, and the Arabs. During the MIDDLE AGES and the RENAISSANCE, storytelling took the forms of beast FABLES, EXEMPLA, folktales, and CHIVALRIC ROMANCES. Giovanni Boccaccio's *The Decameron* was a collection of one hundred tales. It was not, however, until the nineteenth century that the modern short story emerged as a distinct genre in the works of such writers as Washington Irving, Nathaniel Hawthorne, Poe, Prosper Mérimeé, Honoré de Balzac, Guy de Maupassant, Anton Chekhov, E. T. A. Hoffman, and Sarah Orne Jewett. During the twentieth century, the form has been greatly varied, refined, and extended by such modern masters as O. Henry, Katherine Mansfield, Rudyard Kipling, Sherwood Anderson, Somerset Maugham, William Faulkner, Ernest Hemingway, Flannery O'Connor, James Joyce, Katherine Anne Porter, Isak Dinesen, Eudora Welty, Mary McCarthy, Jorge Luis Borges, Heinrich Böll, John Updike, Phillip Roth, J. D. Salinger, John Barth, Bernard Malamud, John Cheever, and Doris Lessing, among many others.

simile. A FIGURE OF SPEECH that uses *like, as,* or *as if* to compare two essentially different objects, actions, or attributes that share some aspect of similarity. In contrast to a METAPHOR, in which a comparison is implied, a simile expresses a comparison directly:

Here and there
his brown skin hung in strips
like ancient wallpaper...

—Elizabeth Bishop

An old man whose black face
shines golden-brown as wet
pebbles under a street light...

—Denise Levertov

Like a small grey
coffee-pot
sits the squirrel.

—Humbert Wolfe

[T]he garbage trucks sped away
gloriously, as if they had been the
Tarleton twins on thoroughbreds
cantering away from the gates
of Tara.

—Annie Dillard

An **epic simile,** or **Homeric simile,** is an extended, elaborated, ornate simile developed in a lengthy descriptive passage.
First used by Homer, epic similes appear in such works as John
Milton's *Paradise Lost* and Matthew Arnold's *Sohrab and Rustum,*
among others. Here is a relatively brief example from Arnold:

As those black granite pillars, once high-reared
by Jemshid in Persepolis, to bear
His house, now 'mid their broken flights of steps
Lie prone, enormous, down the mountainside—
So in the sand lay Rustum by his son.

See FIGURATIVE LANGUAGE, METAPHOR.

situational irony. The contrast that exists between what is intended
and what actually takes place. See IRONY.

Skeltonics. A form of DOGGEREL named after John Skelton. The short VERSES usually have an irregular METER of two or three stresses per line and are arranged in COUPLETS. See DOGGEREL.

slant rhyme. An approximate RHYME, devised by substituting AS-SONANCE or CONSONANCE for TRUE RHYME; also called **near rhyme** and sometimes **half rhyme.** Emily Dickinson and Wilfred Owen both made extensive use of slant rhyme. In the following STANZAS Emily Dickinson uses consonant slant rhyme instead of true rhyme:

> 'T was later when the summer went
> Than when the cricket *came,*
> And yet we knew that gentle clock
> Meant nought but going *home.*

> 'T was sooner when the cricket went
> Than when the winter *came,*
> Yet that pathetic pendulum
> Keeps esoteric *time.*

> See CONSONANCE, RHYME.

slice of life. In FICTION, the extremely detailed, unselective, and re-alistic presentation of a segment of life, without comment or evaluation by the author; the English translation of *tranche de vie,* a phrase used to describe the work of Émile Zola and other French naturalistic novelists. The technique invites the reader to become an invisible spectator of "life as it really is," recorded in minute, almost photographic, detail by an objective observer. In attempting to avoid any sort of idealized or heroic depiction of life, the slice of life technique characteristically focuses on life's seamiest, most sordid side. A method central to NATURALISM, it appears in the works of such writers as Theodore Dreiser, Upton Sinclair, Stephen Crane, Frank Norris, Eugene O'Neill, and James T. Farrell.

See NATURALISM.

socialist realism. A doctrine proposed in 1934 in the Soviet Union by the National Union of Soviet Writers, calling for a "REALISM" in LITERATURE that mirrored the ideals of Marxist socialism by presenting optimistic stories about positive HEROES—happy, disciplined workers. Nikolay Ostrovsky's *How the Steel Was Tempered* (1934) is the classic example of socialist realist FICTION and was lauded by the Soviet writers' union for presenting "the new Soviet man." The penalties for writing "undoctrinaire" fiction were censure, exile, and even death, especially under Zhdanovism, the post–World War II brand of socialist realism, named after Joseph Stalin's cultural adviser Andrey Zhdanov. Two early Soviet writers who managed to write internationally successful fiction that follows the rules of socialist realism were Alexander Fadeyev and Mikhail Sholokhov. Famous rebels against socialist realism have been Boris Pasternak, Alexander Solzhenitzyn, and Anna Akhmatova.

sociological novel.   A NOVEL that is concerned primarily with social issues and problems and that emphasizes the pressures and influences of social, economic, and environmental conditions on CHARACTERS and events. When such a novel focuses on the plight of the working class, it is called a **proletarian novel;** when it concerns the hardships of rural life, a **novel of the soil.** Sociological novels usually recommend reform of the particular social problem they depict. Some well-known examples of the type include Charles Dickens' *Hard Times,* George Eliot's *Middlemarch,* Harriet Beecher Stowe's *Uncle Tom's Cabin,* Upton Sinclair's *The Jungle,* John Dos Passos' *U. S. A.,* John Steinbeck's *The Grapes of Wrath,* Erskine Caldwell's *Tobacco Road,* and Ralph Ellison's *Invisible Man.*

See NOVEL, PROBLEM NOVEL.

sociology of literature.   LITERARY CRITICISM focusing on the social and economic conditions surrounding the production of a literary work—the social and economic status and ideology of the author and of his or her audience. The most prominent sociology of literature is that of MARXIST CRITICISM, which views LITERATURE as inescapably conditioned by the social and economic circumstances under which it is produced. FEMINIST CRITICISM is often also involved with these issues.

See FEMINIST CRITICISM, MARXIST CRITICISM.

Socratic irony. The device of pretending ignorance in order to draw out another's opinions or arguments. See IRONY.

soliloquy. A dramatic CONVENTION in which a CHARACTER in a PLAY, alone on stage, speaks his or her thoughts aloud. Playwrights employ the soliloquy as a device to provide the audience with information about the character's motives, plans, and state of mind, to explain earlier events and actions that have occurred offstage, or to fill in other necessary background. Undoubtedly the most famous soliloquy in all of DRAMA is Hamlet's "To be, or not to be" speech.

See ASIDE.

sonnet. A fourteen-line LYRIC poem in IAMBIC PENTAMETER. The sonnet originated in thirteenth-century Italy, was developed by the Italian poet Petrarch and was brought to England by Sir Thomas Wyatt. The sonnet was modified greatly by the Earl of Surrey and by William Shakespeare and, to a lesser extent, by poets since Shakespeare. The two most important types of sonnets are the **Italian (Petrarchan)** and the **Shakespearean (English).**

The Italian sonnet is organized into two parts—an OCTAVE, consisting of the first eight lines and rhyming *abba, abba;* and a SESTET, the remaining six lines, which usually rhyme *cde, cde.* There may be variations in the RHYME SCHEME of the sestet. The octave establishes a THEME or poses a problem that is developed or resolved in the sestet. John Milton, in his famous sonnet "On His Blindness," uses indentation to emphasize the Italian pattern and begins his new line of thought early in line eight:

When I consider how my light is spent,	*a*
Ere half my days, in this dark world and wide,	*b*
And that one Talent which is death to hide,	*b*
Lodged with me useless, though my Soul more bent	*a*
To serve therewith my Maker, and present	*a*
My true account, lest he returning chide;	*b*
Doth God exact day-labour, light denied,	*b*
I fondly ask; But patience to prevent	*a*
That murmur, soon replies, God doth not need	*c*
Either man's work or his own gifts; who best	*d*

Bear his mild yoke, they serve him best, his state	*e*
Is Kingly. Thousands at his bidding speed	*c*
And post o'er Land and Ocean without rest:	*d*
They also serve who only stand and wait.	*e*

The rhyme scheme of the Shakespearean sonnet, *abab, cdcd, efef, gg,* is looser than that of the Italian sonnet, allowing for seven different RHYMES instead of five. Since rhymes are harder to find in English than in Italian, most writers of sonnets in English have used the Shakespearean form. Although the content of the Shakespearean sonnet sometimes follows the Petrarchan organization, usually it develops through three QUATRAINS, followed by the conclusive, often epigrammatic, comment of the final COUPLET, as in this famous sonnet by Shakespeare:

When to the sessions of sweet silent thought	*a*
I summon up remembrance of things past,	*b*
I sigh the lack of many a thing I sought,	*a*
And with old woes new wail my dear time's waste.	*b*
Then can I drown an eye, unus'd to flow,	*c*
For precious friends hid in death's dateless night,	*d*
And weep afresh love's long since cancell'd woe,	*c*
And moan the expense of many a vanish'd sight	*d*
Then can I grieve at grievances foregone,	*e*
And heavily from woe to woe tell o'er	*f*
The sad account of fore-bemoaned moan	*e*
Which I new pay as if not paid before.	*f*
But if the while I think on thee, dear friend,	*g*
All losses are restor'd and sorrows end.	*g*

The relative brevity and rigidity of the sonnet FORM challenges the poet's concentration of thought, exactness of expression, and skill in working with a rigid rhyme scheme. Among the greatest sonnet writers in English have been Philip Sidney, Edmund Spenser, Shakespeare, John Donne, John Milton, William Wordsworth, John Keats, D. G. Rossetti, Henry W. Longfellow, Elizabeth Barrett Browning, Elinor Wylie, Edna St. Vincent Millay, and W. H. Auden.

sound devices.   Any of the auditory effects employed, especially in POETRY, to communicate MOOD, create feeling, unify ideas, and reinforce meaning; the "verbal music" of poetry achieved through the conscious choice and arrangement of speech sounds and accents. Devices exploiting the sound of words include AL-LITERATION, ASSONANCE, CACOPHONY, CAESURA, CONSONANCE, EUPHONY, ONOMATOPOEIA, REFRAIN, RHYME, STRESS, and repetition.

The artful use of sound devices is evident in the following lines from Edgar Allan Poe's "The Bells." Sound echoes sense and effectively communicates the mood of merriment suggested by silver sleigh bells:

> How they tinkle, tinkle, tinkle,
> In the icy air of night!
> While the stars that oversprinkle
> All the heavens, seem to twinkle
> With a crystalline delight;
> Keeping time, time, time,
> In a sort of Runic rhyme,
> To the tintinnabulation that so musically wells
> From the bells, bells, bells, bells,
> Bells, bells, bells—
> From the jingling and the tinkling of the bells.

speaker. The VOICE of a poem. The poet may be speaking as himself or herself or taking on the role of a fictional CHARACTER, an animal, or even an object. The speaker in Ted Hughes's poem "Hawk Roosting" is the hawk itself, as is revealed in the first STANZA:

> I sit in the top of the wood, my eyes closed.
> Inaction, no falsifying dream
> Between my hooked head and hooked feet:
> Or in sleep rehearse perfect kills and eat.

See PERSONA, VOICE.

Spenserian stanza. A STANZA pattern, created by Edmund Spenser, that consists of nine lines in IAMBIC METER rhyming *ababbcbcc*. The first eight lines are in PENTAMETER and the final line is in HEXAMETER (called an ALEXANDRINE). Spenser invented the form for his long, allegorical poem *The Faerie Queene*. The stanza is noted for the unifying effect of its three interwoven RHYMES, and for the opportunity for summary and TONE of dignity afforded in the added length of the alexandrine. The Spenserian stanza has also been used by Robert Burns in "The Cotter's Saturday Night," by Lord Byron in *Childe Harold's Pilgrimage,* by Percy Bysshe Shelley in *Adonais,* and by John Keats in "The Eve of St. Agnes." Here is an example from Byron:

> Childe Harold had a mother—not forgot,
> Though parting from that mother he did shun:
> A sister whom he loved, but saw her not
> Before his weary pilgrimage begun:
> If friends he had, he bade adieu to none.
> Yet deem not thence his breast a breast of steel:
> Ye, who have known what 'tis to dote upon
> A few dear objects, will in sadness feel
> Such partings break the heart they fondly hope to heal.

See ALEXANDRINE, RHYME SCHEME, STANZA.

spondee. A poetic FOOT consisting of two accented syllables, as in the following combinations: *both wáys; bád lúck.* The spondee is most often used to vary the METER of a line of VERSE. In Thomas Hardy's line,

Ăn ăg|ĕd thrúsh, | fráil, gáunt, | ănd smáll,

"frail, gaunt" is a perfect spondaic foot. Most spondees in English are combinations of monosyllabic words or compounds, such as *héartbréak* and *chíldhóod.* It is rare to find an English word of two syllables or more in which two successive syllables have equal accents.

See METER.

sprung rhythm. A term coined by poet Gerard Manley Hopkins to characterize his experiments in meter by varying IAMBIC PENTAMETER. Hopkins' analysis of sprung rhythm is complicated and not always precise. A simple explanation of sprung rhythm is that it is measured by counting only the accented syllables and by varying the number of unaccented syllables. As the following lines by Hopkins show, the accented syllables can be packed tightly together ("Jésu, heárt's líght"), widely spaced ("Wéll, she has time for the páin, for the"), or placed at regular intervals for swifter pacing ("into the snows she sweeps").

See IAMBIC PENTAMETER, METER.

stage convention. An essentially unrealistic practice, technique, or device in DRAMA, that through custom has become a generally accepted method of communication between actors and audience. Stage conventions include the SOLILOQUY (a character, alone on stage, speaking his or her thoughts aloud); the ASIDE (a character speaking directly to the audience, unheard by others on the stage); the use of VERSE as if it were everyday speech; the invisible "fourth wall" through which the audience watches the action in the three-walled "room" represented on the stage; and dimming the lights or dropping the curtain to indicate shifts in time or place.

See CONVENTION.

stage directions. In a PLAY, the information provided in addition to the DIALOGUE to help a reader visualize the SETTING, CHARACTERS, and action. Stage directions, which are usually printed in italics and are intended for the director, actors, and other readers of the play, vary greatly, ranging from the simple directive, "Exit," found in William Shakespeare's plays, to the elaborate detailing of stage furniture and actors' stage positions of many modern plays. In a class by themselves are the ESSAYS posing as stage directions of George Bernard Shaw. In them he comments sagely on his characters and THEMES.

stanza. A section or division of a poem; specifically, a grouping of lines into a recurring pattern determined by the number of lines, the METER of the lines, and the RHYME SCHEME. For example, the stanza pattern called **rhyme royal** (used by Geoffrey Chaucer in several of his poems) has seven lines of IAMBIC PENTAMETER, rhyming *ababbcc:*

O lady myn, that called art Cleo,	*a*
Thow be my speed fro this forth, and my Muse,	*b*
To ryme wel this book, till I have do;	*a*
Me nedeth here noon othere art to use.	*b*
Forwhi to every lovere I me excuse,	*b*

| That of no sentement I this endite, | c |
| But out of Latyn in my tonge it write. | c |

While a given stanza form is generally repeated as a unit of STRUCTURE throughout a poem, it may sometimes be varied slightly for effect by the substitution of a different FOOT, the lengthening or shortening of a line, or the addition of a line or two. Each stanza in a poem is of interest both as a unit in itself and also as an important element in the development and effect of the whole.

Some stanza FORMS have been used often enough to have acquired names. Among these are **couplet, heroic couplet** (two lines); **tercet, terza rima, villanelle** (three lines); **quatrain, ballad stanza, envoy** (four lines); **cinquain** (five lines); **sestet** (six lines); **rhyme royal** (seven lines); **octave, ottava rima** (eight lines); and **Spenserian stanza** (nine lines).

static character. A CHARACTER who does not change significantly during the course of a story; the opposite of a DYNAMIC CHARACTER. See CHARACTER, CHARACTERIZATION.

stereotype. In LITERATURE, a CHARACTER who represents a trait generally attributed to a social or racial group and lacks other individualizing traits. The term originally referred to a metal mold used for mass-producing duplicates of printer's type. Stereotypes such as the absent-minded professor, the nagging wife, the hardboiled detective, the idealistic student, the cynical businessperson, and the spoiled child are repeated from work to work, or duplicated over and over, like the printer's type.

See CHARACTER, CHARACTERIZATION, STOCK CHARACTER.

stock character. In FICTION, a CHARACTER who represents a STEREOTYPE, or a universally recognizable type, like the hardboiled private eye of DETECTIVE STORIES. See CHARACTER, CHARACTERIZATION.

stock epithet. An EPITHET (descriptive word or phrase used to emphasize a characteristic quality of a person or thing) that is used repeatedly. See EPITHET.

stream of consciousness.   A method and a subject matter of NARRA-TIVE FICTION that attempts to represent the inner workings of a CHARACTER's mind at all levels of awareness, to re-create the continuous, chaotic flow of half-formed and discontinuous thoughts, memories, sense impressions, random associations, images, feelings, and reflections that constitute a character's "consciousness." The method gained currency early in this century as writers moved away from an emphasis on PLOT and intrusive authorial commentary to focus on character and inner thoughts and feelings. It is characterized on the page by fragmented sentences; unusual or nonexistent capitalization, punctuation, and spacing; heavy use of ellipses and dashes, and other typographical devices intended to represent the illogical, disjointed interplay of idea, impression, and emotion in free-flowing thought.

The phrase "stream of consciousness" was coined by William James in his *Principles of Psychology* (1890). Acknowledged masters of the method include Dorothy Richardson (*Pilgrimage*), Virginia Woolf (*Mrs. Dalloway* and *To the Lighthouse*), James Joyce (*Ulysses* and *Finnegans Wake*), and William Faulkner (*The Sound and the Fury*).

Most critics use *stream of consciousness* as an inclusive term to denote a general method and subject matter and reserve the term INTERIOR MONOLOGUE to describe a specific technique by which a stream of consciousness is presented. A few use the terms as synonyms.

See INTERIOR MONOLOGUE, SOLILOQUY, STREAM-OF-CONSCIOUSNESS NOVEL.

stream of consciousness novel.   A type of PSYCHOLOGICAL NOVEL in which a story emerges from and is often limited by the NARRATIVE PERSPECTIVE of the STREAM OF CONSCIOUSNESS of one or more CHARACTERS. In some novels, notably James Joyce's *Ulysses,* Virginia Woolf's *Mrs. Dalloway* and *To the Lighthouse,* and Dorothy Richardson's thirteen-volume *Pilgrimage,* the inner recesses of a character's mind are probed by a third-person omniscient NARRATOR. In *As I Lay Dying* and the first three sections of *The Sound and the Fury,* William Faulkner tells his story through the limited and tortured minds of a series of first-person narrators.

See INTERIOR MONOLOGUE, NOVEL, STREAM OF CONSCIOUSNESS.

stress.   In POETRY, the emphasis placed on a word or a syllable; also called **accent.** In the word *Christmas,* for example, the stress falls on the first syllable. Stress is commonly indicated by the mark (´) and lack of stress by the mark (˘), as in this example from a poem by Christina Rossetti:

> ˘I watched ˘a nest from day to day,
>
> ˘A green nest full of pleasant shade

The regular pattern of stressed and unstressed syllables in a line of poetry determines its METER. For instance, in the Rossetti example each line contains four stressed syllables (TETRAMETER) patterned so that a stressed syllable always follows an unstressed syllable (IAMB). Thus, the meter of the lines (the stress pattern) is iambic tetrameter.

See FOOT, METER, RHYTHM, SCANSION.

structuralism.   In LITERARY CRITICISM, an approach developed from the concepts and methods of structural LINGUISTICS and structural anthropology that analyzes language and LITERATURE as structures. Structuralist critics are primarily interested not in what makes an individual literary work unique but in what it has in common with other literary works. In structuralist terms, they are looking for the "codes" and "conventions" that are in operation within, say, all the works of one GENRE. In *Morphology of the Folk-Tale,* for example, Vladimir Propp reduced the large number of individual CHARACTERS in Russian folktales to a much smaller number of what he called "character functions": HERO, VILLAIN, helper, and so on. He was thus able to conclude that the story element in any of these folktales could be summed up as a sequence of these character functions.

See LITERARY CRITICISM, STRUCTURE.

structure.   The design or arrangement of the parts of a work of LITERATURE to form a unified whole; the planned framework or "architecture" of a literary work. In NARRATIVE FICTION, the arrangement of events from first to last—beginning, middle, ending—is a matter of structure. Structure involves both mechanical and logical arrangement. A PLAY, for instance, is structured mechanically as a sequence of acts and SCENES; it is structured logically as a movement through RISING ACTION, CLIMAX, FALLING ACTION, and DENOUEMENT. The structure of an ITALIAN SONNET consists not only of its mechanical division into eight lines (OCTAVE) followed by six lines (SESTET), but also of its logical division in which a question, problem, or generalization presented in the octave is answered, solved, or made particular in the sestet. Some contemporary critics (NEW CRITICISM) use *structure* and FORM interchangeably, but others (notably the Chicago School) make a careful distinction between the two terms. The consideration of literature as a structure forms the basis of the movement in modern LITERARY CRITICISM known as STRUCTURALISM.

See FORM, STRUCTURALISM.

style. A writer's characteristic way of saying things. Style includes arrangement of ideas, word choice, IMAGERY, sentence structure and variety, RHYTHM, repetition, COHERENCE, EMPHASIS, UNITY, and TONE. One of the two most famous definitions of style, that by Jonathan Swift, emphasizes that style should be appropriate to both the subject matter and the writing occasion or audience. Swift said style is "proper words in proper places." The other famous definition focuses on style as an expression of the writer's attitudes and personality. "Style is the man himself," said Georges-Louis Buffon, an eighteenth-century French naturalist with a particularly vivid style.

See STYLISTICS.

stylistics. A term currently used to identify any of several analytical studies of LITERATURE that apply the techniques and concepts of modern LINGUISTICS. Rejecting the subjective and impressionistic analyses of STYLE they find in traditional criticism, stylisticians attempt to analyze style objectively and "scientifically." Thus, stylistics employs concepts from linguistics to identify, classify, and count the stylistic features characteristic of a given work, author, literary movement, or period. These features include patterns of SOUND DEVICES, METER, or RHYME; types of sentence structures and their frequency; word use, such as the proportion of abstract words to concrete words and the relative frequency of various parts of speech; and elements of RHETORIC, such as the use of IMAGERY, FIGURATIVE LANGUAGE, and SYMBOLISM. Stylisticians involved in the quantitative analysis of style often use computers to compile the statistical "evidence" they need to confirm hypotheses concerning how various stylistic features affect readers' perceptions of a particular style.

See COMPUTATIONAL STYLISTICS, STYLE.

subject. The topic or thing described in a work of LITERATURE. The subject differs from the THEME of a work in that theme is a comment, observation, or insight about the subject. For example, the subject of Kate Chopin's SHORT STORY "Desirée's Baby" is Desirée's life, marriage, and death; the theme is the arbitrariness and irrationality of racial hatred.

See THEME.

subjectivity. Emphasis in writing on the expression of the writer's feelings and personal opinions. Subjectivity is a characteristic of AUTOBIOGRAPHY, autobiographical FICTION (James Joyce's *Portrait of the Artist as a Young Man,* Thomas Wolfe's *Look Homeward, Angel,* or Somerset Maugham's *Of Human Bondage*), INFORMAL ESSAYS, and IMPRESSIONISTIC CRITICISM. Subjectivity is contrasted with OBJECTIVITY, which, in LITERATURE, is the detached, impersonal presentation of situations and CHARACTERS.

See IMPRESSIONISTIC CRITICISM, OBJECTIVE CORRELATIVE, OBJECTIVITY.

subplot. A secondary series of events, subordinate to the main story in a PLAY, SHORT STORY, or NOVEL, that is a story within a story, interesting and complete in itself. A subplot may complement the main PLOT, contrast with it, or simply provide additional action and COMPLICATION. A subplot that presents a contrast to the main story is sometimes called a **counterplot.** Subplots are common in many of William Shakespeare's plays, including *Hamlet* (the Hamlet-Laertes conflict), *King Lear* (the Gloucester story), and *Henry IV, Part I* (the comic incidents centered on Falstaff). One of several subplots in Charles Dickens' *David Copperfield* concerns Steerforth's seduction of Little Em'ly and its tragic consequences for the Peggotty family.

See PLOT.

surrealism.   A movement of poets and painters beginning in France in the 1920s, some of them former Dadaists, who sought to reduce or even eliminate the elements of reason and logic in art and writing as a way of giving expression to the "higher reality" of the unconscious. The term *surrealism*, which means "above reality," was coined by Guillaume Apollinaire. Imbued with the insights of Freudian psychology, Apollinaire and poet André Breton experimented with several ways of releasing the unconscious, including automatic writing and painting under hypnotism. Surrealism influenced many other artists, including painters Max Ernst, Salvador Dali, Giorgio De Chirico, and René Magritte, and writers Samuel Beckett, Jean Genet, William Burroughs, Eugène Ionesco, and Jean Cocteau.

See DADA, REALISM.

suspense.   A state of anxious anticipation, expectation, or uncertainty regarding the RESOLUTION of a CONFLICT, the solution of a problem, the outcome of events, or the eventual well-being of CHARACTERS in a work of LITERATURE. Often stimulated by the author's use of FORESHADOWING, suspense creates tension and maintains interest by leading readers or spectators to ask "What will happen?" or, if the story is a familiar one, "When will it happen?"

syllabic verse.   POETRY in which the lines are measured by the total number of syllables in a line, rather than by the number of stressed syllables alone, as is the case in metered VERSE; characteristic of Japanese verse FORMS.

See HAIKU, METER, TANKA.

symbol.   Broadly, anything that signifies, or stands for, something else. In LITERATURE, a symbol is usually something concrete—an object, a place, a CHARACTER, an action—that stands for or suggests something abstract. In Joseph Conrad's story "The Lagoon," darkness is a symbol of evil and light a symbol of good. A symbol may be universal or private. Darkness and light are universal symbols of evil and good. Climbing is a universal symbol of progress; descending, of failure. The dove is a universal symbol of peace. In contrast, the great white whale in Herman Melville's NOVEL *Moby-Dick* is a private symbol and a complex one. Many books and articles have been written in an effort to explain it, but like many great private symbols in literature and art, its significance is complex and elusive.

A symbol differs from a literal IMAGE, from a METAPHOR, and also from an emblem in an ALLEGORY. Consider a forest, or a wood. In the following lines, *woods* is an image, presented literally as a place one is going through:

Over the river and through the woods
To grandmother's house we go.

If the woods were pictured in more detail—snow-covered pines, elm branches black against the sky—it would still be a literal image, although a more vivid one.

However, in the statement, "From the helicopter, we were able to see the windfarm, a forest of windmills," *forest* is a metaphor. The speaker is not seeing a real forest. A group of windmills is being indirectly compared to a forest. In Dante's allegory, *The Inferno,* Dante awakens to find himself lost in a wood. The wood, the reader is told, is Error. On an allegorical level, Dante is lost in the error of his ways, or in sin. The only way out of the wood is through the hazardous landscape of hell (the recognition of sin) and purgatory (the renunciation of sin). The wood functions as an emblem because its significance is precisely determined by an allegorical CONTEXT, in which abstract concepts have been translated into a kind of picture language.

In William Shakespeare's *As You Like It,* all the main characters turn up sooner or later in the play's principal locale, the Forest of Arden. As the action of the play unfolds, the forest becomes richly symbolic, even though it remains a real forest. It is a place of escape from and banishment from civilization, with both the advantages and disadvantages that that involves; a place of freedom; a dream world, where one can act out one's fantasies; a place of transformation, moral regeneration, and reconciliation; and, ultimately, a place from which one must return. Like many literary symbols, the Forest of Arden both embodies universal suggestions of meaning—the forest as a place of escape from civilization—and takes on private significance from the way it is treated in the play.

See ALLEGORY, IMAGE, METAPHOR, SYMBOLISM, SYMBOLIST MOVEMENT.

symbolism. The conscious and artful use of SYMBOLS, objects, actions, or CHARACTERS meant to be taken both literally and as representative of some higher, more complex and abstract significance that lies beyond ordinary meaning. For example, symbolism is at work when the word *rose* is used not only to signify the flower itself but also to suggest beauty, love, or purity, abstractions that *rose* represents symbolically.

See SYMBOL.

Symbolist movement. A movement in French POETRY and art in the late nineteenth century. Rebelling against REALISM, especially against literally descriptive poetry, and influenced by the poetic theory of Edgar Allan Poe and the ancient doctrine of correspondences between the physical and the spiritual worlds, the Symbolist poets—Charles Baudelaire, Stéphane Mallarmé, Arthur Rimbaud, Paul Verlaine, and others—wrote richly suggestive and musical FREE VERSE that exploited the evocative power of private SYMBOLS. Mallarmé is reported to have proclaimed, "To name is to destroy, to suggest is to create." He defined SYMBOLISM as the art of "evoking an object little by little so as to reveal a mood, or conversely, the art of choosing an object and extracting from it a 'state of soul.'" William Butler Yeats, T. S. Eliot, Dylan Thomas, and James Joyce are among the British and American writers who have been profoundly influenced by the Symbolists.

See SYMBOL, SYMBOLISM.

synecdoche. A FIGURE OF SPEECH in which a part of something stands for the whole thing. In the expression "I've got wheels," *wheels* stands for the whole vehicle, usually an automobile.

See FIGURATIVE LANGUAGE, METONYMY.

syntax. The arrangement and grammatical relation of words, phrases, and clauses in sentences; the ordering of words into phrases, clauses, and sentences. In this sense, syntax is an important element of an author's STYLE: Ernest Hemingway's syntax may be said to be fairly simple, with few complex sentences and few modifying elements. In a more technical sense, *syntax* refers to the study of the "rules" for forming the grammatical sentences of a language. Syntax is one of the three components of grammar, the others being MORPHOLOGY (the study of the processes of word formation) and PHONOLOGY (the study of significant speech sounds).

T

tall tale.   A humorous account of the impossible exploits of a HERO possessing superhuman abilities—for example, Paul Bunyan, Davy Crockett, John Henry, Pecos Bill. The tall tale, typically part of the LITERATURE of the American frontier, is usually narrated in a straight-faced, matter-of-fact STYLE, its realistic SETTING and colloquial DIALOGUE providing the kind of VERISIMILITUDE that almost makes its HYPERBOLE believable. Mark Twain's "The Celebrated Jumping Frog of Calaveras County" is a well-known tall tale.

See HYPERBOLE, VERISIMILITUDE.

tanka.   A FORM of Japanese POETRY consisting of five lines, the first and third with five syllables each, the others with seven syllables. Like the more familiar HAIKU, the tanka is a type of SYLLABIC VERSE, poetry in which lines are measured not by the number of stressed syllables in a line, as is customary in most English poetry, but by the total number of syllables regardless of STRESS.

The tanka, identified for centuries with the Japanese court, uses the strict limitations of its form to compress its subject (most often nature, love, or lament) into a single concentrated IMAGE, MOOD, or event. It has not been as influential on poetry in the West as the haiku has. The CINQUAIN, a five-line VERSE form invented by Adelaide Crapsey, could be considered the American equivalent of the tanka. Perhaps the most successful Western imitator of the form is Amy Lowell. Here is her poem titled "Tanka":

> Roses and larkspur
> And slender, serried lilies;
> I wonder whether
> These are worth your attention.
> Consider it, and if not—

See HAIKU, STRESS.

tension. A term used by Allen Tate and other New Critics for the equilibrium achieved in a poem between opposite tendencies—literal versus metaphorical, abstract versus concrete, serious versus ironic.

See NEW CRITICISM.

tercet. A group, often a STANZA, of three lines usually having the same rhyme; also called a **triplet.** Here is the final tercet of Robert Frost's poem "Provide, Provide":

> Better to go down dignified
> With boughten friendship at your side
> Than none at all. Provide, provide!

The interlocking three-line stanzas in TERZA RIMA are called tercets, as are the three-line stanzas in the VILLANELLE. The term is also used to designate each of the two three-line groups that make up the SESTET of the ITALIAN SONNET.

See SESTET, STANZA, TERZA RIMA, VILLANELLE.

terza rima. A FORM of VERSE composed of three-line STANZAS, or TERCETS, linked by RHYME, as follows: *abc, bcb, cdc, ded,* and so on. The word at the end of the middle line of each stanza rhymes with the words at the ends of the first and third lines of each succeeding stanza. A poem in terza rima concludes with a COUPLET rhyming with the middle line of the previous stanza. Dante composed the entire *Divine Comedy* in terza rima. English examples of the verse form are fairly rare; however, these lines from Percy Bysshe Shelley's "Ode to the West Wind" illustrate both the linking of the terza rima stanzas and the rhyming of the concluding couplet:

> If I were a dead leaf thou mightest bear,   *a*
> If I were a swift cloud to fly with thee;   *b*
> A wave to pant beneath thy power, and share   *a*
>
> The impulse of thy strength, only less free   *b*
> Than thou, O uncontrollable! If even   *c*
> I were as in my boyhood, and could be   *b*
>
> The comrade of thy wanderings over Heaven,   *c*
> As then, when to outstrip thy skiey speed   *d*
> Scarce seemed a vision; I would ne'er have striven   *c*
>
> As thus with thee in prayer in my sore need.   *d*
> Oh, lift me as a wave, a leaf, a cloud!   *e*
> I fall upon the thorns of life! I bleed!   *d*
>
> A heavy weight of hours has chained and bowed   *e*
> One too like thee: tameless, and swift, and proud.   *e*

See RHYME SCHEME.

tetrameter. A line of POETRY composed of four metrical feet. These lines from "The Zoo," a poem by Stevie Smith, are in tetrameter:

> The li | on sits | within | his cage,
> Weeping | tears of | ruby | rage

See FOOT, METER, SCANSION.

textual criticism. A type of LITERARY CRITICISM that attempts to reconstruct the original manuscript or most authoritative text of a literary work. In the cases of early works—William Shakespeare's PLAYS, for example—manuscripts have often been lost and the early printed versions vary greatly. The task of the textual critic is to compare the existing versions and use both scholarship and IMAGINATION to arrive at the most accurate version of the work.

See LITERARY CRITICISM.

texture. A term used, particularly in NEW CRITICISM, to designate those elements and details of INCIDENT, TONE, STYLE, IMAGERY, RHYME, and METER that are considered *not* to be part of the STRUCTURE of a literary work, especially of a poem. Thus, texture, according to New Critics, is everything that remains after the essential meaning (the "argument" or "thesis") of a work has been paraphrased. In a sense, structure is the internal framework of a work; texture, its outer surface.

See FORM, NEW CRITICISM, STRUCTURE.

theme. In LITERATURE, the central or dominating idea, the "message," implicit in a work. The theme of a work is seldom stated directly. It is an abstract concept indirectly expressed through recurrent IMAGES, actions, CHARACTERS, and SYMBOLS, and must be inferred by the reader or spectator. Theme differs from SUBJECT (the topic or thing described in a work) in that theme is a comment, observation, or insight about the subject. For example, the subject of a poem may be a flower; its theme, a comment on the fleeting nature of existence. Not all works have a theme, especially those, like DETECTIVE STORIES, that are written primarily for entertainment.

See MOTIF.

theoretical criticism. An approach to LITERARY CRITICISM that studies individual works to derive general principles of literary excellence and to establish a theory of analyzing, interpreting, or evaluating LITERATURE, usually accompanied by a methodology for applying the theory to individual works. Aristotle's *Poetics* is a work of theoretical criticism, as are I. A. Richards' *Principles of Literary Criticism* and Northrop Frye's *Anatomy of Criticism.*

See APPLIED CRITICISM, LITERARY CRITICISM.

third-person point of view. A method of telling a story in which a person standing outside the action of the story acts as the NARRATOR of events. This passage from Doris Lessing's SHORT STORY "A Mild Attack of Locusts" is an example:

> Margaret sat down helplessly, and thought: Well, if it's the end, it's the end. What now? We'll all three have to go back to town. . . . But at this, she took a quick look at Stephen, the

old man who had farmed forty years in this country, been
bankrupt twice, and she knew nothing would make him go
and become a clerk in the city. Yet her heart ached for him,
he looked so tired, the worry lines deep from nose to mouth.
Poor old man. . . .

The most common third-person method is called the **omniscient point of view**, the narrator being able, by CONVENTION,
to know, see, hear, and reveal everything, even the innermost
thoughts and feelings of the CHARACTERS. The narrator assumes
limited omniscience if he or she reveals the thoughts of a single
character and presents the other characters only externally.

See OMNISCIENT POINT OF VIEW, POINT OF VIEW.

threnody.   A song of death, a DIRGE. See ELEGY.

tone.   The reflection in a work of the author's attitude toward his or
her SUBJECT, CHARACTERS, and readers. Tone in writing is comparable to tone of voice in speech and may be described as
brusque, friendly, imperious, insinuating, teasing, and so on.

See ATMOSPHERE, VOICE.

topic sentence.   A term used in the traditional study of composition
that identifies the sentence that states, directly or indirectly, the
topic to be developed in further detail in a paragraph or sequence
of paragraphs. The first sentence in the following paragraph is
the topic sentence of that paragraph:

> *Statistically, driving at night is far more hazardous than driving dur-
> ing the day.* On the basis of number of miles driven, there are
> nearly three times as many fatal accidents at night as there
> are during the day. This is probably due to decreased visibil-
> ity, driver fatigue, and the increased use of alcoholic bever-
> ages.

The term is useful in analyzing the composition of EXPOSI-
TION and ARGUMENT, the purposes of which are to inform and to
persuade. Even in these types of nonfiction writing, however, not
every paragraph has a topic sentence. The term has no real application in the study of FICTION.

tradition. Broadly, anything handed down from generation to generation, from age to age; the inherited past. A literary tradition is an amalgam of ideas, FORMS, and stylistic traits common to a large number of works over a long period of time—for example, the COURTLY LOVE tradition or the PASTORAL tradition. The word *traditional* is often used to mean old-fashioned and is contrasted with *original* or *new.* T. S. Eliot has disparaged thinking of a traditional writer as one who merely imitates the past. In "Tradition and Individual Talent," Eliot wrote:

> Tradition is a matter of much wider significance. It cannot be inherited, and if you want it, you must obtain it by great labour. It involves, in the first place, the historical sense . . . and the historical sense involves a perception, not only of the pastness of the past, but of its presence; the historical sense compels a man to write not merely with his own generation in his bones, but with a feeling that the whole of the literature of Europe from Homer and within it the whole of the literature of his own country has a simultaneous existence and composes a simultaneous order. This historical sense, which is a sense of the timeless as well as of the temporal and of the timeless and the temporal together, is what makes a writer traditional. And it is at the same time what makes a writer most acutely conscious of his place in time, of his own contemporaneity.

> See INFLUENCE.

tragedy. Broadly, a serious work of FICTION, especially a DRAMA, that presents the downfall of its PROTAGONIST, a person "better than ourselves," who through some error in judgment, weakness of character, or twist of fate suffers crushing defeat or death.

Aristotle, in his *Poetics,* provided the CLASSIC and fundamental definition of tragedy: "the artistic imitation of an action that is serious, complete in itself, and of a certain magnitude" and that involves "incidents arousing pity and fear, wherewith to accomplish the catharsis of such emotions." Exactly what Aristotle meant by CATHARSIS has been the subject of much debate. Most commentators, however, seem to agree that he was attempting to describe the strong emotional response experienced by an audience watching a tragedy, a response that leaves them not depressed but "purged" or "purified" and thus relieved, even exalted.

According to Aristotle, the purpose of tragedy (the arousal of pity and fear) is best accomplished by careful attention to the CHARACTERIZATION of the protagonist and to the STRUCTURE of the PLOT. The tragic HERO should be presented as a person neither entirely good nor entirely evil, who is led by some TRAGIC FLAW, or HAMARTIA, to commit an act that results in suffering and utter defeat. In CLASSIC drama, this tragic flaw is often HUBRIS, an overweening pride, arrogance, or self-confidence. The plot should structure events around a change in fortune from good to bad (REVERSAL) that is precipitated by the RECOGNITION of some awful truth and should progress through COMPLICATIONS to a CATASTROPHE.

While Aristotle's concepts of the nature of tragedy are, on the whole, still applicable, over the centuries each age has adapted tragedy to its own conventions, social structures, and beliefs. During the MIDDLE AGES, tragedies were not dramas but NARRATIVES, brief stories about persons of rank or success who, as a result of bad luck or vice, fall from prosperity and high estate to poverty and wretchedness. Such tragic tales appear in Geoffrey Chaucer's "The Monk's Tale."

The ELIZABETHAN Age saw the introduction of **revenge tragedies,** PLAYS featuring murders and other sensational horrors, quests for revenge urged on by ghosts, suicides, and feigned or real insanity. Thomas Kyd's *The Spanish Tragedy,* Christopher Marlowe's *The Jew of Malta,* and William Shakespeare's *Titus Andronicus* and *Hamlet* represent the type. Most Elizabethan tragedies differed radically from the classical tragedy described by Aristotle. They ignored the UNITIES of action, time, and place and employed SUBPLOTS and SCENES of COMIC RELIEF.

Before the eighteenth century, almost all tragedies were written in VERSE about protagonists of high rank. The **domestic tragedy,** written in PROSE about middle-class protagonists suffering commonplace disasters, emerged during the eighteenth century and was followed in the nineteenth century by middle-class tragedies focusing on social issues and problems (notably those by Henrik Ibsen). One of the best-known tragedies of the twentieth century, Arthur Miller's *Death of a Salesman,* presents the destruction of Willy Loman, not a classical hero, but an ordinary man who embodies the failure of hard-sell capitalism to achieve the American dream.

See CATASTROPHE, CATHARSIS, COMEDY, COMIC RELIEF, HAMARTIA, RECOGNITION, REVERSAL, TRAGIC IRONY.

tragic flaw. The error, misstep, frailty, or flaw that causes the downfall of the HERO of a TRAGEDY. As a translation of Aristotle's term HAMARTIA, "tragic flaw" is misleading. Hamartia in a tragic hero might be a character flaw, but it could just as easily be an error in judgment, ignorance, an inherited weakness, or pure misfortune.

See HAMARTIA, TRAGEDY.

tragic irony. In TRAGEDY, those instances in which a CHARACTER, ignorant of the true situation, says or does something that contrasts ironically with what the audience knows to be the truth; a form of DRAMATIC IRONY. For example, in Sophocles' famous tragedy, Oedipus vows to bring the murderer of his father to justice, not knowing (as the audience does) that he himself is the evildoer. In William Shakespeare's PLAY, Othello, unaware that Iago has falsely accused Desdemona of infidelity, calls him "honest Iago."

See DRAMATIC IRONY, IRONY, TRAGEDY.

transcendentalism. A philosophical and literary movement ishing between 1835 and 1860 in New England. The A⸍ version of ROMANTICISM, transcendentalism held that something in human beings that transcended humar spark of divinity. This idealistic philosophy of b⸍ stood in opposition to the pessimism of Puritan ⸍ dominant in New England. It led to an empha⸍ ism in religion and the arts, stressing particu⸍ individual conscience as a guide to behavic⸍ of intuition in the discovery of truth and ⸍ spiration. These and other transcende⸍ most articulate expression in Ralph V⸍ Henry David Thoreau's *Walden.*

Emerson, Thoreau, and m⸍ including Bronson Alcott, Ma⸍ Elizabeth Peabody, and Jones ⸍

228

abolitionists, feminists, and early ecologists. They shared their views on social reform in articles in *The Dial,* a transcendentalist magazine edited first by Fuller, then by Emerson. Some of them participated in an experiment in communal living at Brook Farm in Massachusetts.

See ROMANTICISM.

transferred epithet.   An adjective linked to a noun that it would not normally modify, as in "cold war" and "blind mouths." See EPI-THET.

transition.   A word, phrase, sentence, paragraph, or longer passage of writing that serves as a link in writing. Words such as *however, therefore, then,* and *here* are often used as transitions. Short SCENES in PLAYS or movies and short chapters in books sometimes function merely as transitions between longer sections. In Chaim Potok's *The Chosen,* for example, Chapter 5, a mere five pages long, mirrors the transition in Reuven's life between an INCIDENT that put him in the hospital for surgery and nearly blinded him, and the resumption of his life. In Chapter 5, Reuven is shown seeing his home with new eyes.

translation.   The process of changing the language in which a work was written to another language. A **literal translation** renders the text of a work word for word, without regard for differences in idiom and IMAGERY between the two languages. A **loose translation** attempts to preserve the TONE, spirit, and effect of a work, at the expense of an exact or precisely accurate parallel of the original. An **adaptation,** the loosest of all translations, derives its inspiration from a work in another language but represents a rewriting, a version that retains broad and general features of PLOT, CHARACTER, and tone but makes no attempt at a faithful rendering of the language.

Various critics and writers who insist that FORM and content are inseparable question the possibility of translation. Others, notably poets, feel that the essence of POETRY is lost in translation. Nevertheless, although it is true that, because of the obvious differences among languages, something of the original sense and feeling of a work is different in translation, it seems reasonable that an interested reader should be deprived of *War and Peace* because he or she cannot read Russian. Among the famous translations in English that stand as great pieces of LITERATURE in their own right are the King James Bible, Edward FitzGerald's *Rubáiyát of Omar Khayyám,* Thomas North's *Plutarch's Lives,* and George Chapman's *Iliad.*

travesty.   An especially GROTESQUE form of low BURLESQUE; a satiric imitation of a literary or dramatic GENRE. See BURLESQUE.

trilogy.   Originally, a group of three TRAGEDIES performed in competition at dramatic festivals in ancient Greece; by extension, any three literary or musical works (NOVELS, PLAYS, operas) that are related in THEME or sequence closely enough to form a group but that are also capable of standing alone. Sophocles' tragedies *Oedipus Rex, Oedipus at Colonus,* and *Antigone* form a trilogy, as do the three parts of William Shakespeare's *Henry VI,* and John Dos Passos's three novels *The 42nd Parallel, 1919,* and *The Big Money* (brought together in *U. S. A.*).

trimeter.   A line of POETRY consisting of three metrical feet. These lines from "The Night Wind" by Emily Brontë are in trimeter:

I sat | in si|lent musing,

The soft | wind waved | my hair;

It told | me Heaven | was glorious,

And sleep|ing Earth | was fair.

See FOOT, METER, SCANSION.

triple rhyme.   A RHYME of three syllables, the first accented and the following two unaccented: *beautiful/dutiful.* See FEMININE RHYME.

triplet.   A group of three lines of POETRY, often having the same RHYME but sometimes unrhymed; also called a **tercet.** The three-line STANZAS in TERZA RIMA are triplets. See TERCET.

trochee.   A metrical FOOT consisting of two syllables, an accented syllable followed by an unaccented syllable, as in the word *fortune.*

This line from Sir John Suckling contains four trochees, or **trochaic feet:**

Whý so | pále and | wán, fŏnd | lóvĕr?

See FOOT, METER, SCANSION.

true rhyme. Also called **exact rhyme,** RHYME in which the accented syllables and all succeeding sounds are identical between two words (*fountain/mountain*). Rhyme that is not true is called SLANT RHYME. See RHYME.

Tudor. The name of the royal family that ruled England from 1485 to 1603. The Tudor kings and queens were Henry VII (1485–1509), Henry VIII (1509–1547), Edward VI (1547–1553), Mary (1553–1558), and Elizabeth I (1558–1603). The period of Tudor reign coincided with and greatly fostered the English RENAISSANCE.

See ELIZABETHAN, RENAISSANCE.

turning point. A term used to describe that point in the PLOT of a PLAY, NOVEL, or SHORT STORY when the PROTAGONIST's situation changes for the better or for the worse; that EPISODE or INCIDENT during which the action begins its movement toward a final RESOLUTION, when RISING ACTION peaks and turns to FALLING ACTION; also called **crisis** or **climax.** The term *climax,* however, is also used to refer to the point of highest interest or most intense emotional response for the reader or audience. Thus, the turning point (crisis) and the climax in any given work do not always coincide.

See CLIMAX, FREYTAG'S PYRAMID, PLOT.

type. A literary CHARACTER who represents a typical class of persons or type of behavior, rather than being a fully realized individual. See ARCHETYPE, FLAT CHARACTER.

U

understatement. A type of verbal IRONY in which something is purposely represented as being far less important than it actually is; also called **meiosis**. A comically ironic example of understatement is Mark Twain's famous remark "The reports of my death are greatly exaggerated." See LITOTES, MEIOSIS, SATIRE.

unities. The three unities of DRAMA—unity of action, unity of time, and unity of place—are sometimes attributed to Aristotle, although he articulated only one, unity of action, and mentioned the others only in passing. Neoclassical critics in the RENAISSANCE, studying his works, created the impression that he had laid down three rules for the construction of a drama. As a result, the three unities prevailed for a time, especially in France and Italy. As understood by the Renaissance critics and the dramatists who followed their dictates, the three unities were:

1. Unity of action. The PLOT should be a single line of action (no SUBPLOTS) with no unnecessary SCENES or CHARACTERS.

2. Unity of time. The time period covered by the drama should not exceed "one revolution of the sun" (in Aristotle's words) and should correspond as closely as possible to the time required to perform the play.

3. Unity of place. The action of the play should be confined to one locale, or to one city, so that, conceivably, the actors would be able to visit any scene in the time required to perform the play.

William Shakespeare generally disregarded the unities, following them only in *Comedy of Errors* and *The Tempest*. Ben Jonson's *Volpone* and, in the modern theater, Tennessee Williams' *Cat on a Hot Tin Roof* are other examples of plays that observe the unities.

See DRAMA, NEOCLASSICISM, PLOT.

unity. That quality of oneness in a literary work, in which all parts are related by some principle of organization so that they form an organic whole, complete and independent in itself. A work has unity when all of its parts work together to create one main impression or effect. If any part is changed or removed, the whole is drastically altered. The source of unity—it may be PLOT, CHARACTERIZATION, FORM, THEME, MOOD, IMAGERY, SYMBOLISM— varies from work to work.

See UNITIES.

utopia. An imaginary ideal society or political state. The term, a PUN on two Greek words, *outopia* ("no place") and *eutopia* ("the good place"), was coined by Sir Thomas More for his work *Utopia,* which described a perfect political state as he envisioned it. The first and greatest utopia was Plato's *Republic.* Other notable examples of utopian LITERATURE include Tommaso Campanella's *City of the Sun,* Francis Bacon's *The New Atlantis,* William Morris's *News from Nowhere,* Edward Bulwer-Lytton's *The Coming Race,* Samuel Butler's *Erewhon,* Edward Bellamy's *Looking Backward,* W. D. Howells' *Traveler from Alturia* and *Through the Eye of the Needle,* H. G. Wells's *Modern Utopia,* James Hilton's *Lost Horizon,* and Charlotte Perkins Gilman's *Herland.*

The term **dystopia,** meaning "bad place," is applied to undesirable imaginary societies, as portrayed in Aldous Huxley's *Brave New World,* Yevgeny Zamyatin's *My,* George Orwell's *1984,* and Arthur Koestler's *Darkness at Noon.*

See SCIENCE FICTION.

verbal irony. A FIGURE OF SPEECH in which there is a meaningful contrast between what is said and what is actually meant. See IRONY.

verisimilitude. The appearance of truth, actuality, or reality; what *seems* to be true in FICTION. For example, Daniel Defoe achieved such verisimilitude in his *Journal of the Plague Year,* a fictional account of the outbreak of bubonic plague in England in 1665 that many believed it to be an eyewitness report of actual events. And the verisimilitude of Orson Welles's 1938 radio dramatization of H. G. Wells's novel *War of the Worlds,* in which Earth is invaded by spaceships from Mars, was so strong that it caused widespread panic in the United States.

vernacular. The everyday spoken language of the people in a particular locality; by extension, writing that imitates or suggests that language.

See DIALECT.

verse. In its most general sense, a synonym for POETRY. However, *verse* is often used more specifically to denote metrical and rhymed compositions of lesser literary value (as in LIGHT VERSE,

NONSENSE VERSE, and OCCASIONAL VERSE), the words *poetry* or *poem* being reserved for serious verse of high quality and merit. The term is also sometimes used to refer to a single line of poetry, or as a synonym for STANZA.

See POETRY.

Victorian. Referring to the reign of Queen Victoria of England (1837–1901), sometimes dated from 1832, when the first Reform Bill was passed. The year 1870 is considered the dividing point between the Early Victorian Period and the Late Victorian Period. Scientific and economic progress coupled with philosophical optimism imbued the early days of Victoria's reign with the kind of confidence, even complacency, expressed in Robert Browning's famous lines: "God's in his heaven;/All's right with the world." But as the period wore on, the Industrial Revolution brought social problems. New scientific theories—particularly Charles Darwin's theory of evolution—raised religious and philosophical doubts. Karl Marx personally brought socialism to London, and in the 1870s, Germany became a threatening international power. All of these events undermined the celebrated Victorian optimism.

Literary activity in Victorian England was intense and prolific, with much of the writing concerned with social problems. The great age of the English NOVEL (Charles Dickens, William M. Thackeray, George Eliot, George Meredith, Charlotte Brontë, Emily Brontë, Anthony Trollope, Thomas Hardy), it was also a great age of the ESSAY (Thomas Carlyle, John Ruskin, Thomas Huxley, J. S. Mill, Matthew Arnold, Walter Pater) and of POETRY (Alfred, Lord Tennyson; Robert Browning; Elizabeth Barrett Browning; D. G. Rossetti; Christina Rossetti; Charles Swinburne; Rudyard Kipling; Robert Louis Stevenson; Edward Lear; Thomas Hardy; G. M. Hopkins).

The term *Victorian* is often used to evoke the attitudes of moral earnestness, complacency (even smugness), respectability, prudery, and hypocrisy typical of the Victorian middle classes.

viewpoint. The stance or vantage point from which the action and SETTING of a work are viewed and commented on by the NARRATOR. See POINT OF VIEW.

villain. An ANTAGONIST (CHARACTER in conflict with the HERO) that has no admirable qualities; often found in MELODRAMAS, westerns, DETECTIVE STORIES, and ROMANCES. See CHARACTER.

villanelle. A LYRIC poem made up of five STANZAS of three lines (TERCETS), plus a final stanza of four lines (QUATRAIN). In the tercets, the RHYME SCHEME is *aba;* in the quatrain, it is *abaa.* The villanelle also includes a REFRAIN, a repetition of the first and third lines of the first stanza. A familiar villanelle is Dylan Thomas's "Do not go gentle into that good night":

Do not go gentle into that good night,	*a*
Old age should burn and rave at close of day;	*b*
Rage, rage against the dying of the light.	*a*
Though wise men at their end know dark is right,	*a*
Because their words had forked no lightning they	*b*
Do not go gentle into that good night.	*a*
Good men, the last wave by, crying how bright	*a*
Their frail deeds might have danced in a green bay,	*b*
Rage, rage against the dying of the light.	*a*
Wild men who caught and sang the sun in flight,	*a*
And learn, too late, they grieved it on its way,	*b*
Do not go gentle into that good night.	*a*
Grave men, near death, who see with blinding sight	*a*
Blind eyes could blaze like meteors and be gay,	*b*
Rage, rage against the dying of the light.	*a*
And you, my father, there on the sad height,	*a*
Curse, bless, me now with your fierce tears, I pray.	*b*
Do not go gentle into that good night.	*a*
Rage, rage against the dying of the light.	*a*

See RHYME SCHEME, STANZA, TERCET.

voice. A term used in LITERARY CRITICISM to identify the sense a written work conveys to a reader of its writer's attitude, personality, and character. As is the case with the closely related term TONE, *voice* reflects the habit of thinking of writing as a mode of speech. Inexperienced writers are often instructed to "get more of your own voice into your writing." The concept of voice is sometimes compared to Aristotle's concept of *ethos,* the personal image projected by an orator.

See PERSONA, TONE.

willing suspension of disbelief. The circumstance in which the reader or viewer of a FICTION, such as a NOVEL or a PLAY, temporarily withholds doubt about truth or actuality and willingly accepts the make-believe world invented by the author. The expression first appeared in Samuel Taylor Coleridge's *Biographia Literaria,* a volume of ESSAYS on LITERARY CRITICISM, philosophy, and AESTHETICS, in which he discusses "that willing suspension of disbelief for the moment, which constitutes poetic faith."

wit. The ability to make brilliant, imaginative, or clever connections between ideas—quickly, and with verbal deftness. Wit differs from HUMOR in being intellectual and verbal. Wit finds expression in PUNS, METAPHORS, PARODOXES, and EPIGRAMS, while humor amiably presents INCONGRUITIES of CHARACTER and situation.

Originally meaning "knowledge" and then "intellect," *wit* arrived, in the seventeenth century, at something like its present meaning, but with emphasis on IMAGINATION—or FANCY, as it was then called. The METAPHYSICAL POETRY of John Donne, Andrew Marvell, and others was a poetry of wit—full of fanciful, often paradoxical, and strikingly brilliant connections. The eighteenth-century neoclassicists distrusted fancy in their worship of reason and distinguished *true wit* (wit of judgment and fancy or of judgment alone) from *false wit* (merely fanciful wit). For the romantics, rebelling against NEOCLASSICISM, wit was associated with reason and judgment and had lost its connection with imagination. In the nineteenth century wit also suffered the misfortune of being linked to levity. For Matthew Arnold, the wittiness of Geoffrey Chaucer and Alexander Pope disqualified them from being included among the greatest poets. They lacked "high seriousness." In the twentieth century, T. S. Eliot came to the rescue of both wit and seriously witty poets when he rediscovered John Donne.

See HUMOR, METAPHYSICAL POETRY, NEOCLASSICISM.

Z

zeitgeist. From German, the "spirit of the age"; the moral, emotional, or intellectual climate or tendency characteristic of a period or era. For instance, moral earnestness, restraint, respectability, smugness, and hypocrisy could be said to constitute the zeitgeist of Victorian England.